SUICIDE OF THE WEST

BOOKS BY JAMES BURNHAM

THE MANAGERIAL REVOLUTION

THE MACHIAVELLIANS

THE STRUGGLE FOR THE WORLD

THE COMING DEFEAT OF COMMUNISM

CONTAINMENT OR LIBERATION?

THE WEB OF SUBVERSION

SUICIDE OF THE WEST

INTRODUCTION TO PHILOSOPHICAL ANALYSIS
(with Philip Wheelwright)

THE CASE FOR DE GAULLE
(with André Malraux)

CONGRESS AND THE AMERICAN TRADITION

Suicide of the West

AN ESSAY ON THE MEANING AND
DESTINY OF LIBERALISM

James Burnham

WITH A NEW FOREWORD BY
John O'Sullivan

AND INTRODUCTION BY
Roger Kimball

A WILLIAM F. BUCKLEY, JR. PROGRAM AT YALE BOOK

Encounter Books  New York • London

First hardcover edition published in 1964 by John Day Co.
First paperback edition published in 1985 by Regnery Publishing.
Second paperback edition published in 2014 by Encounter Books,
an activity of Encounter for Culture and Education, Inc.,
a nonprofit, tax exempt corporation.
Encounter Books website address: www.encounterbooks.com

Manufactured in the United States and printed on
acid-free paper. The paper used in this publication meets
the minimum requirements of ANSI/NISO Z39.48-1992
(R 1997) (*Permanence of Paper*).

SECOND AMERICAN PAPERBACK EDITION

LIBRARY OF CONGRESS CATALOGING-IN-PUBLICATION DATA
Burnham, James, 1905-1987.
Suicide of the West : an essay on the meaning and destiny of liberalism / by
James Burnham.—Revised paperback edition.
pages cm
ISBN 978-1-59403-783-2 (paperback)—ISBN 978-1-59403-784-9 (ebook)
1. Liberalism—United States. 2. United States—Politics and government—
20th century. I. Title.

JK271.B728 2014
320.51'30973—dc23

2014025111

I dedicate this book to all liberals of good will

CONTENTS

Foreword, by John O'Sullivan   ix

Introduction, by Roger Kimball   xiii

Preface   xxxiii

1. The Contraction of the West   1

2. Who Are the Liberals?   17

3. Human Nature and the Good Society   39

4. The Universal Dialogue   61

5. Equality and Welfare   77

6. Ideological Thinking   103

7. A Critical Note in Passing   133

8. Do Liberals Really Believe in Liberalism?   157

9. The Liberal's Order of Values   177

10. The Guilt of the Liberal   211

11. Pas d'Ennemi à Gauche   231

12. Dialectic of Liberalism   251

13. Again: Who Are the Liberals?   271

14. The Drift of U.S. Foreign Policy   287

15. Liberalism vs. Reality   319

16. The Function of Liberalism   341

Index   353

FOREWORD

JAMES BURNHAM IS USUALLY seen as a cool and unsentimental analyst of world politics and ideological movements in the twentieth century. This description is certainly one that fits most of his major works, such as *The Machiavellians* (his best book, in my judgment) and *The Struggle for the World* (his most consequential book). It also accords with his advice in these works for assessing and dealing with global politics and ideologies. And it probably reflects his own image of himself as a sober realist warning people not to trust the idealistic slogans that mask the cruel realities of all power.

In most of his works, he seems to be saying, like the Prophets: This world is a vale of tears. Don't expect justice in it. The wicked flourish like a green bay tree. The good are doomed to be continually betrayed and disappointed. The best we can hope for is that a balance between different masters, between greater and lesser evils, will allow the humble to enjoy a moderate temporary prosperity. Analyze your way to that clearing in the jungle as best you can.

His famous maxims at *National Review*—where he is remembered by Linda Bridges and Rick Brookhiser as a quiet, authoritative, exacting editor and a kindly colleague beneath a restrained, gentlemanly exterior—exude the same dry, unillusioned tone of rebuke to human self-deception. For instance: You can't invest in retrospect.

Some of Burnham's critics, notably George Orwell, accept this self-portrait of the artist as a self-consciously scientific, even amoral, analyst of power politics. Orwell's criticism, indeed, includes the accusation that Burnham displays altogether too much relish when he is describing the remorseless necessities that drive men to oppress and murder others in uncertain times. He comes close, writes Orwell, to the worship of power under a mask of realism.

All these aspects of Burnham's literary personality, except perhaps the last, support the picture of him as a realist, almost passionless, analyst. But this impression is blown away by reading even a few pages of *Suicide of the West*. There can be no real doubt that this is the work of an engaged and passionate writer responding fiercely to events in the world that strike him as something between a tragedy and an outrage.

The realism is there still, as it always is. So is the cold logical reasoning. But they are not expressed coldly—and not indignantly either, since a Lear-like raging at the political weather is for Burnham the mark of modern American liberalism. On the contrary, the realism and logic are expressed sarcastically, wittily, savagely, and at times with a kind of despairing enjoyment at the repeated follies of his inveterate opponents in the liberal camp.

Suicide of the West is the first book in which Burnham grabs his readers by the lapels and shakes them hard rather than merely pointing quietly to obvious facts they have managed to avoid noticing. His arguments are as strong as ever, but not always as minutely documented. He builds his case against liberalism with bold insights as much as with his usual logical deductions.

His tone is prophetic rather than professorial. Injustice and folly no longer amuse him; they enrage him. This is the unbuttoned Burnham. And the result may not be his best book, but it surely is his most inspired.

What inspired him, then? Let me suggest three things.

First, as Roger Kimball's fine and informative introduction establishes, Burnham's life was a succession of different moral, political, and artistic commitments until he reached a permanent haven in the 1950's. He was an aesthete in the 1920's, a Trotskyist in the 1930's, a theorist of oligarchic collectivism (see Orwell) in the first half of the 1940's, an anti-communist strategist in the second half, and a founder of a new American conservatism in the 1950's. These are the conversions of a man highly attuned to the spirit of the age even when he was sharply opposed to it. As such, he divined in the early 1960's what was to happen in the later Sixties. And this shaman-like sensitivity transformed the tone of his arguments even when he was re-hashing older material from his lecturing days.

Second, the contradiction between the objective realities of the early 1960's and the response of liberal policymaking must have been infuriating to an observer of Burnham's insight and ability. Though the West and in particular the United States were dominant economically, militarily, and morally, they were everywhere faltering, uncertain, or even in retreat—over Hungary, Suez, Algeria, Vietnam, the Bay of Pigs, and so on. Burnham had argued for a form of political warfare designed to undermine the Soviets; he thought containment inadequate, and even that was being feebly enforced.

Third, even while he was helping to found the Congress for Cultural Freedom in the 1940's to win Europe's liberal intelligentsia to the side of anti-communism, he had glimpsed that liberal intellectuals on both sides of the Atlantic would bolt toward a morally equivalent "neutralism" as soon as the United States had to take some action internationally that could not be justified in simplistic liberal terms.

He knew by now that the Western order of global power was the freest, most prosperous, and most just order available to mankind in that era. He had looked into the soul of American liberalism and seen the vacancy there. He could guess what was coming. And in response, he cast aside his customary restraint and indicted liberalism as the doctrine that reconciled the West to its own needless defeats and eventual dissolution.

We should probably read Burnham's other works in the light of *Suicide of the West*. But we should also follow the light that it casts forward to illuminate his final years. On his deathbed, Burnham returned to the Catholic Church that he had left in his twenties without, as Kimball notes, any apparent soul-searching. What prompted his return to faith? Any man's reasons for turning to faith can only be known fully to God. But it would hardly be surprising if someone who saw clearly that injustice is the way of this world while also finding injustice intolerable should seek—and find increasingly necessary—a world in which the wicked no longer flourish and the good no longer suffer and the intelligent analyst can find more pleasurable pursuits than indicting crime and folly for what they really are.

—*John O'Sullivan*

INTRODUCTION

I put for a general inclination of all mankind, a perpetual and restless desire of power after power, that ceaseth only in death.
—*Thomas Hobbes,* Leviathan

The common-place critic...believes that truth lies in the middle, between the extremes of right and wrong.
—*William Hazlitt, 'On Common-Place Critics'*

Americans have not yet learned the tragic lesson that the most powerful cannot be loved—hated, envied, feared, obeyed, respected, even honored perhaps, but not loved.
—*James Burnham,* Containment or Liberation?

'WHO IS JAMES BURNHAM?' How often did I field variants of that question while pondering this essay! My informal survey suggests that almost no one under the age of sixty has even heard of him ("James who?"). And for most people over that magic age, Burnham is but an attenuated presence, a half-remembered, even vaguely embarrassing fashion that has failed to return— fins on the back of a model that was discontinued long ago for lack of sales. "Ah, yes," speak the glimmers of remembrance, "author of *The Managerial Revolution*"—Burnham's first and most famous book, published in 1941—"ardent Cold Warrior, helped organize the Congress for Cultural Freedom (remember that?), and...wasn't he a supporter of Joseph McCarthy?" The answer to that last question is No—more on this below—but even the hint of an adumbration of a suspicion of "McCarthy-ite" leanings is sufficient to expel one from the ranks of civilized recollection, as Burnham learned to his cost.

The most notable exception to the oblivion surrounding Burnham is among people associated with *National Review*, the conservative fortnightly that Burnham helped start in 1955, when he was fifty. For more than two decades, Burnham enlivened the magazine's pages with his spare but unsparing prose and editorial intelligence. He ranged widely, dilating on everything from foreign policy—his specialty—to (early on) the movies. William F. Buckley, Jr., the founding editor and perpetual *genius loci* of *NR*, called Burnham "the number one intellectual influence on *National Review* since the day of its founding." In a just world, that would be patent enough for continued interest and recognition. But in this world, the combination of Burnham's ferocious intellectual independence and unclubbable heterodoxy long ago consigned him to the unglamorous limbo that established opinion reserves for those who challenge its pieties too forcefully.

In 2002, the late Daniel Kelly published *James Burnham and the Struggle for the World*, a meticulous and thoughtful biography of this sage political gadfly. If any book could resuscitate Burnham's reputation, this was it. But Burnham is too idiosyncratic, too polemical, and too faithful to the dictates of intellectual integrity to enjoy anything like a general renaissance. As I write, in the summer of 2014, all of Burnham's ten or so books are listed as "Out of Print" or being of "Limited Availability," i.e., more limited than available.

I am doubly grateful, therefore, that the William F. Buckley, Jr. Program at Yale suggested bringing out a new edition of Burnham's classic admonition, *Suicide of the West: An Essay on the Meaning and Destiny of Liberalism*. First published in 1964, *Suicide of the West* provides an acute anatomy of that species of self-infatuated sentimentality we continue to misname "liberalism" (is there anything *less* liberal than contemporary liberalism?). The book also, fifty years on, speaks powerfully to a broad range of current deformations, moral or existential as well as political.

James Burnham (who died in 1987 after a decade's incapacity) was an astonishing writer. Subtle, passionate, and irritatingly well read, he commanded a nimble style that was sometimes blunt but unfailingly eloquent. Burnham was above all a *rousing* writer. Immanuel Kant paid homage to David Hume for awakening him from his "dogmatic slumbers" about metaphysical questions. Burnham performed a similar service for the politically complacent. If he occasionally exaggerated the extent or imminence of the evils he described—Burnham was liberally endowed with what Henry James called "the imagination of disaster"—he was fearless in opposing and exposing the totalitarian temptation. Which is to say that he was fearless in opposing and exposing the most corrosive, most addictive, most murderous ideology of our time: communism.

Today, Burnham is best known—to the extent that he is known at all—as an anti-communist crusader. He was that. But he did not confine his criticism to communism. On the contrary, he understood that the impulse to totalitarian surrender comes in many guises. That is part of what underwrites his contemporary relevance. The "managerial revolution" that he warned about in the book of that title was a revolution aiming to repel freedom for the sake of bureaucratic efficiency and control. That revolution has not—not yet—succeeded in the monolithic fashion that Burnham envisioned. He did not, as his subtitle promised, so much tell us "what is happening in the world" as what *might* happen should certain tendencies be left unchecked. But who can gaze upon the ever-increasing routinization of life and regulation of individual liberty in our society without acknowledging the pertinence of Burnham's gloomy analysis?

Over his long career, Burnham changed his mind about many things. He went from being a sort of philosophical aesthete to having a serious infatuation with Trotskyism—a form of Marxism peculiarly seductive to intellectuals—emerging in the 1940's as a prominent spokesman for an astringent species of democratic realism. But throughout the evolution of his opinions, Burnham remained unwavering in his commitment to freedom. This commitment had two sides: an infrequently exercised celebratory side, which he reserved for freedom's genuine triumphs, and an oppositional side, which he lavished with cordial hostility on those opinions, policies, sentiments, and personalities that worked to stymie freedom.

This dual commitment made Burnham an equal-opportunity scourge. He was almost as hard on what Tocqueville called democratic despotism—the tendency of democracies to barter freedom for equality—as he was on communism. Burnham was a connoisseur of insidiousness, of the way benign—or seemingly benign—intentions can be enlisted to promulgate malevolent, illiberal policies. He descried this process as accurately in Western democracies as he did in communist tyrannies, and he was tireless in his excoriation of what he called "that jellyfish brand of contemporary liberalism—pious, guilt-ridden, do-goody—

which uses the curious dogma of 'some truth on both sides' as its principal sales line."

Kelly observes in his biography that Burnham was "the living embodiment of what would later come to be known as political incorrectness." Kelly is right. Consider, to take just one example, Burnham's observation that most African nations were really "half-formed pseudo nations." Now, as then, that is indisputably the case, but how many accredited intellectuals have the forthrightness to apprise Robert Mugabe of this inconsiderate fact? (Burnham was refreshing on many subjects, not least the United Nations and its disapproving resolutions about U.S. policy: "Why in the world," he wondered, "should any sensible person give a damn what some spokesman for cannibalistic tribes or slave-holding nomads thinks about nuclear tests?")

It would be easy to multiply such crisp interventions. Nevertheless, I hesitate to apply the label "politically incorrect" to so insightful and spirited a critic as James Burnham. In many quarters, calling someone "politically incorrect" has become a popular method of discounting his opinions without the inconvenience of allowing them a hearing. It is a clever, if cowardly, rhetorical trick. It allows you to ignore someone by the simple expedient of declaring his arguments to be beyond the pale, "extreme"—that is, unworthy of a place in the forum of public exchange. At bottom, the procedure is a form of political ostracism. The goal is to silence someone not by forbidding him to speak but by denying him an audience. This technique is especially effective with writers, like Burnham, who specialize in telling truths that most people would rather not hear.

James Burnham cut an odd figure in the world of intellectual polemics. He impressed his peers as both unusually pugnacious and curiously disengaged. His background had a lot to do with the mixture. The eldest of three sons, he was born in 1905 to a prosperous Chicago railway executive. His father, Claude, was a classic American success story. At fourteen, he was a poor English immigrant delivering newspapers at the head office of James J. Hill's Great Northern Railway. Two decades later he was a vice president of the Chicago, Burlington & Quincy Railroad (among other lines), traveling with his family in a private railway car. In later life, Burnham objected to the description of his father as a "minor railway magnate," but the epithet does seem to cover the facts.

Even moderate wealth can be a segregating force, and it was one factor that set Burnham apart from many of his fellows. Religion was another. Burnham's father (who died of pneumonia in his late forties in 1928) was Protestant but his mother, in Kelly's phrase, was a "rigorous Catholic." Burnham grew up Roman Catholic in a world still mildly suspicious of papist influence. Society did not snub the Burnhams, exactly, but neither did it welcome them without reserve. And if Catholicism was grounds for distance, so was culture. The Burnhams were a cultivated family. Art, literature, and argument were staple goods in the Burnham household. Young James was musical, like his mother, and delighted throughout life in playing the piano. He enjoyed an expensive education. When the Burnhams understood that their local parochial schools discouraged their charges from applying to Ivy League colleges, they decided to send James and his brother David to the Canterbury School, a tony Catholic institution in New Milford, Connecticut. Burnham performed well, brilliantly in English and math, and matriculated at Princeton in 1923. He majored in English, graduated at the top of his class, and went to Balliol to study English and medieval philosophy. Among his teachers were an unknown professor of Old English called J.R.R. Tolkien—I wonder if Burnham ever recorded his opinion of Hobbits? I doubt that it was flattering—and the suave Jesuit philosopher Martin D'Arcy, who had a magnetic effect on nonbelievers such as Evelyn Waugh. But while Burnham gloried in theological argument, D'Arcy's example and tutelage did not salvage Burnham's religious commitments, which he shed without noticeable struggle while at Balliol.

Being an ex-Catholic is not the same thing as being a non-Catholic, and an ex-Catholic with a taste for theological argumentation is a decidedly strange hybrid. Burnham did not return to the Church until the very end of his life, but his Catholic upbringing and intellectual training served to inflect his intelligence in distinctive ways. In 1929, he went to teach philosophy at New York University—a task he discharged for some two decades—and he stood out not only because of his brilliance but also because of his tone, a combination of passion, polish, and polemic. One of Burnham's students, Joseph Frank, the future biographer of Dostoevsky, remembered him as "very sophisticated, very serious, and very intense."

Among Burnham's early colleagues at NYU was the philosopher Philip E. Wheelwright, whose book *The Burning Fountain: A Study in the Language of Symbolism* made a deep impression on generations of students. Wheelwright had been one of Burnham's teachers at Princeton. The two had corresponded for some time about starting a new literary-philosophical magazine, and in January 1930 (one year after the debut of Lincoln Kirstein's *Hound and Horn*) the first issue of *Symposium: A Critical Review* appeared. The first issue of the quarterly contained essays by John Dewey, Ramon Fernandez (the French literary critic who is probably best known today as a figure in Wallace Stevens's poem "The Idea of Order at Key West"), and the

philosopher Morris R. Cohen. Burnham contributed a long review of I.A. Richards's *Practical Criticism*. It is a canny essay.
Burnham judged Richards's book to be "the most considerable
and the most formidable study of poetry...which has appeared
in America during the past year." But he also noted that he
could "not help feeling...that Mr. Richards's Defense of Poetry
is more 'inspired,' more 'stirring,' and more *desperate* than any
Sidney's or Shelley's."

> To those of us who, however ardent may be our affection for
> poetry, do not look to it so entirely for the organization of
> our lives, Mr. Richards's defense may seem most damaging to
> poetry itself; and poetry may appear through his efforts, as in
> the old twist of Pope's, faint with damned praise.

That is pretty good stuff.

Symposium had a run of three years. It was an impressive,
if sometimes discursively academic, achievement. Burnham
and Wheelwright snagged essays by Lionel Trilling (on D.H.
Lawrence), Frederick Dupee (on Edmund Wilson's *Axel's Castle*),
Allen Tate (on Emily Dickinson), and Sidney Hook (on Marxism).
Ezra Pound wrote for *Symposium*, as did Herbert Read, John
Middleton Murry, Harold Rosenberg, and G. Wilson Knight.
The first bit of Ortega y Gasset to appear in English—a portion
of *The Dehumanization of Art*—appeared in *Symposium*, as did
important essays on Eliot (a major influence on Burnham's think-
ing at the time), Valéry, and other modernist figures.

In general, the magazine lived up to its announced ambition
"not to be the organ of any group or sect or cause," which may
be one reason that Burnham let it fold in 1933. In one of the last
issues, Burnham contributed a long review of Trotsky's *History*

of the Russian Revolution. He was deeply impressed. That "re-markable book," the reading of which was "an exciting experi-ence," had strengthened his conviction that "a major transition [was] taking place" in the world. As for the lineaments of that transition—perhaps "revolution" is the apt word—Burnham was more and more coming to see it in Marxist terms.

Whatever the internal logic that propelled Burnham toward Marxism in the 1930's, there were also two important external factors. One was the Great Depression. Burnham looked around and saw the institutions of American society in crisis. The lib-eral nostrums seemed useless at best; more likely, their effect was positively malevolent. Burnham loathed the paternalistic, big-government policies of Roosevelt, describing the New Deal as "Fascism without shirts." The second factor was the philos-opher Sidney Hook, who was Burnham's entrée into the world of "pragmatic" Marxism—Marxism with a human face (or so Hook thought at the time).

Burnham was an idiosyncratic Marxist. It's not that he lacked fervency. On the contrary, as Kelly reports, he fell "head-over-heels" for Marxism and "labored mightily for the Trotskyist cause." Under Hook's guidance, he joined the American Work-ers Party and petitioned, agitated, organized, and above all wrote to further its aims. He helped edit and contributed innumera-ble broadsides to publications like *The New Militant, Socialist Appeal,* and *The New International.* His efforts did not go un-noticed. Before long he was in regular correspondence with "the Old Man," with Trotsky himself; and although they never met, Burnham became a trusted lieutenant in Trotsky's left-wing anti-Stalinist movement.

At the same time, Burnham always regarded the utopian strain of Marxism with a suspicion bordering on contempt. He had too low—too accurate—an opinion of human nature to be seduced by the promise of perfection. And while he did not repudiate violence, he was always alert to Marxism's (or any bureaucracy's) sweet tooth for totalitarian strategies. Burnham was also a social oddity among the comrades. In 1934 he married Marcia Lightner—like him, a Midwesterner—and moved from New York's Greenwich Village (bohemian paradise) to Sutton Place (adult respectability), where he entertained in a style appropriate to that address. (For her part, Burnham's wife always seemed to regard her husband's adventures in Trotskyist radicalism with bemused distaste.) It is likely, as Kelly notes, that Burnham was "the only Trotskyist to own a tuxedo." When he summered with his family in Biarritz, he perused Marx and Engels during the day and played chemin de fer at night. His acquisition of a summer house in Kent, Connecticut, completed the contrast.

Of course, Burnham was hardly the only privileged beneficiary of capitalism to embrace communism while holding fast to his bank account. But his intellectual independence made him an unreliable militant. Burnham happily immersed himself in Aquinas, Dante, and the Renaissance one moment, Marx and bulletins from Comrade Trotsky the next. It was a giddy but unstable amalgam. Unwilling, as Kelly puts it, to sacrifice intellect to militancy, Burnham became an increasingly restless recruit. The break came in 1939 when the Soviets, fortified by the Hitler-Stalin Pact, attacked Poland. Trotsky justified the action as a step toward the abolition of private property (and how!), but Burnham saw it for what it was: a brutal land grab by a totalitarian power. He wrote as much and in short order found himself expelled from the Socialist Workers Party and the object of Trotsky's rage: overnight Burnham went from being a favored if sometimes wayward collaborator to being an "educated witch-doctor," "strutting petty-bourgeois pedant," and (the coup de grâce) an "intellectual snob." Burnham's response was to gather his correspondence with Trotsky and dump it into the incinerator.

By the end of the 1930's, Burnham was a minor but respected public intellectual. In 1938 he began a long association with *Partisan Review*, the premier intellectual organ of the anti-Stalinist left. But he did not become an intellectual celebrity until 1941, when *The Managerial Revolution: What Is Happening in the World* became a runaway bestseller—much to the surprise of its publisher and the chagrin of the several houses that had turned it down. Written at the moment when Hitler's army seemed poised to overrun Europe, the book is a grim exercise in dystopian prognostication. It is not, I think, one of Burnham's better books. As he himself later admitted, it is full of "remnants of Marxism," above all the depressing aroma of economic determinism and praise for the superiority of central planning. But *The Managerial Revolution* certainly is a bold, an impressive book. Its vision of the rise of an oligarchy of experts and alignment of world powers into three competing superstates made a deep impression on many readers, not least on George Orwell.

Orwell wrote about Burnham at least three times, reviewing *The Managerial Revolution* in 1944 and then in long essays about his work in 1946 and 1947. As Kelly notes, Orwell found *The Managerial Revolution* both "magnetic and repellent." Orwell criticized Burnham for "power worship," for being "fascinated by the spectacle of power" (and hence contenting himself with analyzing rather than condemning Hitler's early military successes). Burnham's essential intellectual failing, Orwell thought, was in "predicting *a continuation of the thing that is happening.*" Nazi power is on the rise, *ergo* it will continue irresistibly; American capitalism is in crisis, *ergo* it will necessarily disintegrate—except that the rude, unkempt force of reality intervenes, transforming those *ergos* into "might have beens."

With hindsight, we can see that Orwell was right that Burnham underestimated "the advantages, military as well as social, enjoyed by a democratic country." His neat, schematic intelligence lulled him into believing that the (apparently) better-organized nation was going to be the victorious nation. Burnham undervalued the advantages of the ad hoc, the unexpected reversal, the sudden inspiration. His "besetting sin," Orwell said, was to overstate his case: "He is too fond of apocalyptic visions, too ready to believe that the muddled processes of history will happen suddenly and logically." (Orwell makes the arresting observation that during the Second World War, the smarter Brits were often the more pessimistic: "their morale was lower because their imaginations were stronger.") At the same time, Orwell repeatedly underscored Burnham's "intellectual courage" and willingness to deal with "real issues." And it is clear that, whatever his criticisms, Orwell was deeply influenced by *The Managerial Revolution*. In 1984, he adopted wholesale Burnham's idea that the world was reorganizing itself into three rival totalitarian states. *The Managerial Revolution* itself appears in Orwell's novel under the title *The Theory and Practice of Oligarchic Collectivism*.

From 1939 to 1941, the communists worked mightily to keep America "neutral." Good Trotskyist that he aspired to be, Burnham, too, was opposed to America's entry into the war. His opposition persisted after his break with Trotsky. But it did not survive Pearl Harbor. The Japanese attack on the Pacific Fleet precipitated a political metanoia. Overnight, Burnham became a vociferous supporter of all-out war against the Axis powers.

This hardening, or clarifying, is evident in his next book— considered by many critics to be his best—*The Machiavellians:*

Defenders of Freedom. Published in 1943, *The Machiavellians* is ostensibly an exposition of, and homage to, some modern followers of Machiavelli. Its larger purpose is to distinguish between the sentimental and the realistic in politics. Dante (in *De Monarchia*), Rousseau, and the architects of the French Revolution are prime examples of the former; they represent "politics as wish": noble, optimistic, ultimately futile—indeed, ultimately "reactionary and vicious" in Burnham's judgment.

Machiavelli and his heirs belong to the latter camp. They saw things as they really were and faced up to unpleasant facts about human nature. Because they saw humanity as it was—in its imperfection, its treachery, its unceasing desire for power—they were the true friends of liberty. They did not exchange real freedoms for pleasant-sounding but empty idealities. They understood that all political freedom is imperfect freedom, won through struggle, preserved with difficulty, constantly subject to assault and diminution.

Burnham's political thought is often described as "hard-boiled." *The Machiavellians* is the cauldron in which the promised firmness is achieved. "All societies," he writes, "including societies called democratic, are ruled by a minority." Although the minority, the ruling "élite," naturally seeks to legitimize its power in the eyes of society, in the end "the primary object of every élite, or ruling class, is to maintain its own power and privilege," an aim that is sought largely on "force and fraud." Burnham had high hopes for "an objective science of politics"; at the same time, he believed that "logical or rational analysis plays a relatively minor part in political and social change." The true friends of freedom budget heavily for the imperfection of humanity and acknowledge the relative impotence of reason in political affairs. Above all, they understand that the possession of power is inseparable from its intelligent exercise.

In terms of the evolution of Burnham's thought, *The Machiavellians* is perhaps most important not for its exposition of power politics but for its implicit recognition of the value of freedom, "that minimum of moral dignity which alone can justify the strange accident of man's existence." As the 1940's and the Second World War unfolded, Burnham came more and more to understand that the preservation of freedom was primarily a salvage operation. And as the war hurried to its end, he looked on aghast as the West timidly made concession after concession to the Stalinist tyranny. In 1944, Burnham wrote a paper on postwar Soviet ambitions for the Office of Strategic Services. In 1947, an expanded version of this document appeared as *The Struggle for the World*. It is with this book, I believe, that Burnham comes into his own, for it is here that he first clearly articulates the opposition between the West as a precious heritage to be defended and communism as a murderous tyranny to be defeated.

Was Burnham's opposition "oversimplified," as many critics charged? Doubtless it was. But it was also right in essentials and was, moreover, a salutary corrective to the naive—and therefore deluded—advice of good-hearted liberals. Burnham understood with searing clarity two fundamental facts. First, that communism was an expansionist ideology bent on world domination. And, second, that its triumph would entail the destruction of every liberty, intellectual as well as political, that we in the West held sacred and yet (perilously) took for granted—above all, "the absolute value of the single human person." Communism, Burnham saw, was opportunism elevated to a position of absolute power. Unchecked, no human good, not even the commitment to truth, can withstand its assault. Anyone who has leafed through Marxist-inspired writings will remember attacks on "mechanical logic." But this, Burnham notes, is at bottom an attack on "the rules of objective inference and proof, the rules that permit us to test for truth and falsity." The alternative, what is called "dialectical logic," is simply a device that declares "whatever serves the interest of communist power is true."

In terms of foreign policy, the fight against communism required neither appeasement—appeasement was merely a prelude to capitulation—nor containment—containment was merely appeasement on the installment plan. What was required was a concerted campaign to undermine, to roll back, the communist juggernaut. In domestic terms, the fight against communism had to begin with the recognition that communists used and abused democratic freedoms in order to destroy them. Their aim was the subversion of democracy. Therefore, Burnham argued, their capacity to subvert must itself be subverted. In the end, he thought, this meant that communism would have to be outlawed. In the near term, it required that serious restraints be placed upon communist sympathizers and agents. Would this be a violation of their civil rights—the right to free speech, for example? Doubtless it would. But, Burnham argued,

> Democracy in practice has never, and could never, interpret the right of free speech in an absolute and unrestricted sense. No one, for example, is allowed to advocate, and organize for, mass murder, rape, and arson. No one feels that such prohibitions are anti-democratic. But why not? Why cannot some purist tell us that any restriction whatsoever is, logically, counter to the absolute democratic principle of free speech?

Burnham's point was that because "Communism, in democratic nations, makes use of free speech in order to abolish free speech," its own right of free speech had to be curtailed. (Burnham stressed later that great care would have to be taken to avoid lumping real communists together with "socialists, liberals, honest progressives," and other "legitimate" critics and reformers.)

Burnham's point, as pertinent today as when he uttered it, is that free speech cannot be understood in isolation, but only in the context of that which makes it possible, that is, in the context of democratic government and the functioning social community that supports it. "The principles of an organized society," he argued,

> cannot be interpreted in such a way as to make organized society impossible.... Any individual right or freedom is properly extended only to those who accept the fundamental rules of democracy. How...could any society survive which deliberately nursed its own avowed and irreconcilable assassin, and freely exposed its heart to his knife?

The publication of *The Struggle for the World* happened to coincide with President Truman's speech announcing what came to be known as the Truman Doctrine, according to which the United States sought to "support free peoples who are resisting attempted subjugation by armed minorities or by outside pressures." This coincidence garnered a great deal of publicity—much of it negative—for the book. It also aroused the interest of the fledgling Central Intelligence Agency. Burnham, recommended by his Princeton classmate Joseph Bryant III, worked as a consultant to the Political and Psychological Warfare division (which Bryant headed) of the Office of Policy Coordination, a semi-autonomous covert branch of the agency. He took a leave from New York University—to do "research," the university explained—and moved to Washington.

Perhaps Burnham's greatest contribution while working for the

CIA was to help found the Congress for Cultural Freedom. This organization, covertly funded by the CIA, was established to provide a liberal but also anti-communist alternative to the communist-controlled propaganda initiatives for "peace and friendship." The liberal element of the Congress cannot be overemphasized: this was an effort to win over the liberal intelligentsia—forgive the pleonasm—to the cause of anti-communism. Accordingly, in 1950 at the Congress's inaugural conference in Berlin, patrons and speakers included Bertrand Russell, John Dewey, Benedetto Croce, Karl Jaspers, Jacques Maritain, Herbert Read, A.J. Ayer, Ignazío Silone, Sidney Hook, and Arthur M. Schlesinger, Jr. Burnham was one of the few hardliners. In his talk, Burnham directly tackled "neutralism" (what we have come to call "moral equivalence"), the "denunciation on equal terms of American and Soviet barbarism." Burnham admitted the demotic nature of American pop culture. But tawdriness was better than tyranny: Coca-Cola might be bad, he said, but "not quite in the same league with Kolyma," the Soviet labor camp.

Burnham's tenure with the CIA (which, we tend to forget, was and is a deeply liberal institution) came to an end over the issue of "McCarthyism." Burnham was ambivalent about the Wisconsin senator: he was not, he explained, a McCarthyite but an "anti-anti-McCarthyite." He understood that anti-McCarthyism was often "a screen and cover for the Communists and...a major diversion of anti-Communist efforts." Reflecting on the phenomenon after McCarthy's death, Burnham noted that

> McCarthy became the symbol through which the basic strata of citizens expressed their conviction...that Communism and Communists cannot be part of our national community, that they are beyond the boundaries: that, in short, the line must

be drawn somewhere. This was really at issue in the whole McCarthy business, not how many card-carrying members were in the State Department. . . . The issue was philosophical, metaphysical: what kind of community are we? And the Liberals, including the anti-Communist Liberals, were correct in labeling McCarthy the Enemy, and in destroying him. From the Liberal standpoint—secularist, egalitarian, relativist—the line is not drawn. Relativism must be Absolute.

Burnham's stand on McCarthy precipitated his deportation to political Siberia. Overnight, this influential public commentator became persona non grata. Philip Rahv, his colleague at *Partisan Review*, put it well: "The Liberals now dominate all the cultural channels in this country. If you break completely with this dominant atmosphere, you're a dead duck. James Burnham had committed suicide." The irony is that Burnham, so astute about the workings of power, should have become a casualty of this skirmish: one might have expected him to negotiate the battlefield more cannily.

It was *National Review* that rescued Burnham and provided a home for his intellectual energies and a platform for broadcasting his insights in the final decades of his career. "Every aspect of the magazine interested him," William F. Buckley, Jr. recalled at the magazine's twenty-fifth anniversary banquet. "Its typography—just for instance." But also its coverage of culture, the length of its book reviews, and, above all, its stance with respect to America's foreign policy. Burnham saw with ferocious clarity that, as he puts it in the present volume, civilizations generally collapse because of internal failures, not attacks from outside. "Suicide," he wrote, "is probably more frequent than murder as the end phase of a civilization." Contemplating the expansionist threat of Soviet communism, Burnham warned that "The primary issue before Western civilization today, and before its member nations, is survival."

In some ways, *Suicide of the West* is a period piece. It is a product of the Cold War, and many of its examples are dated. But in its core message it is as relevant today as ever. The field of battle may have changed; the armies have adopted new tactics; but the war isn't over—it is merely transmogrified. Burnham promises "the definitive analysis of the pathology of liberalism." At the center of that pathology is an awful failure of understanding which is also a failure of nerve, a failure of "the will to survive." Burnham admits that his invocation of "suicide" may sound hyperbolic. " 'Suicide,' it is objected, is too emotive a term, too negative and 'bad.' " But it is part of the pathology that Burnham describes that such objections are "most often made most hotly by Westerners who hate their own civilization, readily excuse or even praise blows struck against it, and themselves lend a willing hand, frequently enough, to pulling it down."

Burnham offered this still-pertinent reflection about facing down the juggernaut of communism: "just possibly we shall not have to die in large numbers to stop them; but we shall certainly have to be willing to die." The issue, Burnham saw, is that modern liberalism has equipped us with an ethic too abstract and empty to inspire real commitment. Modern liberalism, he writes,

> does not offer ordinary men compelling motives for personal suffering, sacrifice, and death. There is no tragic dimension in its picture of the good life. Men become willing to endure, sacrifice, and die for God, for family, king, honor, country, from a sense of absolute duty or an exalted vision of the meaning of history.... And it is precisely these ideas and institutions that

liberalism has criticized, attacked, and in part overthrown as superstitious, archaic, reactionary, and irrational. In their place liberalism proposes a set of pale and bloodless abstractions—pale and bloodless for the very reason that they have no roots in the past, in deep feeling and in suffering. Except for mercenaries, saints, and neurotics, no one is willing to sacrifice and die for progressive education, medicare, humanity in the abstract, the United Nations, and a ten percent rise in social security payments.

In his view, the primary function of liberalism was to "permit Western civilization to be reconciled to dissolution," to regard weakness, failure, even collapse not as a defeat but "as the transition to a new and higher order in which Mankind as a whole joins in a universal civilization that has risen above the parochial distinctions, divisions, and discriminations of the past."

It's a mug's game, worthy of all those "friends of humanity" whose sentimentality blinds them to the true realities of human life. Like the poor, such dubious friends seem always to be with us. Which is another reason that the teachings of James Burnham are as relevant today as they were when Nikita Khrushchev came to the UN to bang his shoe on the table and warn the West that "we will bury you." "But," says the Friend of Humanity, "that didn't happen. We overreacted, don't you see?" As the great Oxford don Benjamin Jowett observed, "Precautions are always blamed. When successful, they are said to be unnecessary." James Burnham would have liked Jowett.

—*Roger Kimball*

PREFACE

THIS BOOK IS A BOOK, and not a collection of articles, papers or lectures. Some of the material from which it has been made had a first form as three lectures on "American Liberalism in Theory and Practice" that I gave as the 1959 Maurice Falk Lecture Series at Carnegie Institute of Technology. Considerably transmuted and grown during four intervening years, there next emerged a set of papers on "Liberalism as the Ideology of Western Suicide" that for six evenings at Princeton, early in 1963, suffered the slings and arrows of a Christian Gauss Seminar in Criticism. So, in the third generation, this book.

What franticke fit (quoth he) hath thus distraught
    Thee, foolish man, so rash a doome to give?
    What justice ever other judgement taught,
    But he should die, who merites not to live?
    None else to death this man despayring drive,
    But his owne guiltie mind deserving death.
    Is then unjust to each his due to give?
    Or let him die, that loatheth living breath?
Or let him die at ease, that liveth here uneath?
    . . . .

    What if some little paine the passage have,
    That makes fraile flesh to feare the bitter wave?
    Is not short paine well borne, that brings long ease,
    And layes the soule to sleepe in quiet grave?
    Sleepe after toyle, port after stormie seas,
Ease after warre, death after life does greatly please.

SUICIDE OF THE WEST

ONE

The Contraction
of the West

I

WHILE WORKING ON THIS BOOK one morning, I happened to
come across, lingering on a remote shelf, an historical atlas left
over from my school days long, long ago. I drew it out and began idly turning the pages, for no particular reason other than to
seize an occasion, as a writer will, to escape for a moment from
the lonely discipline of his craft. We Americans don't go in much
for geography, but I suppose nearly everyone has seen some sort
of historical atlas somewhere along the educational line.

This was an old-timer, published in 1921 but carried through
only to 1929. It begins in the usual way with maps of ancient
Egypt under this, that and the other dynasty and empire. There
is Syria in 720 B.C. under Sargon II, and in 640 B.C. under
Assurbanipal. Persia "prior to 700 B.C." appears as no more
than a splotch in the Middle East along with the Lydian Empire,
Median Empire, Chaldean Empire and the territory of Egypt.
But by 500 B.C. Persia has spread like a stain to all the Near and

Middle East and to Macedonia. Thereafter, it shrinks in rapid stages. Macedonia in turn pushes enormously out in no time; then as quickly splits into the fluctuating domains of Bactrians, Seleucids and Ptolemies.

Then Rome, of course, with dozens of maps, beginning with the tiny circle of "About 500 B.C." around the seven hills themselves plus a few suburban colonies; flowing irresistibly outward over Italy, Sicily, Asia Minor, Macedonia and the Balkans, Greece, North Africa, Spain, Switzerland, Dalmatia, Gaul, Britain, Egypt…; then ineluctably receding, splitting, disintegrating until by the end of the fifth century A.D. the Eastern Empire is left stewing in its own incense while the Western lands are fragmented into inchoate kingdoms of Goths, Vandals, Burgundians, Franks, Angles, Saxons and lesser bandits.

The successive maps of Islam are also there, rushing headlong out of the Arabian desert in all directions, to India, the Danube valley, around North Africa into Spain and the middle of France; then falling back, phase by declining phase. The ebb and flow of Mongol Hordes and Ottoman Turks are duly translated into their space-time coordinates. Because this atlas was made when the Westernized, straight-line "ancient-medieval-modern" historical perspective still prevailed over the historical pluralism made familiar by Spengler and Toynbee, it makes only minor display of the civilizations that flourished far from the Mediterranean Basin. But successive maps of the empires and civilizations of China, India and Central America would have shown the same general forms and space-time cycles.

Leafing through an historical atlas of this sort, we see history as if through a multiple polarizing glass that reduces the infinite human variety to a single rigorous dimension: effective political control over acreage. This dimension is unambiguously represented by a single clear color—red, green, yellow, blue...—imposed on a particular segment of the outline world. The red on Italy, Gaul, Spain, Egypt means Roman Rule; the blue means Parthian Rule; the uncolored fringes mean the amorphous anarchy of barbarism.

What of our own Western civilization, then, viewed through this unsentimental lens? More than half the pages of this old atlas of mine are used to chart its course. In the seventh and eighth centuries its birth pangs can be seen succeeding hard on Rome's death agonies, until the West is shown plainly alive and breathing in the compact purple that marks "The Carolingian Empire About 814 A.D." From then on it moves unceasingly outward over the globe from its west European heartland. In the fifteenth century it bursts from western Europe and the Mediterranean into Africa, Asia, the Americas, Oceania and all the seas. The last map in my atlas' Western series—a double-size inserted page is needed for it—is entitled, "Colonies, Dependencies and Trade Routes, 1914"; and there before your eyes you can see at once that in A.D. 1914 the domain of Western civilization was, or very nearly was, the world.

True enough, in many regions the Western dominance was only external; the local societies had not been Westernized, or only superficially so; the peoples were subjects rather than citizens of the West. But, still, the West held the power. It held the power in western Europe itself, original home of the civilization, and in central Europe; in both Americas; over all Africa, Oceania and much of Asia. Japan was outside the Western domain, though there had been Western intrusions. China, too, was largely outside; though the system of concessions and enclaves had turned many of the most important areas of China into at least semidependencies of the West. The case of Russia is harder to classify. Peter the Great, the Napoleonic Wars, the Holy Alliance and the influence of Western ideas and technology had brought her in some measure within the Western concert of nations. But the combination of Byzantine, Asiatic and barbarian strains in her culture had prevented her from becoming organically a part of the West, while her strength and remoteness had fended off Western conquest. With these exceptions, or partial exceptions, plus a few oddities like Afghanistan and Ethiopia—all of which together would have seemed to a galactic observer almost too trivial to note—the planet, water and land, at the start of the First World War belonged to the West.

My atlas ended there; but as I closed it that morning and replaced it in its dark corner, my imagination was automatically carrying the series of maps forward over the intervening five decades: Territories and Possessions of the Major Powers in 1920, at the Founding of the League of Nations; Eastern Europe at the Conclusion of the Second World War; Asia and Oceania in 1949, after the Communist Conquest of Mainland China; Decolonization of Africa in the Period 1951-196X . . .

The trend, the curve, is unmistakable. Over the past two generations Western civilization has been in a period of very rapid decline, recession or ebb within the world power structure. I refer here to the geographic or what might be called "extensive" aspects only. I ignore the question whether this decline is a good thing or a bad thing either for the world as a whole or for Western civilization itself; whether the decline in extensive power may be accompanied by a moral improvement like the moral rejuvenation of a man on his deathbed. I leave aside also the question of increases in material power and wealth that may have come about within the areas still remaining under Western control. I want to narrow my focus down to a fact so obvious and undeniable that it can almost be thought of as self-evident;

4

and, having directed attention to this undeniable fact, to accept it hereafter as an axiom serving to define, in part, the frame of reference for the analysis and discussion that are to follow.

IT WAS WITH RUSSIA that the process of the political and geographic disintegration of the West began. However we may describe Russia's relation to the West prior to 1917, the Bolsheviks at the end of that year broke totally away. What we mean by "Western civilization" may be defined in terms of the continuous development through space and time of an observable social formation that begins (or is revived—the distinction is irrelevant to the present purpose) about the year A.D. 700 in the center of western Europe; in terms of certain distinctive institutions; in terms of certain distinctive beliefs and values, including certain ideas concerning the nature of reality and of man. In the years 1917-21 most of the huge Russian Empire, under the command of the Bolsheviks, became not merely altogether separate from Western civilization but directly hostile to it in all these senses, in the moral, philosophical and religious as well as the material, political and social dimensions. The separateness and hostility were symbolized by the sealing of the borders that has continued ever since, often under such grotesque forms as the Berlin Wall, to be a conspicuous feature of Bolshevik dominion. The new rulers understood their initial territory to be the base for the development of a wholly new civilization, distinguished absolutely not only from the West but from all preceding civilizations, and destined ultimately to incorporate the entire earth and all mankind.

During the years between the first two world wars, through a process completed in 1949 except for a few small islands off her southeast coast, China shook off what hold the West had established on her territory. With the end of the Second World War, the rate of Western disintegration quickened. The communist enterprise conquered all eastern and east-central Europe, which had always been the march and rampart of the West against the destroying forces that periodically threatened from the steppes and deserts of Asia. Western power collapsed in the great archipelago of the South Seas, leaving only a few isolated enclaves that are now being picked off one by one. The Indian subcontinent fell away, and step by step the Arab crescent that runs from Morocco to Indonesia, along with the rest of the Near and Middle East.

In 1956 the Isthmus of Suez, the bridge between Asia and Africa, fell; and thus all Africa was left exposed and vulnerable. From 1957 on it has been the turn of sub-Saharan Africa. In 1959 communism's anti-Western enterprise achieved its first beachhead within the Americas. It is like a film winding in reverse, with the West thrust backward reel by reel toward the original base from which it started its world expansion.

IT MAY BE RIGHTLY POINTED OUT that this shrinking of the West comprises two phenomena that are in at least one respect different in content: *a)* the ending of Western dominion over a non-Western society; *b)* the ending of Western domination within a society and region that have been integrally part of Western civilization. Undoubtedly the distinction can be drawn; and it may be important within some contexts. For example, there are many Westerners who find this distinction to be a proper criterion for moral judgment: the ending of Western rule over a non-Western society ("liberation" or "decolonization," as it is usually called), they deem right and good; but they are less happy, even grieved, at the collapse of Western rule within a plainly Western area.

I am not sure that the line is quite so plain in practice as these persons feel it to be. Civilization is not a static condition but a dynamic development. The first stage of Western civilization in any area of the globe's surface is, by the nature of the case, Western dominion over a non-Western society; and there must be an analogous first stage in the case of any other civilization also. The society is not created Western, Indic, Sinic, Babylonian, Incaic or Moslem *ex nihilo*, but becomes so. Moreover, the society over which the dominion of a given civilization is extended is not necessarily that of another civilization that is conquered and then in time replaced; often it is, as in New Guinea, eastern South America or sub-Saharan Africa, a primitive, pre-civilized social order, in which case the moral differentiation becomes rather blurred.

Still, this distinction between the two kinds of recession, whatever its relevance for some purposes, has none for my own. A greater refinement in definition will not alter the main point that I am making. I am referring to what can be seen in the changing colors of maps. These show that over the past two generations Western civilization has undergone a rapid and major contraction—it still continues—in the quantitative terms of the relative amount of area and population it dominates. This is the fact on which I want to fix attention; and it is a fact that, taken at its barest, the past history of mankind seems to endow with considerable significance. We may once more review, to that point, the successive maps of Rome, which also had its colonies, dependencies and subject nations.

Moreover, recession of both types has been taking place: from areas where Western civilization was not only dominant but integral as well as from others where it was merely dominant. Russia has already been mentioned as a special case, since it was never fully part of the West; though in the nineteenth and early twentieth centuries it acquired enough Westernism to make it a net quantitative loss for the West when the Bolshevik triumph took Russia altogether out of Western civilization. But most of those regions of eastern and east-central Europe acquired by the communist enterprise at the end of the Second World War—the Baltic nations, Poland, Hungary, East Germany, Bohemia—had undoubtedly been an integral, and very important, part of the West. So too were at least much of the coastal plain of Algeria, and of Tunisia and Morocco also for that matter; and, indeed, the Western communities in a number of other colonial or subject regions, where these communities were much more than a band of proconsuls and carpetbaggers. Let us not omit Cuba.

The mode of the Western withdrawal is not everywhere identical, nor is the resultant condition of the abandoned territory. Where the communist enterprise takes fully over, it inflicts an outright defeat on the West and destroys or drives out the representatives of Western power. It then consolidates the territories, resources and peoples inside the counter-system of its own embryonic civilization.

But in many of the regions breaking away from the West, communism has not had the sole or major direct role, at least in the early stages. In some of these, too, the West has been defeated in outright military struggle. In most—perhaps indeed in all—military battles have been a secondary factor. In some of these regions, the withdrawal of the West is still not total: in parts of the vanished British Empire, for example, and even more notably in what was France's sub-Saharan empire. It is still conceivable that such regions are not altogether lost to the West. Though the political interrelationship has now sharply changed, their internal development may, conceivably, be such as to make them part of the West in a deeper sense than in their colonial past. However, that would alter only details and fragments of the moving picture.

As in every great historical turn, the symbols are there to be seen by all who are willing to look: the Europeans fleeing by the hundreds of thousands from Morocco, Tunisia, Algeria; the

8

British Viceroy's palace in Delhi taken over by a Brahman mass leader posing as a parliamentarian; the crescent replacing the cross over the cathedrals of Algiers and Constantine; the mass rape of European women in central Africa, the elaborate killing of European men, the mass feasts on dismembered bodies of European seminarists and airmen; the ostentatious reversion of non-Western leaders, in public, to non-Western clothes; the Western warships abandoning Dakar, Bombay, Suez, Trincomalee; the many conferences and palavers from which the representatives of the West but not the communists are excluded; the deliberate public insolence to soldiers, diplomats and wandering citizens of the West.

MODERN RESEARCH INTO PAST civilizations and its systematization into theory or poetry, as by Spengler and Toynbee, have made us familiar with this flow and ebb, the growth, climax, decline and death of civilizations and empires, whose morphological pattern, unclouded by the abstractions and metaphors of the theories, can be so plainly seen by turning the colored pages of the atlas. From precedents and analogues we learn that the process of shrinking, when once it unmistakably sets in, is seldom if ever reversed. Though the rate of erosion may be slow, centuries-long, the dissolution of empires and civilizations continues, usually or always, until they cease altogether to exist, or are reduced to remnants or fossils, isolated from history's mainstream. We are therefore compelled to think it probable that the West, in shrinking, is also dying. Probable, but not certain: because in these matters our notions are inexact, and any supposed laws are rough and vague. Even from the standpoint of perfect knowledge the outcome might be less than certain; for it may be dependent, or partly dependent, on what we do about it, or fail to do.

I have, perhaps, been putting too heavy a burden of adornment on the modest premise which it is the business of this chapter to lay down. The premise is itself so very simple and makes such a minimum assertion that I would not want it called into question because of possible implications of the elaborating gloss. For the past two generations Western civilization has been shrinking; the amount of territory, and the number of persons relative to the world population, that the West rules have much and rapidly declined. That is all the premise says.

I would like to state this proposition in language as spare and neutral as possible, so that it cannot smuggle any unexamined cargo. To speak of the "decline" of the West is dangerous. It calls to mind Spengler, via the English translation of his title; and almost unavoidably suggests a psychological or moral judgment that may be correct but is irrelevant to my purposes. It is not self-evident that in shrinking quantitatively the West is morally deteriorating. Logically, the contrary might equally well be the case. There are similar confusions with words like "ebb," "break-up," "waning," "withering," "decay," "crumbling," "collapse" and so on. It may be of some significance that nearly all words referring to quantitative decrease have a negative feel when applied to human beings or society. But let us try to be neutral.

Let us say only: "Western civilization has been contracting"; and speak of "the contraction of the West."

Reduced to so small a minimum, my premise would seem to be so easily verified, so much a part of common knowledge, as to be unquestionable. Yet I know, from the experience of many discussions and debates on these matters, that it is questioned; or, more exactly, is avoided. As soon as it is formulated, someone (I mean some Westerner; non-Westerners have no difficulty with this premise) will say: "Isn't it a good thing that the West should put an end to the injustice, tyranny and exploitation of colonialism?"

And another: "It is deceptive to put things as you do because actually the West has become stronger by liquidating its overseas empires." Still another will add: "Surely the West is much better off dealing with non-Western peoples on the basis of freedom, equality and friendship." And again: "Colonial oppression and exploitation were in reality not an expression of Western civilization, but a betrayal of Western ideals, so that the West has not truly lost anything but in fact gained by getting out of Asia, Africa, etc. And as for Eastern Europe, communism is just a temporary excess that will soften in good time, to permit Poland, Hungary and the others, and Russia itself, to take their place within a broadened Western framework." Or in still another variant: "That purely quantitative way of putting things misses the important factors. By basing its relations with the rest of the world on concepts of equality, mutual respect, the rule of law, the search for peace, etc., and by dropping the old ideas of Western superiority and rightful domination, Western civilization has in reality improved its standing and increased its global influence in spite of superficial appearances."

Maybe so. Later on there will be occasion to examine more closely comments of this sort, the ideas and attitudes that give rise to them, and the functions they fulfill. Whatever their merits, they do not negate the assertion that, in the simple, straightforward atlas sense, the West has, for two generations, been contracting.

So much, then, for my structural premise.

II

WHY HAS THE WEST BEEN contracting? This is a question that I shall not try to answer, now or later. I raise it here only to reject two answers that are surely false.

The contraction of the West cannot be explained by any

lack of economic resources or of military and political power. On the brink of its contraction—that is, in the years immediately preceding the First World War—the West controlled an overwhelming percentage of the world's available economic resources, of raw materials, of physical structures, and of the physical means of production—tools, machines, factories. In advanced means of production it had close to a monopoly. And the West's superiority in politico-military power was just as great, perhaps even more absolute. In terms of physical resources and power there just wasn't any challenger in the house.

Even today, when the Western dominion has been cut to less than half of what it was in 1914, Western economic resources—real and available resources—and Western military power are still far superior to those of the non-Western regions. The disparity has lessened—though not nearly so much as masochistic columnists would lead us to think—but it is large enough to define a different order of dimension. In sheer power, the ratio in favor of the West was probably at its height long after the contraction started: in the seven or eight years following the Second World War, when the West had a monopoly of nuclear weapons.

So it cannot be the case that the West is contracting because of any lack of physical resources and power; there neither was nor has been nor is any such lack. (This is a point, by the way, that might well be pondered, though it will not be, by those of our leaders who believe the answer to defeats in the Cold War to be one after another colossal weapons system heaped on the armament pile, or a compound growth rate for our economic plant.)

Bolshevism was launched as a practical enterprise in 1903, when Lenin pieced together the Bolshevik faction during the course of the convention of the Russian Social Democratic Party that met first at Brussels, and then, on the suggestion of the

Belgian police, adjourned to London. Its armament consisted of a dozen or so revolvers, possessed mostly by men who didn't know much about using them. Its treasury was a few hundred pounds borrowed from the first bourgeois fellow traveler. Lenin—in spite of a professed belief in a materialist theory of history—didn't allow himself to be fooled into thinking that physical resources and power were going to decide the twentieth-century destinies of empires and civilizations.

Nor did the West suffer from any other of the sort of material deficiency that has in the past sometimes choked off the initially dynamic growth of a civilization or empire. Besides the resources and arms, the West had, at the beginning of the twentieth century, a big enough population, a large enough extent of land, an abundance of strategic positions—in fact, every key strategic post on earth outside the inner Asiatic heartland. There was no possibility that a purely external challenger could pose a serious direct threat. There *was* no external challenger to be taken seriously, if his assault against Western civilization were mounted solely from the outside.

We must therefore conclude that the primary causes of the contraction of the West—not the sole causes, but the sufficient and determining causes—have been internal and non-quantitative: involving either structural changes or intellectual, moral and spiritual factors. In one way or another the process involves what we rather loosely call, by a kind of metaphor, "the will to survive." The community of Western nations has possessed the material means to maintain and even to extend still further its overwhelming predominance, and to beat off any challenger. It has not made use of those means, while its position, instead of being maintained or extended, has drastically shrunk. The will to make use of the means at hand has evidently been lacking.

Under these circumstances we shall not be straining our

metaphor too much by speaking of the West's contraction as "suicide"—or rather, since the process is not yet completed and the West still some distance short of nothingness, as "potential suicide" or "suicidal tendency." *If* the process continues over the next several decades more or less as it has gone on during the several decades just past, *then*—this is a merely mathematical extrapolation—the West will be finished; Western civilization, Western societies and nations in any significant and recognizable sense, will just not be there any more. In that event, it will make a reasonable amount of sense to say: "The West committed suicide." In an analogous way, one might say that the Aztec and Incaic civilizations were murdered: destroyed, that is, not by inner developments primarily, but by an external assault from an outside source possessing power that was overwhelming compared to their own. It may be added that suicide is probably more frequent than murder as the end phase of a civilization.

I know, again from direct experience of discussion, argument and conversation, that my use of the word "suicide" to describe what is happening to the West is even more disturbing to many persons than the use of such words as "contraction." "Suicide," it is objected, is too emotive a term, too negative and "bad." Oddly enough, this objection is often made most hotly by Westerners who hate their own civilization, readily excuse or even praise blows struck against it, and themselves lend a willing hand, frequently enough, to pulling it down.

All words carry an emotive and normative load of one sort or another, though we are less likely to notice this when we are in accord with the feelings and evaluation than when these go against our grain. But it is always possible to disregard the non-cognitive meanings, and to confine our attention to the cognitive assertion and its logical properties. My intention in using the word "suicide" is purely cognitive. It seems to me an appropriate and convenient shorthand symbol for dealing with the set of facts I have just reviewed, the facts showing that: *a)* Western civilization is contracting rapidly; *b)* this contraction cannot be accounted for by the material power of any agency external to Western civilization; *c)* it cannot be accounted for by any Western deficiency in material power or resources; *d)* it must therefore derive from structural or non-material internal factors.

It remains possible to believe that Western civilization, assuming that it disappears, will be conquered, succeeded or replaced by another civilization or civilizations that might be judged superior to it. If so, the suicide of the West might be considered good riddance; or might be looked on as the immolation of the phoenix, or the free sacrifice of the god who dies that man may live. These are indeed ways in which many persons—many Westerners among them—do in fact feel about the present troubles of the West. From such a point of view, a decidedly positive, not negative, emotion and moral estimate attaches to the idea of Western suicide. But however we feel about them, the facts are still there.

This book is a set of variations on a single and simple underlying thesis: that what Americans call "liberalism" is the ideology of Western suicide. I do not mean that liberalism is—or will have been—responsible for the contraction and possible disappearance of Western civilization, that liberalism is "the cause" of the contraction. The whole problem of historical causation is in any case too complex for simple assertions. I mean, rather, in part, that liberalism has come to be the typical verbal systematization of the process of Western contraction and withdrawal; that liberalism motivates and justifies the contraction, and reconciles us to it. But it will not be until the final pages that my thesis can be both amply and clearly stated.

TWO

Who Are the Liberals?

EVERYONE WHO HAS BEEN subjected to an elementary course in philosophy has run up against some of the tricky paradoxes that have been used by philosophy teachers since the time of the Greeks to try to provoke the minds of students into active operation. One well-known example goes like this: Epimenides, the Cretan, declared that all Cretans are liars. Run through a computer, that will block the circuits. Then there are the famous paradoxes of Zeno, which prove that change and motion are impossible. At any given moment an arrow must be either where it is or where it is not. But obviously it cannot be where it is not. And if it is where it is, that is equivalent to saying that it is at rest. Zeno invented three or four others along the same line, proving that Achilles could never catch the tortoise, and so on.

Socrates was especially concerned with one other of these classical paradoxes which, as a matter of fact, can be understood as a starting point for Plato's philosophical system. In a number of the Platonic dialogues, Socrates proves, apparently to his own satisfaction, that it is impossible to learn, or to teach, the scientific truth about anything. His reasoning, in brief, is this. Unless you knew the truth beforehand, you would have no way of recognizing it when you found it.

Let me translate this into a practical problem. Suppose that I want to find out the scientific truth about dogs. I will get it, presumably, by studying a lot of dogs: by observing their behavior, dissecting them, performing experiments on and with them. It sounds straightforward enough. But suppose someone asks me: how do you know those creatures you have assembled for study are really dogs? Maybe they are coyotes or wolves or cats or a missing link. You are just reasoning in a circle. Unless you *already* knew the truth about dogs, unless you had *in advance* of your observations a scientific definition of what a dog is, you would have no basis for bringing these particular creatures rather than others into your laboratory. Let us add that this is not just juggling with words. There is a very difficult philosophical issue at stake here, which has come up repeatedly in the history of thought from Socrates' day to our own.

In the analysis of American liberalism that we here begin, we face the same initial problem as our student of dogs. We have got to get our dogs into the laboratory, even though we haven't yet learned exactly what a dog is. That is to say: we, author and reader, setting out on a scientific examination—as I hope it will prove to be—of the meaning and function of liberalism, have got to place before our mental eye examples—specimens, we might call them—of individual liberals and of particular liberal ideas, writings, institutions and acts, *before* we have defined what a liberal or liberalism is. How do we know that Eleanor Roosevelt—let us say—was really a liberal, if we don't yet know what liberalism is? Maybe, scientifically examined, Mrs. Roosevelt was a fascist or reactionary, a communist or conservative or a political missing link. How can we talk, in short, if we don't know what we are talking about?

Whether in pursuit of dogs or liberals, it is best to take a rather crude, common-sense way out of this logical blind alley. The plain common-sense fact is that everybody knows Eleanor Roosevelt was a liberal, just as everybody knows that Fido, who runs around the yard next door, is a dog. We all know that Mrs. Roosevelt was a liberal even if we have no idea what liberalism is. *Whatever* liberalism is, she was *it*. That's something we can start with.

And this is our usual procedure in inquiries of this kind. In learning, we never really start from scratch. We always know something about the subject-matter to begin with, whether dogs or liberals or chemical compounds. Plato expressed this fact through his beautiful myth of recollection. The soul, he said, knows the truth in an existence before the birth of the body, so that all learning in this life is in reality only remembering. In humbler terms, we can note that day-by-day experience provides us with preliminary, rough-and-ready ideas. The job of rational thought and science is to take these over in order to refine, clarify and systematize them. In doing so, science may conclude that common sense had made some mistakes: that this particular Fido is in truth a wolf and not a dog; this supposed fish, a whale; and this particular avowed liberal, a communist in free speech clothing.

WELL, THEN, EVERYBODY KNOWS that Mrs. Roosevelt was a liberal; and that Democratic Senators Hubert Humphrey, Paul Douglas, Wayne Morse, Joseph Clark, Maurine Neuberger, Stephen M. Young, Eugene McCarthy, yes, and Republican Senators Jacob Javits, Thomas Kuchel and Clifford Case are liberals; Supreme Court Justices William O. Douglas, Arthur

J. Goldberg and Hugo Black, and Chief Justice Earl Warren; Chester Bowles, Arthur M. Schlesinger, Jr., John Kenneth Galbraith, Orville Freeman, Averell Harriman, Adlai Stevenson, Thomas Finletter, Edward R. Murrow, G. Mennen Williams, Theodore Sorensen, James Loeb; Ralph McGill, Drew Pearson, James Wechsler, Dorothy Kenyon, Roger Baldwin, William L. Shirer, David Susskind, James Roosevelt, Herbert H. Lehman; Harold Taylor, Norman Cousins, Eric Goldman, David Riesman, H. Stuart Hughes, Henry S. Commager, Archibald MacLeish; cartoonists Herblock and Mauldin; the editors of *The Progressive, The New Republic, Harper's, Look, Scientific American, The Bulletin of the Atomic Scientists, Washington Post, New York Post, St. Louis Post-Dispatch, Baltimore Sun*; the larger part of the faculties—especially within the humanities—of Harvard, Yale, Princeton, of the other Ivy League colleges and their sister institutions, Vassar, Smith, Bryn Mawr, Radcliffe, Barnard, Bennington, Sarah Lawrence, and in fact the majority of all the larger colleges and universities outside the South; the officers, staffs, directors and members of the American Civil Liberties Union, Americans for Democratic Action, the Committee for an Effective Congress, the Center for the Study of Democratic Institutions and its parent, the Fund for the Republic, the National Association for the Advancement of Colored People, the League of Women Voters, the Association for the United Nations, the Committee for a Sane Nuclear Policy...

Everyone knows, and no one will dispute, that all these are liberals. But the line stretches further out. These that I have been naming are the purebred, pedigree-registered, blue-ribboned, Westminster liberal champions. We must include in the species not only these show performers but all the millions of others who may be a little long in the haunch or short in the muzzle for the prize ring, or may show the marks of a bit of crossbreeding, but are honest liberals for all that.

The *New York Times* may not have quite the undiluted liberal blood line of the *Washington Post*, and it admits a few ideological deviants to its writing staff, but no one who reads it regularly—as do most of those persons who run the United States—will doubt its legitimate claim to the label; and its owners would have cause to bring suit if you called it anti-liberal. There may be more Democratic Party liberals than Republican liberals; but Republicans like Jacob Javits, Clifford Case, Paul Hoffman, the late perennial New York City Councilman Stanley Isaacs, Representative John Lindsay, and a good many of those who have followed Professor Arthur Larson's suggestion to call themselves "modern Republicans" can hardly be denied entrance at the liberal gate.

It can be argued, with some cogency, that certain parts of Roman Catholic dogma are not easy to reconcile with liberal doctrine. Nevertheless, California Governor Pat Brown, New York Mayor Robert Wagner, at least a few Kennedys, Supreme Court Justice William Brennan and many another prominent Catholic are surely to be numbered, as they number themselves, in the liberal army. The best-known magazine published by Catholic laymen, *The Commonweal*, describes itself, accurately, as "liberal."

Though few other daily papers are so quintessentially and uniformly liberal as the *Washington Post*, few of the larger papers outside the South, except for the *Wall Street Journal*, *New York Daily News* and *Chicago Tribune*, stray very far from the liberal reservation; and even in the South there is the *Atlanta Constitution*. The mass weeklies do not use quite the same doctrinaire rhetoric as *The New Republic*; but among them only *U.S. News and World Report* is openly and consistently anti-liberal—though, it must be granted, no prudent liberal could regard *Time* and *Life* as the staunchest of allies. Some teachers at the big state universities may not repeat the liberal ritual with quite the practiced fervor of an Arthur Schlesinger, Jr. in his Harvard days, a John P. Roche at Brandeis, a Henry Commager at Amherst or Eric Goldman at Princeton; but in the liberal arts faculties you will not find many confessed heretics to the liberal faith—though a few more today, perhaps, than a decade ago. In book publishing, radio-TV, professional lecturing, theater, movies and the rest of the "communicative arts," there are a few non-liberals, but you could make plenty of money by giving five to one that any name drawn at random would be a liberal's.

In sum, then: liberalism rather broadly designated—ranging from somewhat dubious blends to the fine pure bonded 100 proof—is today, and from some time in the 1930's has been, the prevailing American public doctrine, or ideology. The predominant assumptions, ideas and beliefs about politics, economics, and social questions are liberal. I do not mean that a large majority of the population is, by count, liberal. Perhaps a majority is liberal, but that is hard to determine accurately. What is certain is that a majority, and a substantial majority, of those who control or influence public opinion is liberal, that liberalism of one or another variety prevails among the opinion-makers, molders and transmitters: teachers in the leading universities—probably the most significant single category; book publishers; editors and writers of the most influential publications; school and college administrators; public relations experts; writers of both novels and non-fiction; radio-TV directors, writers and commentators; producers, directors and writers in movies and the theater; the Jewish and non-evangelical Protestant clergy and not a few Catholic priests and bishops; verbalists in all branches of government; the staffs of the great foundations that have acquired in our day such pervasive influence through their relation to research, education, scholarships and publishing.

When I state that liberalism is the prevailing American doctrine, I do not, of course, suggest that it is the only doctrine, even among those who make or influence public opinion. In order to understand what a thing is, as Spinoza insisted, we must know what it is not. In trying to understand what liberals and liberalism are, it is useful to take note of the unambiguous examples around us of non-liberals and non-liberalism. We are not quite all liberals, not yet at any rate.

Senators Barry Goldwater, John Tower and Harry F. Byrd maintain their non-liberal seats alongside Hubert Humphrey and Jacob Javits. David Lawrence and John Chamberlain write their daily columns as well as Marquis Childs, James Wechsler and Doris Fleeson. Fulton Lewis, Jr. continues, on the provincial air at any rate, and no one has ever accused him of liberalism. Lewis Strauss, who has never even pretended to be a liberal, occupied several of the nation's highest appointive posts under both Democratic and Republican Presidents—though it is worth noting that even when he was supported by all the power of the Presidential office and the seldom-broken tradition of American governmental procedures, his liberal critics won a majority in the Senate for his dismissal. *U.S. News and World Report* does exist and even flourish among the mass weeklies; among the magazines of opinion, as they are somewhat deprecatingly called, there is also William F. Buckley, Jr.'s *National Review*; and the quarterly, *Modern Age*, founded by the unapologetic conservative, Russell Kirk, manages to penetrate a number of academic ramparts. The *Richmond Times-Dispatch*, *Arizona Republican* and *Indianapolis News* provide contrasting if provincial background for the *Washington Post*.

Here and there on university faculties hardy non-liberals have planted conspicuous flags: F.A. Hayek, Leo Strauss, Milton Friedman at Chicago; David Rowe at Yale; Warren Nutter at Virginia; Karl Wittfogel at Washington; Robert Strausz-Hupé at Pennsylvania; Hugh Kenner at California; Walter Berns at Cornell; at Harvard itself, Edward C. Banfield. The company of retired generals and admirals seems to be rather an assembly point for non-liberals: Generals Douglas MacArthur, Albert C. Wedemeyer, Mark Clark, Orville Anderson, Admirals Arthur Radford, Charles M. Cooke, Arleigh Burke—indeed, a random gathering of ex–general officers, even with a number of active generals and admirals included, would be one of the few occasions on which a liberal might not feel altogether at home: a fact that perhaps has a certain symptomatic importance. He would be lonely, too, though not isolated, at conventions of the National Association of Manufacturers or the United States Chamber of Commerce. At the extreme wings there are small sects of communists, anarchists, fascists, racists and crackpots outside both liberal and conservative boundaries.

And finally—though I should perhaps have listed it first—there is the Deep South, much of which is still, in a more general and institutionalized way, non- and indeed anti-liberal. There are liberals in the South, and their tribe has been increasing, as there are non-liberals in the North, East and West; and a fair amount of liberal doctrine has seeped gradually into the Southern mind, a good deal of it in fact on matters other than the South's peculiar problem. But the South as a whole, or at any rate the Deep South, remains for elsewhere ascendant liberalism a barbarian outpost, under heavy siege but not yet conquered, in spite of manifestos, court orders, freedom riders and paratroops.

I I

IN ASSEMBLING THIS SIZABLE mass of particular data, both positive and negative, I have stayed within American national limits. The ideology that Americans call "liberalism" is, however, by no means confined to the United States. It, and the typical sorts of persons who believe it—"liberals," that is to say—are found in every nation outside the communist empire; and no doubt liberals are present, if silent, within the communist regions also.[1] The ideology and its adepts bear different names in different places. Except where the American usage has become accepted, they are usually not called "liberalism" and "liberals," terms that retain elsewhere a greater portion of their nineteenth-century laissez-faire, limited-government meaning. Still, the type, the species, is easily enough recognizable across the barriers of geography and language.

In political and ideological range, the tendency that Americans call "liberalism" corresponds roughly to what the French call "*progressisme*" and bridges what are known in Europe and Latin America as "the Left" and "the Center." It covers most of the Left except for the communist parties and those dogmatic socialist parties that have not, like the German Social Democratic Party and the British Labour Party, abandoned orthodox Marxism. In the other political direction, it covers the left wing and much of the center of the Christian Democratic parties and the modernized (welfarist) Conservative parties like the British. The

---

1. There are persons in every country who may be appropriately called "liberals," and who regard themselves as liberals (or the equivalent). I shall show later on, in the discussion of the dialectics of liberalism, that the existential meaning of the liberalism found in the new and underdeveloped nations is radically different from liberalism within older and more advanced nations.

similarity between American liberalism and the corresponding tendencies found elsewhere is indicated by the interchangeability of rhetoric. No reader of the American *New Republic* would feel uneasy with a copy of the British *New Statesman* or the French *L'Express*. A *Washington Post* or *New York Times* editorial writer would need no more than a week's apprenticeship to supply leading articles for the London Sunday *Observer* or, if he knew French, for the Paris *Le Monde*. At the international gatherings on all conceivable subjects that have become a feature of our era, the liberal professors, writers, journalists and politician-intellectuals from North America discover quickly that they speak the same ideological language as their progressive confreres from other continents, however many simultaneous translations must be arranged for the vulgates.

The American variety of this worldwide ideology—whatever name we may choose to give it—has certain special features derived from the local soil, history and intellectual tradition. It is somewhat more freewheeling, less doctrinaire, than the European forms; it bears the imprint of more recent frontiers, and of the Americanized pragmatism of William James and John Dewey. But the differences are secondary in terms of either basic doctrine or historical consequence. With only a few exceptions, which I shall note in each case, the analyses that I shall be making hold for the global ideology, not merely for the American variety. This is natural enough, because the categories of the ideology are universalistic, without local origin or confinement.

Though most of the analysis and the conclusions will thus be unrestricted, most (though not all) of the specific examples and references will be American, in order that we may not get lost in trackless mountains of data. I have stated as my underlying hypothesis the proposition that liberalism is the ideology of

Western suicide. My Americanized procedure might suggest narrowing the proposition to: liberalism is the ideology of American suicide. On two grounds I think that the wider assertion may be retained: first because of the fact just noted, that American liberalism is only a local variety of an ideology (and historical tendency) present in essentials in the other Western nations; and second, because Western civilization could not survive as a going concern, as more than a remnant, without the United States. I take it to be too obvious to require discussion that, if the United States collapses or declines to unimportance, the collapse of the other Western nations will not be far behind—if it won't have occurred beforehand.

III

HAVING GATHERED TOGETHER a laboratory load of specimens, it becomes my duty to get out the scalpels and begin more refined dissection. What, more exactly, is this "liberalism" that I have been writing about rather cavalierly so far, this prevailing doctrine which, I must have been assuming, all these many individual liberals and liberal institutions share?

The individual liberals I have named—I should more properly say, the individuals whom I have named as liberals—do not, certainly, share identical ideas on all things, even on matters political, economic and social. They differ among themselves, and they are notably fond of debates, panels, discussions and forums in which they air their divergencies. Some of them feel that a 91 percent top limit on the American progressive income tax is about right; some, that it should be 100 percent above a certain maximum income; others, that it might be lowered to, say, 60 percent. But all liberals, without any exception that I know of, agree that a progressive income tax is a fair, probably the fairest, form of taxation, and that the government—all governments—ought to impose a progressive tax on personal incomes.

Liberals dispute just how speedy ought to be the deliberate speed with which schools in the United States should, under the Supreme Court's order, be racially integrated; whether the next summit meeting to negotiate with the Kremlin should be held before or after a Foreign Ministers' meeting; whether private schools should or should not be granted tax exemption; whether the United Nations should or should not retain the veto power in the Security Council; whether the legislature, courts or executive should play the primary role in guaranteeing equal rights to all citizens in housing, employment, voting, education and medical care; whether Communist Party spokesmen deserve equal time with Republican and Democratic Party spokesmen in public forums; whether the legal minimum wage should be $1.25 or $1.50 or $1.75 an hour.

All liberals agree, without debate, that racial segregation in any school system is wrong and that government ought to prevent it; that in one way or another, whether at the summit or the middle, we *ought* to negotiate with the Kremlin, and keep negotiating; that, whether private schools are to be permitted to exist or not, the basis of the educational system should be universal, free—that is, tax-supported—public schooling; that whatever changes may be theoretically desirable in its charter and conduct, the United Nations is a worthy institution that deserves financial, political and moral support; that all citizens possess equal rights and deserve equal treatment guaranteed by the central government; that whatever the times and forums made available to communists, they should be allowed to speak their piece freely; that government should define and enforce *some* minimum level of wages.

In short, liberals differ, or may differ, among themselves on application, timing, method and other details, but these differences revolve within a common framework of more basic ideas, beliefs, principles, goals, feelings and values. This does not mean that every liberal is clearly aware of this common framework; on the contrary, most liberals will take it for granted as automatically as pulse or breathing. If brought to light, it is likely to seem as self-evident and unquestionable as Euclid's set of axioms once seemed to mathematicians.

It is a matter of what seems open to rational discussion, to discussion among reasonable men. It is rational that Leon Keyserling, let us say, should dispute with John Kenneth Galbraith or Walter Heller whether the initial appropriation under a newly proposed federal school program should be $2.3 billion or $3.2 billion. Reasonable men, that is to say liberals, differ on such points, and negotiate their differences through the discussion process. But it is a waste of time for Mr. Keyserling, Ambassador Galbraith, Mr. Heller or other reasonable men to try to argue a contention by, say, Senator Tower that there should not be any federal school program at all. That sort of talk is reactionary nonsense, eighteenth-century thinking, outside the limits of rational discussion. In such cases there is no sense relying on persuasion; it will have to be settled by rounding up the votes, and, if the reactionaries keep asking for trouble long enough, by calling out the paratroops. "In our day," it seems to a liberal, "nobody but a madman, fascist or crackpot would *really* question whether democracy is better than aristocracy and dictatorship, whether there ought to be universal education and universal suffrage, whether all races and creeds deserve equal treatment, whether government has a duty to the unemployed, ill and aged, whether we ought to have a progressive income tax, whether trade unions are a good thing, or peace better than war."

Whether or not all liberals understand the principles behind their own judgments, attitudes and actions—and some of them undoubtedly do—and whether these principles are self-evidently true or just plain true or even plain false, the principles are nevertheless *there*, logically speaking. They can be brought to light by a consideration of what is logically entailed by liberal words and deeds: by answering the question, "What *would* a liberal have to believe, in order to make logical sense of the way he talks, judges, feels and acts about political, economic and social affairs?"

Present-day American liberalism is not a complete system of thought comparable to, say, dialectical materialism, Spinozism, or Christian philosophy as taught by the Thomist wing of the Roman Catholic Church. Liberalism has no single, accepted and authoritative book or person or committee that is recognized as giving the final word: no Bible, Pope nor Presidium. Liberalism is looser, vaguer, harder to pin down; and permits its faithful a considerable deviation before they are pronounced heretic. Nevertheless, liberalism does constitute in its own terms a fairly cohesive body of doctrine, cluster of feelings and code of practice. This is indirectly demonstrated by the fact that usually— not always, but usually—it is easy enough to tell the difference between a liberal on the one hand and a conservative on the other; between a liberal proposal in politics or economics and a conservative proposal. (And still easier, it goes without saying, to tell the difference between a liberal and an outright reactionary.) There are troublesome intermediary cases, but surprisingly few, really. A political journalist seldom has any trouble identifying the public figures he writes about as liberal or not. The ideological spectrum between the leftmost wing of liberalism and the rightmost wing of conservatism is not an evenly graduated gray continuum. The L's and the C's are bunched; and we can usually tell the difference intuitively. A connoisseur, in fact, can tell the difference intuitively just from a momentary sample of rhetoric at a Parent-Teacher meeting or a cocktail party, even without a specific declaration or proposal to go by, much as a musical connoisseur can distinguish intuitively a single phrase of Mozart from a phrase of Brahms.

IV

IT IS NOT TOO DIFFICULT TO DEVISE a fairly accurate diagnostic test for liberalism. In individual and group experiments over the past several years I have often used, for example, the following set of thirty-nine sentences. The patient is merely asked whether he agrees or disagrees with each sentence—agrees or disagrees by and large, without worrying over fine points.[2]

1. All forms of racial segregation and discrimination are wrong.

2. Everyone is entitled to his own opinion.

3. Everyone has a right to free, public education.

4. Political, economic or social discrimination based on religious belief is wrong.

5. In political or military conflict it is wrong to use methods of torture and physical terror.

6. A popular movement or revolt against a tyranny or dictatorship is right, and deserves approval.

---

2. Readers of this book might be interested, or amused, to give themselves the test.

7. The government has a duty to provide for the ill, aged, unemployed and poor if they cannot take care of themselves.

8. Progressive income and inheritance taxes are the fairest form of taxation.

9. If reasonable compensation is made, the government of a nation has the legal and moral right to expropriate private property within its borders, whether owned by citizens or foreigners.

10. We have a duty to mankind; that is, to men in general.

11. The United Nations, even if limited in accomplishment, is a step in the right direction.

12. Any interference with free speech and free assembly, except for cases of immediate public danger or juvenile corruption, is wrong.

13. Wealthy nations, like the United States, have a duty to aid the less privileged portions of mankind.

14. Colonialism and imperialism are wrong.

15. Hotels, motels, stores and restaurants in the Southern United States ought to be obliged by law to allow Negroes to use all of their facilities on the same basis as whites.

16. The chief sources of delinquency and crime are ignorance, discrimination, poverty and exploitation.

17. Communists have a right to express their opinions.

18. We should always be ready to negotiate with the Soviet Union and other communist nations.

19. Corporal punishment, except possibly for small children, is wrong.

20. All nations and peoples, including the nations and peoples of Asia and Africa, have a right to political independence when a majority of the population wants it.

21. We always ought to respect the religious beliefs of others.

22. The primary goal of international policy in the nuclear age ought to be peace.

23. Except in cases of a clear threat to national security or, possibly, to juvenile morals, censorship is wrong.

24. Congressional investigating committees are dangerous institutions, and need to be watched and curbed if they are not to become a serious threat to freedom.

25. The money amount of school and university scholarships ought to be decided primarily by need.

26. Qualified teachers, at least at the university level, are entitled to academic freedom: that is, the right to express their own beliefs and opinions, in or out of the classroom, without interference from administrators, trustees, parents or public bodies.

27. In determining who is to be admitted to schools and universities, quota systems based on color, religion, family or similar factors are wrong.

28. The national government should guarantee that all adult citizens, except for criminals and the insane, should have the right to vote.

29. Joseph McCarthy was probably the most dangerous man in American public life during the fifteen years following the Second World War.

30. There are no significant differences in intellectual, moral or civilizing capacity among human races and ethnic types.

31. Steps toward world disarmament would be a good thing.

32. Everyone is entitled to political and social rights without distinction of any kind, such as race, color, sex, language, religion, political or other opinion, national or social origin, property, birth or other status.

33. Everyone has the right to freedom of thought, conscience and expression.

34. Everyone has the right to freedom of opinion and expression.

35. The will of the people shall be the basis of the authority of government.

36. Everyone, as a member of society, has the right to social security.

37. Everyone has the right to equal pay for equal work.

38. Everyone has the right to form and to join trade unions.

39. Everyone has the right to a standard of living adequate for the health and well-being of himself and of his family, and the right to security in the event of unemployment, sickness, disability, widowhood, old age or other lack of livelihood in circumstances beyond his control.

A FULL-BLOWN LIBERAL WILL mark every one, or very nearly every one, of these thirty-nine sentences, *Agree*. A convinced conservative will mark many or most of them, a reactionary all or nearly all of them, *Disagree*. By giving this test to a variety of groups, I have confirmed experimentally—what is obvious enough from ordinary discourse—that the result is seldom an even balance between *Agree* and *Disagree*. The correlations are especially stable for individuals who are prepared to identify themselves unequivocally as either "liberal" or "reactionary": such self-defined liberals almost never drop below 85 percent of *Agree* answers, or self-defined reactionaries below 85 percent of *Disagree*; a perfect 100 percent is common. Certain types of self-styled conservatives yield almost as high a *Disagree* percentage as the admitted reactionaries. The answers of those who regard themselves as "moderate conservatives" or "traditional conservatives" and of the rather small number of persons who pretend to no general opinions about public matters show considerably more variation. But in general the responses to this list of thirty-nine sentences indicate that a liberal line can be drawn somewhere—even if not exactly along this salient—and that most persons fall fairly definitely (though not in equal numbers) on one side of it or the other.

These sentences were not devised arbitrarily. Many of them are taken directly or adapted from the writings of well-known liberals, the French Declaration of the Rights of Man, or the liberal questionnaires that have been put out in recent years by the American Civil Liberties Union. The last eight are quoted verbatim from the United Nations' "Universal Declaration of Human Rights," adopted in 1948 by the United Nations General Assembly. That entire document is an impressive proof of the global nature of liberalism and its prevalence that I have remarked among opinion-makers.

A number of articulate liberals—university professors, as it happens—who have become acquainted with this set of thirty-nine sentences have objected to it. I am not sure that I have understood just exactly what the objection comes down to; actually, it is rather mild compared to objections that have been made to other portions of this book. No one has stated that these thirty-nine, give or take a couple and disregarding verbal details, are not liberal sentences—that is, sentences that most liberals would agree to. I gather that some critics feel the sentences are not *distinctively* liberal: that not only liberals but *all* normal and reasonable persons nowadays agree with them; that they express no more than the "universal modern consensus," or something of that sort.[3]

Of course it will seem so, if one is interpreting and judging

---

3. In the *New York Times Magazine*, April 19, 1959, Chester Bowles, one of the most forthright of liberal oracles, declared: "To paraphrase a Victorian Tory statesman, we are all liberals now."

them as a liberal, from the perspective of liberalism. It will seem so because the conceptions of a "normal" and "reasonable" person, of "rationality," are then derived from the implicit basic assumptions of liberalism. I must report, however, that though these sentences are undoubtedly agreed to by the presently prevailing trends of opinion in the United States and in most other advanced Western nations—less widely so in some, perhaps, than in the United States and Britain—there nevertheless remains a fair number of persons, doubtless irrational but still not quite the fascist mad dogs of Herblock's or Low's cartoons, who disagree with many, with a majority, even in some cases with all of these thirty-nine self-evident truths.

The evidence seems to show that liberals share a common stock of ideas and that they agree on at least the main lines of practical programs: and that many or most of these liberal ideas and programs are recognizably different from non-liberal ideas and programs. We might thus call liberalism a *Weltanschauung*, a world-view and life-view; the dominant *Weltanschauung* of the United States and much of the West in the past generation. Or we may use a now familiar term and call liberalism, as I have been doing, an "ideology." It might be still more convenient, as I have suggested elsewhere,[4] to borrow a term from medicine, and to call liberalism a "syndrome"; more specifically, an "ideological syndrome." A syndrome is a set of symptoms or elements that are observed to occur together, as a group. Thus doctors find it useful to define certain diseases as syndromes— Parkinson's disease, for example. It is not necessary that every element or symptom should be present in each instance of a given

---

4. In *Congress and the American Tradition* (Chicago: Henry Regnery Co., 1959).

syndrome. It is enough if most of them are there, in a certain relation to each other.

By designating liberalism a syndrome we avoid trying to assign it more systematic order and rigidity than it actually displays. There is the further advantage of leaving open the question of causation. As a pattern or collection of symptoms, a syndrome may be observed to exist and recur, even if we have no idea what causes it.

We can verify by observation that each of the persons whom I earlier listed as typical liberals exhibits all or most of a certain cluster of symptoms. Suitably analyzed, we may call this cluster or set the "liberal syndrome." When we discover it latent in the ideas, words and acts of a hitherto unobserved individual, we may call him a "liberal." In a similar way, we might also discover different clusters—different not in every symptom but in most, and very different in general pattern—that we might name "the conservative syndrome," "the fascist syndrome," "the communist syndrome," and so on.

THREE

Human Nature
and the Good Society

I

AMONG THE ELEMENTS OF AN ideological syndrome there
are feelings, attitudes, habits and values as well as ideas and theories. My direct concern in this and the two following chapters
will be the ideas and theories of the liberal syndrome: the "cognitive" meanings of liberalism that can be stated in the form of
propositions accepted by liberal ideology as *true*. The distinction suggested here between cognitive meanings and emotive or
affective meanings is considerably less clear in content than in
form, and it will be necessary to qualify it later on; but it provides a convenient framework for exposition.

My present objective, then, is to exhibit modern liberalism as
a more or less systematic set of ideas, theories and beliefs about
society.[1] Before proceeding, I pause for a prefatory comment on
liberalism's intellectual ancestry.

---

1. In Chapter VIII, I shall consider the question whether the system of

Modern liberalism, as is well known, is a synthetic, or eclectic, doctrine with a rather elaborate family tree. Without trying to carry its line back to the beginning of thought, we can locate one undoubted forebear in seventeenth-century rationalism. Professor Michael Oakeshott, the successor of Harold Laski in the chair of political science at London University, uses the term "rationalism" as the genus of which liberalism and communism are the most prominent contemporary species. In *Rationalism and Politics* he names both Francis Bacon and René Descartes as "dominating figures" in its early history.[2]

The lines to the eighteenth century are fuller and more direct: to the Enlightenment in general, to Voltaire, to Condorcet[3] and his co-fathers of the idea of Progress, and to Jacobinism. From utilitarianism and the older doctrine that was called "liberalism" in the nineteenth century, as it still is in parts of Europe, modern liberalism has taken some of its theory of democracy, its critical emphasis on freedom of speech and opinion, and certain of its ideas about the self-determination of nations and peoples. Genes from the Utopian tradition—both of the Enlightment's kind of utopianism and of Utopian pre-socialism like that of Saint-Simon, Fourier and Robert Owen—are manifestly part of the heritage.

A somewhat different line intermarried more lately; some of Karl Marx's spiritual offspring, particularly such cousins from the

---

ideas that I shall have by then made explicit "really is" liberalism, whether liberals believe in liberalism. Meanwhile, I note that my endeavor in these three chapters is in no respect to distort, misstate, libel, caricature or refute liberalism considered as a system of ideas, but merely to understand and describe it.

2. Michael Oakeshott, *Rationalism and Politics* (New York: Basic Books, 1962), p. 14.

3. Professor Charles Frankel, *The Case for Modern Man* (New York: Harper & Bros., 1956), p. 7, lists Voltaire, Condorcet and John Stuart Mill as "the great names" attached to the philosophy of history standing behind liberal ideas.

collateral revisionist branch as Eduard Bernstein, Karl Kautsky, Jean Jaurès and the British Fabians; William James, John Dewey and others from the American pragmatist and utilitarian wing; and the most influential economist of the twentieth century, John Maynard Keynes.

Although these make up a large and seemingly mixed lot, the lineage is not so arbitrarily linked as it might at first glance seem. These forebears share certain features of historical posture as well as theoretical doctrine, a fact which, as we shall be able to see more specifically later on, helps solve a paradox in the way modern liberalism functions in practice.

Having named these multiple roots, I might almost seem to be saying that the intellectual source of liberalism is the entire body of post-Renaissance thought. It is natural enough that this should almost be the impression. Our modern liberalism is in truth the contemporary representative, the principal heir, of the main line (or lines) of post-Renaissance thought, the line that has the right to consider itself most distinctively "modern" and most influential in both shaping and being shaped by the post-Renaissance world.

Still, this main line is not the only line, even if the rest consists of poor relations. From its undoubted and acknowledged forebears, liberalism has inherited only a portion of the estates; a part and in some cases a major part of the entireties, liabilities along with assets, has been assigned elsewhere. If the modern liberal can press his claim to the legacies of Descartes, Diderot, Rousseau, Adam Smith, Locke, Bentham, Ricardo, John Stuart Mill, William James and Kautsky by bringing before the court many a confirming page and chapter, a disputant will be able to present a contrary file substantial enough to cast a cloud on at least some of the titles. It can even be argued, and has been, that today's liberals maintain their hold on some of the properties—those tracing, for obvious example, back to John Stuart Mill or John Locke—only by what lawyers would call "adverse possession," backed by their present control of the intellectual records office.

And, granted all these many prominent figures among the ancestors, direct, collateral and adopted, of modern liberalism, not everyone is hung in its gallery even from the post-Renaissance epoch—not to mention those dark centuries before science and democracy, as to which liberalism's family records are on any account somewhat skimpy and blurred.

The entire tradition of Catholic philosophy, especially its primary Aristotelian wing, which after all did live on after Renaissance and Reformation and even Isaac Newton, has little part, or none, in liberalism's lineage. Nor do we find among its ancestors Thomas Hobbes or Thomas Hooker, Blaise Pascal, David Hume, Edmund Burke, John Adams, Alexis de Tocqueville, Henry Maine, Jacob Burckhardt, Fustel de Coulanges or Lord Acton. Niccolò Machiavelli and Michel de Montaigne had only minor flirtations, without issue on the chart. And for the most part, though it has an emotional attraction for some contemporary liberal intellectuals, liberalism has in its blood little of the dark infusion that flows from the nineteenth century's irrational springs: from Soren Kierkegaard (back to Pascal, really, with his heart's reasons of which Reason knows nothing), to Dostoevsky's underground man and Friedrich Nietzsche.

As a way of thinking for moderns, liberalism is out in front, but it is not alone in the field.

II

CLOSING THAT PARENTHESIS, I shall now describe the basic ideas and beliefs that compose the formal structure of the ideological syndrome of modern liberalism.

1. The logical starting point for liberalism, as for most other ideologies, is a belief about the nature of man. On this point as on many of the others it is unwise to try to be too precise in formulation. Liberalism is not an exact and rigid doctrine, in either its psychological and social function or its logical structure. Its beliefs are not like theorems in geometry or Spinoza, *questiones* in scholastic philosophy or theses in Hegel. We must understand them in a looser, more flexible sense, with plenty of modifiers like "on the whole," "more or less" and "by and large." Some of the beliefs of liberalism should be thought of as expressing tendencies or presumptions rather than as attempting to state laws or precise hypotheses. Nevertheless, even if rough or vague, a belief can be meaningful, significantly different from contrasting beliefs, and exceedingly important from a practical standpoint.

That disclaimer recorded, we may assert that liberalism believes man's nature to be not fixed but changing, with an unlimited or at any rate indefinitely large potential for positive (good, favorable, progressive) development. This may be contrasted with the traditional belief, expressed in the theological doctrines of Original Sin and the real existence of the Devil, that human nature had a permanent, unchanging essence, and that man is partly corrupt as well as limited in his potential. "Man, according to liberalism, is born ignorant, not wicked," declares Professor J. Salwyn Schapiro,[4] writing as a liberal on liberalism.

The traditional view of human nature came under indirect attack by Bacon, Descartes and even earlier Renaissance thinkers.

---

4. J. Salwyn Schapiro, *Liberalism: Its Meaning and History* (Princeton: D. Van Nostrand, 1958), p. 12. This small volume is, so far as I know, the only attempt to present modern liberalism in a more or less systematic textbook.

In the eighteenth century, Rousseau, Condorcet, Diderot and other French philosophers of the Enlightenment made a frontal assault. They openly rejected the dogma of Original Sin and its attendant philosophical theory. In their rhetorical enthusiasm, they taught that man is innately good, not bad or corrupt, and held that man's potentialities are unlimited: that man, in other words, is perfectible in the full sense of being capable of achieving perfection.

On this as on many issues, modern liberalism puts matters more cautiously and vaguely. Innately and essentially, human nature is neither pure nor corrupt, neither good nor bad; and is not so much "perfectible" in a full and literal sense as "plastic." There may be *some* limit, short of perfection, to what men might make of themselves and their society; but there is no limit that we can see and define in advance. If a limit exists, it is so distant and so far beyond anything that man has yet accomplished that it has no practical relevance to our plans and programs.

The decisive distinction is probably this: Modern liberalism, contrary to the traditional doctrine, holds that there is nothing intrinsic to the nature of man that makes it impossible for human society to achieve the goals of peace, freedom, justice and well-being that liberalism assumes to be desirable and to define "the good society." Liberalism rejects the essentially tragic view of man's fate found in nearly all pre-Renaissance thought and literature, Christian and non-Christian alike.

There exist individuals whom no one would hesitate to call "liberals" but who do not seem to believe this doctrine concerning human nature that I here attribute to liberalism. Specifically, there are Roman Catholics who regard themselves as liberals and are so regarded, but who as Catholics are committed to the theological dogma of Original Sin. And there are others known as liberals who hold Freudian or similar views in psychology—Max Lerner would seem to be a prominent American example; but it is difficult to reconcile the psychoanalytic account of human nature with a doctrine of man's indefinitely benign plasticity.

These apparent anomalies will be dealt with more thoroughly in Chapter VIII. I here comment on them briefly.

(a) Though it is true that some Catholics and Freudians (or post-Freudians) are to be numbered in the liberal army, there is often a little uneasiness, on both sides, on this score. On a mass scale, Catholics are comparatively recent recruits to liberalism. The older generation of bluestocking liberals are glad to welcome such impressive contingents to the camp of virtue, but they can't help remaining just a bit suspicious; and this is in part because of a feeling that there is something wrong, from a liberal standpoint, with the Catholic theory about human nature and man's fate. This feeling is strong enough to lead some liberals—like Paul Blanshard and his Committee for the Separation of Church and State—to steer altogether clear of Catholics. Nearly all liberals keep their ideological fingers crossed when they observe such a group as the Jesuits beginning to sound like liberals, as the American Jesuits have often done of late in the pages of their principal magazine, *America.* The wisest liberals are not surprised, and reassured in their own faith, when, after saying all the proper things about social reforms and right-wing extremists, *America* suddenly reverts, as it did in 1962, to reactionary prejudice when it has to comment on a Supreme Court decision banning prayer in public schools.

It is noteworthy that Americans for Democratic Action, one of the leading congregations of liberal fundamentalism, was at first most unhappy about the prospect of the nomination of the Catholic John F. Kennedy to the Presidency—even though scores of ADA members were soon to find themselves occupying high posts in the Kennedy administration. Joseph L. Rauh, Jr., an ADA founder and leader, estimated that less than 10 percent of the ADA membership was pro-Kennedy at the start of 1960. In September 1959, a memorandum by Allen Taylor, director of the New York State ADA chapter, recorded: "Religion is the major element in the liberals' doubt about Kennedy."[5]

A Freudian, too, can disturb the liberal waters. Max Lerner is in practice a somewhat maverick ranger in the liberal formation, far less reliable than, say, his columnar teammate, James Wechsler. Occasionally Mr. Lerner gets way out of line with the liberal consensus.

(b) Many individuals professing belief in a religious doctrine of Original Sin, or such theories of human nature as Freud's, give their view a modified or metaphorical interpretation that brings it sufficiently into accord with the requirements of liberal theory and practice—rather as believers in the Bible have been able to reinterpret their understanding of Genesis to reconcile it, psychologically at least, with the theory of evolution. This process is eased by the fact that general beliefs about human nature are not precise anyway; their meaning may be more to express attitudes toward life than to make verifiable assertions.

(c) Nonetheless, there undoubtedly are many cases where a given individual is logically committed by his religion or by

5. Clifton Brock, *Americans for Democratic Action* (Washington: Public Affairs Press, 1962), pp. 177, 185.

psychological or biological theory to one view of human nature and by his liberalism to an incompatible view. Of such cases, we can only note that human beings are like that. They are seldom fully consistent in their beliefs; and are often committed to many a contradiction. To most people this is not particularly troublesome; they are usually not aware of the contradictions, and in any case they don't take logical precision very seriously.

(d) However varied may be the combination of beliefs that it is *psychologically* possible for an individual liberal to hold, it remains true that *liberalism* is logically committed to a doctrine along the lines that I have sketched: viewing human nature as not fixed but plastic and changing; with no pre-set limit to potential development; with no innate obstacle to the realization of a society of peace, freedom, justice and well-being. Unless these things are true of human nature, the liberal doctrine and program for government, education, reform and so on are an absurdity. To this logical necessity, Chapter VIII will return.

2. The liberal ideology is rationalist. Professor Oakeshott, as I have mentioned, classifies liberalism as simply a special case of what may be called in general, "rationalism." Reason, according to rationalism, is not only what distinguishes man in logical definition from other species, as Aristotle stated (though meaning something rather different by "reason"); reason is man's essence, and in a practical sense his chief and ultimately controlling characteristic. Liberalism is confident that reason and rational science, without appeal to revelation, faith, custom or intuition, can both comprehend the world and solve its problems.

The liberal as rationalist is described by Professor Oakeshott: "He stands...for independence of mind on all occasions, for thought free from obligation to any authority save the authority of 'reason.' His circumstances in the modern world have made him contentious: he is the *enemy* of authority, of prejudice, of the merely traditional, customary or habitual. His mental attitude is at once skeptical and optimistic: skeptical, because there is no opinion, no habit, no belief, nothing so firmly rooted or so widely held that he hesitates to question it and to judge it by what he calls his 'reason'; optimistic, because the rationalist never doubts the power of his 'reason' (when properly applied) to determine the worth of a thing, the truth of an opinion or the propriety of an action."[6]

The rationalism enters into the definition of human nature, as Professor Schapiro explains: "In general, liberals have been rationalists [holding] the conviction that man is essentially a rational creature....What is known as rationalism endeavors, by using reason, to subject all matters, religious as well as nonreligious, to critical inquiry. The rationalist looks primarily to science for enlightenment. Reason...is his mentor. Hence, what cannot stand the test of reason is not to be accepted."[7] Professor Sidney Hook has squeezed the entire definition of liberalism into a single unintentionally ironic phrase: "faith in intelligence."

3. Since there is nothing in essential human nature to block achievement of the good society, the obstacles thereto must be, and are, extrinsic or external. The principal obstacles are, specifically, as liberalism sees them, two: ignorance—an accidental

---

6. Oakeshott, *op. cit.*, pp. 1, 2.
7. Schapiro, *op. cit.*, p. 12.

and remediable, not intrinsic and essential, state of man; and bad social institutions.

4. From these doctrines of human plasticity and rationality and of the external, remediable character of the obstacles to the good society, there follows belief in progress: what might be called *historical optimism.*

The idea of progress had its purest expression during the eighteenth-century Enlightenment, but it is present in one form or another, along with one or another degree of historical optimism, throughout the family history of liberalism, from Francis Bacon and René Descartes to Senator Hubert Humphrey. If mankind would employ his method, Bacon promised, it would be able to "extend the power and dominion of the human race itself over the universe"; disdaining "the unfair circumscription of human power, and...a deliberate factitious despair," human life will "be endowed with new discoveries and power."[8] By *his* method, Descartes explained, any man, merely using the reason native to him as a human being, could discover all truths.[9] The Marquis de Condorcet explains his purpose with aristocratic candor: "The aim of the book that I have undertaken to write, and what it will prove, is that man by using reason and facts will attain perfection....Nature has set no limits to the perfection of the human faculties. The perfectibility of mankind is truly indefinite; and the progress of this perfectibility, henceforth to be free of all hindrances, will last as long as the globe on which nature has placed us."[10]

---

8. *Novum Organum*, Book I, Aphorisms 129, 88, 81.

9. *Discourse on Method, passim.*

10. *Esquisse d'un Tableau historique des progrès de l'esprit humain* ("Outline of the Progress of the Human Mind").

As it took charge of the French Revolution, the Jacobin Club announced "the reign of Virtue and Reason" not only over France but soon to spread over the entire globe; and Robespierre actually crowned the Goddess Reason in Notre Dame Cathedral. (The young girl who was the Goddess' fleshly avatar for the occasion subsequently disappointed her worshipers by marrying a rather ordinary fellow and producing several bouncing babies.) Robert Owen proposed a world convention that would "emancipate the human race from ignorance, poverty, division, sin and misery." The British Fabian Society launched itself in 1883 "for the reconstruction of society according to the highest moral principles."

In our own day, Americans for Democratic Action keeps the torch alight. The 1962 Program offers ADA's self-definition as "an organization of liberals, banded together to work for freedom, justice and peace. Liberalism, as we see it, is a demanding faith [and] the goals of liberalism are affirmative: [not only] the fulfillment of the free individual in a just and responsible society [at home but] a world where all people may share the freedom, abundance, and opportunity which lie within the reach of mankind—a world marked by mutual respect, and by peace."

There is a double aspect to this historical optimism. The peaceful, just, free, virtuous, prosperous and so on society is, on the one hand, the desirable goal for mankind. But in addition, the good society is to be the actual outcome of historical development: either inevitably, as Condorcet and many other pre-liberals and liberals have believed and even tried to prove, or scheduled to come about on the condition that human beings behave rationally—that is, accept the liberal ideology, program and leadership.

It is the second, predictive aspect that is the more distinctive attribute of liberalism. There are others who agree with liberals about the specifications of the good society—though not everyone; there are some persons who have favored, some who still do favor, quite different social arrangements, and still others who do not have any goal at all for secular society, either because their goal is not of this world or because they think that a general social goal is silly. But even among those non-liberals who do share the liberal goal, many would look on it not as an attainable target but merely as a somewhat obscure ideal that can sometimes provide rough guidance for social conduct or inspiration for social effort.

That is to say: it is characteristic of liberals—and perhaps of all ideologues—to believe that there are solutions to social problems. Most liberals, and nearly all their intellectual forebears, have believed that there is a general solution to *the* social problem: that "the good society" or a reasonable facsimile thereof can actually be realized in this world. "The twentieth-century liberal, like his eighteenth-century forebears...believes that free men have the intellectual capacity and moral resources to overcome the forces of injustice and tyranny," was the way Hubert Humphrey restated the tradition in 1959.[11]

More sophisticated liberal intellectuals of our day—Arthur Schlesinger, Jr., for example, Sidney Hook or Charles Frankel—usually keep the old-fashioned optimism out of sight when company is present. They drop most of the eighteenth-century metaphysics and concede that progress may not be "automatic" or "inevitable." But in the end, by the back door if not the front,

---

11. "Six Liberals Define Liberalism," *New York Times Magazine*, April 19, 1959, p. 13. It should be recalled that Senator Humphrey was a professor of political science before turning professional politician.

they return to their heritage. "To hold the liberal view of history," Professor Frankel writes as if passing impersonal judgment on the naive beliefs of yesteryear, "meant to believe in 'progress.' It meant to believe that man could better his condition indefinitely by the application of his intelligence to his affairs." But five pages later he is recommitted: "Can we, amidst the collapse of our hopes, still maintain the essential elements of the liberal outlook on history? I think we can."[12]

If they reduce the odds (Professor Frankel quotes them as "a fighting chance") on mankind's realizing *the* good society in general, they continue to believe that there is indeed a solution to every particular social problem, even to the large and difficult problems: the problems—liberals are prone to speak in terms of "problems"[13]—of war, unemployment, poverty, hunger, prejudice, discrimination, crime, disease, racial conflict, automation, the population explosion, urban renewal, recreation, underdeveloped nations, unwed mothers, care of the aged, Latin America, world communism and what not. "The vision behind liberalism," Professor Frankel sums up from this perspective, though why "behind" is somewhat obscure, "is the vision of a world progressively redeemed by human power from its classic ailments of poverty, disease, and ignorance."

"ADA's most fundamental tenet," proclaimed a 1962 Statement issued by Americans for Democratic Action, echoing therein its *philosophes*, many of whom are also members, "is faith in the democratic process. Faith in its capacity to find solutions to the problems that challenge twentieth-century so-

---

12. Frankel, *op. cit.*, pp. 36, 41.

13. Professor Frankel remarks: "To put it starkly, but I think exactly, liberalism invented the idea that there are such things as 'social problems.'" (*Ibid.*, p. 33.)

ciety. *We have faith that* [their italics], with major efforts, we can find solutions to the old but continuing problems of... " and then comes a sample list of the usual problems. ADA is cited here much as a medical textbook seeking to define schizophrenia would refer in the first instance to well-developed clinical cases rather than to the incipient or partial schizoid behavior common to so many of us. As a liberal fundamentalist group, ADA often puts these matters in conscious, explicit and unequivocal terms. But this faith in the existence of solutions to social problems is present right across the entire liberal spectrum, overlapping in fact a large segment of the band that names itself "conservative" but actually shares many of the underlying liberal axioms. Few indeed are the editorial writers, columnists, professors, speakers, elected or appointed officials in the United States[14] who flatly declare of a pending political, economic or social problem that it is not going to be solved, that it is just plain insoluble. Professor Oakeshott comments on this feature of liberalism ("rationalism," in his terminology). The liberal, he writes, "is not devoid of humility; he can imagine a problem which would remain impervious to the onslaught of his own reason. But what he cannot imagine is politics which do not consist in solving problems, or a political problem of which there is no 'rational' solution at all. Such a

---

14. This faith in the solubility of social problems has been so prominent and widespread in the United States, that in the American context it should probably be considered more a national than an ideological trait. In American speeches, reports or articles on political, economic or social problems, a "positive" ending is *de rigueur* in nearly all circles. This is one of the senses in which Professor Louis Hartz and other intellectual historians are almost correct when they state that "the liberal tradition" is the only American tradition. In Europe the conservatives and many religious tendencies have never shared this social optimism.

problem must be counterfeit. And the 'rational' solution of any problem is, in its nature, the perfect solution.... Of course, the Rationalist is not always a perfectionist in general, his mind governed in each occasion by a comprehensive Utopia; but invariably he is a perfectionist in detail."[15]

5. The ignorance and bad social conditions that cause the world's evils and block progress are the legacy of the past; "the product," Professor Schapiro puts it, "of the errors and injustices of the past."[16] There is therefore no reason to favor ideas, institutions or modes of conduct merely because they have been long established, because our ancestors accepted them; their ancient lineage is, if anything, a ground for suspicion. We should, rather, be ready to undertake prompt, and even drastic and extensive, innovations, if these recommend themselves from a rational and utilitarian standpoint. Thus liberalism is *anti-traditional*.

I rather think that the attitude toward tradition furnishes the most accurate single shibboleth for distinguishing liberals from conservatives; and still more broadly, the Left from the Right, since with respect to change the revolutionary and the reactionary are merely pushing the respective attitudes of liberal and conservative toward their limits. In the *New York Times Magazine* article on the definition of "liberalism," to which I have already referred, Senator Humphrey particularly insists on "change" as the key: "It is this emphasis on changes of chosen ends and means which most sharply distinguishes the liberal from a conservative in a democratic community.

---

15. Oakeshott, *op. cit.*, p. 5.
16. Schapiro, *op. cit.*, p. 12.

The dictionary defines a liberal as 'favorable to change and reform tending in the direction of democracy.'... In the political
lexicon of 1959, liberals recognize change as the inescapable
law of society, and action in response to change as the first
duty of politics."

We may put the question this way: does the fact that a particular idea, institution or mode of conduct has been established
for some while create a presumption in favor of continuing it?
To this question a conservative will answer with a definite *Yes*;
and a liberal, with *No*, or "very little." This does not mean
that a conservative never, and a liberal always, wants to change
what is. It is the revolutionary nihilist, not the liberal, who
thinks everything to be wrong; and the reactionary, not the
conservative, who wants nothing altered (unless, perhaps, in
order to return to the past). For the conservative there might be
some new circumstance cogent enough to call for a change in
the prevailing ways, in spite of his presumption in their favor;
and the liberal is on occasion content to let well enough alone.
But the difference in presumption, bias, trend, remains.

The innovations favored by the liberal he usually calls "reforms," and liberals may be described in general as "reform-
ists." "Belief in progress," writes Professor Schapiro, "has inspired liberals to become the ardent advocates of reforms of all
kinds in order to create the good society of the future. Reform
has been the passion of liberalism."[17] In situations where both
conservatives and liberals agree that reforms are in order, the
conservative will want the reforming to be less extensive and
more gradual than what the liberal will believe to be necessary,
desirable and possible. This difference is plainly illustrated by

---

17. Schapiro, *op. cit.*, p. 13.

the present "racial problem" in the United States. Nearly all conservatives agree with all liberals that there ought to be reforms in existing race relations. But the conservatives, as compared to the liberals, wish the reform program to be more piecemeal, involving at any given stage less sharp a break with existing conditions. In the "deliberate speed" that the Supreme Court set as the proper pace for changes, conservatives would stress the "deliberate," and liberals the "speed."

Let us consider another example more fully. In the American Congress the chairmen of standing committees are named from the majority party on the basis of seniority. Although some rational arguments can be offered in favor of this practice, they are on the whole less convincing—judged strictly from an abstract, purely rational point of view—than the many arguments that can be and often have been brought against it. It is a practice, however, of ancient lineage, which, without being formally debated or much thought about, became fixed very early in the history of the Congress; fixed also—though this is less seldom remarked—in the practice of all other legislative bodies (state and municipal) in the United States; fixed as a rule, in truth, in most legislative bodies at all times and places, once they have been established for a number of years.

To the conservative mind this venerable habit or custom, appearing or reappearing in so many times and conditions, seems to wield some legitimate authority. Not deliberate reasoning, granted, but long practical experience seems to have led men to adopt or to fall into these seniority rules and other procedures of the same sort. This might seem to suggest that from the practical experience itself men gradually learn certain things about conducting assemblies and making laws that cannot be derived from principles and reason alone, or from books; much as practical experience, habit, apprenticeship and direct acquaintance seem to be necessary to the proficient practice as well as the genuine understanding of painting, carpentry, music and indeed all the arts and crafts—maybe, even for adequate understanding of philosophy and the sciences themselves.

Nevertheless, most liberals in and out of Congress do not feel in this matter of committee chairmanships, which is a very critical point in the American governmental system, that such considerations of experience, habit, custom and tradition have any appreciable weight as against the clear-cut arguments derived from democratic theory and reformist goals; and the liberals are certainly correct in holding that seniority and similar rules in legislative assemblies are logically counter to democratic theory, and in practice are brakes to the rapid achievement of major social reforms.

Liberals, moreover, when seized with the "passion" for reform to which Professor Schapiro readily confesses, do not reflect unduly on the fact that no social innovation takes place in a vacuum. When we alter item A, especially if it is changed deliberately and abruptly instead of by the slow molding of time, we will find items B and C also changed, and to some degree the entire social situation, sometimes in most unexpected ways. We may be successful in achieving our sought-for reform; but there will be other, unintended and perhaps undesired changes arriving along with it; and there will also and inevitably be something lost—at the minimum, what the reform has replaced; so that on net the loss may more than counterbalance the gain on the scale of Progress.

In the case we have been considering and in general, this possibility does not greatly worry the liberal in advance because he will have reached his decision about the desirability of the reform by derivation from his ideology—which comprises a ready-made set of desirable goals—and not from slow, painstaking and rather pedestrian attention to the actual way in which assemblies, or whatever it may be, function. Thus in every session of Congress in these recent decades since liberalism has become a pervasive influence there are proposals to abolish the seniority and allied non-democratic rules. On this matter it is revealing to note that in spite of the generally prevailing liberal climate of opinion in the United States, the liberal innovations have made slow headway in Congress: a fact that confirms the liberal judgment and condemnation of Congress as the most conservative of our national political institutions.

The liberal attitude toward tradition and change can be illustrated from every sphere of social life, and toward a thousand issues ranging from divorce to Peace Corps, from patriotism to the school curriculum. Bertrand Russell, one of the early if somewhat eccentric prophets of twentieth-century liberalism, expresses it without qualification in his book *Why Men Fight*. The task of education, he insists, should be not to uphold but to destroy "contentment with the status quo....It should be inspired, not by a regretful hankering after the extinct beauties of Greece and the Renaissance, but by a shining vision of the society that is to be, of the triumphs that thought [or reason, as we have been using the term] will achieve in the time to come."[18] John Stuart Mill was no less categorical in his most influential essay, "On Liberty": "The despotism of custom is everywhere the standing hindrance to human advancement, being in unceasing antagonism to that disposition to aim at something

---

18. Quoted from *Selected Papers of Bertrand Russell* (New York: The Modern Library, 1927), pp. 99, 110.

better than customary, which is called, according to circum-stances, the spirit of liberty, or that of progress or improve-ment.... The progressive principle, however, in either shape, whether as the love of liberty or of improvement, is antagonistic to the sway of Custom, involving at least emancipation from that yoke; and the contest between the two constitutes the chief interest of the history of mankind."[19]

19. John Stuart Mill, "On Liberty." Quoted from Bantam Books edition of *Essential Works of John Stuart Mill*, edited and with an Introduction by Max Lerner (New York, 1961), p. 318.

FOUR

The Universal Dialogue

I

INSIDE THE LIBERAL SYSTEM OF IDEAS, we have so far found, human nature is changing and plastic, with an indefinitely large potential for progressive development. Through reason, freed from superstition, authority, custom and tradition, human beings can discover the truth and the road toward the betterment of society. There is nothing inherent in human nature that prevents the attainment of peace, freedom, justice and well-being—of, that is, the good society. The obstacles are ignorance and faulty social institutions. Because both these obstacles are extrinsic and remediable, historical optimism is justified. Social problems can be solved; the good society can be achieved, or at any rate approximated.

Let us proceed to the liberal beliefs that explain the means and the rules by which the progress that is possible will be brought about in practice.

6. In order to get rid of the ignorance that is one of the two factors blocking progress toward the good society, what is needed,

and the only thing needed, is universal, rationally grounded education. It was Maximilien de Robespierre, leader of the Jacobin Club, who—in the midst of the Terror, as it happened—put forward the first law, modeled on a project of Condorcet's, instituting a system of free (that is, state-financed), universal education. This has been an inviolate article of the liberal creed ever since; and obviously must be, for it follows with syllogistic simplicity from the other liberal principles.

We should stop to note that there is implicit here a particular view of education that is not the only view. By liberal principles strictly applied, the specific function of education is to overcome ignorance; and ignorance is overcome by, and only by, acquiring rational, scientific knowledge. All the myriad beliefs within the range that liberalism regards as non-rational or irrational, as the debris of superstition, prejudice, intuition, habit and custom, would be admitted to the curriculum only as miscellaneous data to be studied objectively by psychology, history, anthropology and the social sciences; and so, too, religion, or rather, religions. As Lord Russell and John Stuart Mill so unconditionally assert in the quotations given at the end of the last chapter, the purpose of genuine education as understood by liberalism is, precisely, to liberate the mind from the crippling hold of custom and all non-rational belief.

For liberalism, the direct purpose of education cannot be to produce a "good citizen," to lead toward holiness or salvation, to inculcate a nation's, a creed's or a race's traditions, habits and ceremonies, or anything of that sort. Nor is there any need that it should be, for the logic of liberalism assures us that, given the right sort of education—that is, rational education—the pupil, in whose nature there is no innate and permanent defect or corruption, will necessarily become the good citizen; and, with the right sort of education universalized, the good citizens together will produce the good society.

The child, for liberalism, approaches the altar of education—for the school is, in truth, liberalism's church—in all his spiritual nakedness as a purely rational, or embryonically rational, being, shorn of color, creed, race, family and nationality: the Universal Student before the universal teacher, Reason. This is the conception, gradually crystallized out of the logic of liberalism, that makes intelligible the liberal position on the multitudinous educational issues that are presently of so much public concern in the United States, and on the typical educational programs that are put forward for the new and underdeveloped nations.

7. In order to get rid of the bad institutions that constitute the second of the two obstacles to progress, what is needed, along with education, is democratic reform, political, economic and social. Properly educated, and functioning within a framework of democratic institutions, human beings will understand their true interests—which are peace, freedom, justice, cooperation and material well-being—and will be able to achieve them.

Bertrand Russell summed up this encouraging outlook in another of his essays, called "The World As It Could Be Made," originally published as part of a book entitled *Proposed Roads to Freedom*—the two titles are themselves unmistakable symptoms from the liberal syndrome. Men, he wrote, are beset by three types of evil: from physical nature (death, pain, tough soil); from character (chiefly ignorance); from power. "The main methods of combating these evils are"—and I now quote his words directly—"for physical evils, science; for evils of character [that is, for ignorance], education...; for evils of power, the reform of the political and economic organization of society."

But I want to stress especially the words of a spokesman still more significant for the liberalism of present-day America. Robert Maynard Hutchins is intelligent, learned and eloquent in his own person. Though he has been a liberal all his public life, his liberalism is not excessively doctrinaire and sectarian, except perhaps on the matter of free speech. In his ideas about the content of education Mr. Hutchins has deviated from liberal orthodoxy: in particular when, on revising a university curriculum, he treated pre-Renaissance philosophy as not merely a historical artifact but part of rational knowledge, and therefore part of what would help overcome ignorance.

Mr. Hutchins has reflected carefully on the meaning of the doctrines he believes, not just picked them off the ideological shelf. Our society has marked his eminence by the high posts, many distinctions and abundant publicity it has bestowed on him, and the large sums of money it has placed at his disposal. After his years as head of the Rockefeller-endowed University of Chicago, he directed the Ford-endowed Fund for the Republic, and has more lately shifted his primary attention to an offshoot of the Fund that has become something of a magnet for liberal fundamentalists, the Center for the Study of Democratic Institutions—tax exempt, of course, like the parent Fund, *its* parent, the Ford Foundation, and the University. The Center, both Funds and the University of Chicago are all among our active and influential opinion-forming institutions. The voice of Mr. Hutchins is not that of a prophet crying in the wilderness; it is more nearly that of a herald proclaiming the sovereign's will.

On January 21, 1959, Mr. Hutchins received, with due ceremony, the Sidney Hillman Award for Meritorious Public Service. As so often, the very name is symptomatic—honoring the career of a member of a minority that is the classic target of discrimination, who achieved fame first by building one of the major organizations of the advancing labor movement and then by becoming integrated into the power structure of the Rooseveltian New Deal, the regime that marked the rise of the liberal ideology to national predominance. On the occasion of this award, Mr. Hutchins delivered an address that is a condensation of much of the theoretical side of the liberal ideology. He called it, "Is Democracy Possible?"—meaning by "democracy" what we are calling "liberalism."

Let me quote from that address a few sentences that bear on the seven symptoms that I have so far listed, very directly on the last two. I shall return to it later on.

"The democratic [i.e., liberal] faith is faith in man, faith in every man, faith that men, if they are well enough educated and well enough informed, can solve the problems raised by their own aggregation." Mr. Hutchins then added a comment admitting with surprising candor that liberalism is not a scientific theory nor a cognitive assertion of any kind, and is immune to fact, observation or experience: "One advantage of this faith is that it is practically shock-proof."

He went on: "Industrialization can sweep the world. Nationalism and technology can threaten the extinction of the human race. Population can break out all over. Man can take off from this planet as his ancestors took off from the primordial ooze and try to make other planets to shoot from. Education can be trivialized beyond belief. The media of communication can be turned into media of entertainment. The [democratic] dialogue [made possible by the right of free speech] can almost stop because people have nothing to say, or, if they have something to say, no place to say it. And still it is possible to believe that if democracy and the dialogue can continue, if they can be expanded, freedom, justice, equality, and peace will ultimately be achieved."

I cannot forbear taking a moment to taste the irony of this moving declaration of faith. The doctrine that begins by proclaiming its emancipation from all prejudice, superstition and dogma, from all beliefs sanctioned by time, habit and tradition, that opens up *every* question to free inquiry by every questing mind, that declares its total readiness to follow reason, science and truth wherever they may beckon: it is *this* doctrine that, we discover at last, is so fixed an absolute that no possible happening now or in any conceivable future could trouble its eternal certainty by so much as a surface tremor!

Still, Mr. Hutchins is not willing merely to anchor his ship to so secure a rock, and rest his oars. Over and over again, he tells us how much educating there is still to be done.

"If our hopes of democracy are to be realized, every citizen of this country"—every one, note—"is going to have to be educated to the limit of his capacity." (It is tiresome to harp on details of language, but surely there must be some significance in the fact that ideologues use words so imprecisely. Anybody in his right mind knows after an instant's reflection that *every* citizen of this country is *not* going to be "educated to the limit of his capacity," ever; that, in fact, very few citizens, in the best of cases, will ever be educated to that limit, which, according to the psychologists, is rather formidable. Now it follows from the logic of Mr. Hutchins' assertion that if even one single citizen is not educated to the limit of his capacity, then our hopes for democracy are not going to be realized. The only possible conclusion is that these must be pretty silly hopes.) And toward the end of his address, Mr. Hutchins is drawn irresistibly to the problem of tradition, which we have found to be so crit-

66

ical. Today, he finds, the democratic dialogue, education and therefore progress, are "impeded by obsolescent practices and institutions from the long ballot to the Presidential primary, from the electoral college to the organization of cities, counties and states.... The political anatomy is full of vermiform appendices, many of them, like Arkansas [Mr. Hutchins was speaking after the Little Rock episode], inflamed.... One thing is certain, and that is that if our hopes of democracy are to be realized, the next generation is in for a job of institutional remodeling the like of which has not been seen since the Founding Fathers."

8. According to the doctrine we have reviewed, what liberalism notices as the evils of society—crime, delinquency, war, hunger, unemployment, communism (if this is judged an evil), urban blight, etc.—are the results of ignorance and faulty social institutions or arrangements. The effective method for getting rid of the evils is therefore to eliminate the ignorance (by education) and to reform the institutions.

It follows as a corollary that we have no rational basis for "blaming" criminals for their crimes, teen-agers for their muggings and rumbles, soldiers for wars, the poor of India or Egypt for their hunger, the non-working for their joblessness, the city dwellers for the decay of their city, or the Communist Party for communism. They cannot be blamed for being ignorant, for not having been given a proper education; nor for the faulty institutions into which they were born. Since no one is to blame—except society, with her shady past— there is no ground for a retributive theory of punishment, for "vengeance," as liberals call it. Our aim in the treatment of delinquents, criminals, soldiers and communists must be to educate, or re-educate, them into good, that is liberal, citizens; and meanwhile to improve the bad conditions—slums, poverty, lack of schoolrooms, lack of democracy—that produced them.

These conceptions lead quite naturally to what we may describe as a "permissive" attitude toward erring members of the community—particularly when they belong to racial, religious, caste or economic groups less privileged than the general average (i.e., suffering more, as liberalism would explain it, from the faulty arrangements)—and to a "social service" mentality. Eleanor Roosevelt was a supreme example of both this attitude and this mentality. Time and again her newspaper column offered the kindest of sociological explanations for the derelictions of some poor devil—rather, some poor victim—who had run afoul of a parole officer, congressional committee, Southern sheriff or Northern court. And in her descriptive prose, the entire globe was spread out like a gigantic slum eagerly awaiting the visit of an international legion of case workers: a vision which, as things have been developing in recent years, proves to have been by no means an idle fancy.

These same ideas underly the liberal approach to the Cold War, underdeveloped countries, the world communist enterprise and international relations more generally, as we shall consider in another context later on. Communism, dictatorship, Mau Mau and other political badnesses are explained as the results of hunger and poverty. Foreign aid plus democratic reforms (the equation was made explicit in the program for the Alliance for Progress) will bring a rise in the standard of living which will in turn do away with the tendencies toward tyranny, aggression and war. In fact, a higher standard of living is going to transform the Soviet Union itself into a satisfied and peaceful country, as Professor Walt Whitman Rostow, who was President Kennedy's selection to head the State Department's Policy Planning staff, has proved by an elaborate liberal sorites in his very influential book, *Stages of Growth*. The yearly programs of Americans for Democratic Action are at pains to protest that our real "enemies" are not wicked people or nations or creeds, and certainly not the Soviet Union or communism, but hunger and racial discrimination; the real war is the "war against want."[1]

It must be confessed, however, that the point of view of liberalism in this respect is not wholly consistent. If ignorance and bad social arrangements explain crime, war, hunger, racial riots, urban blight and so on, and thereby relieve the individual mugger, soldier, jobless adult, berserk Negro and unwed mother of direct responsibility for their behavior and its consequences, then the well-to-do citizen who gets mugged, the generals, landlords, merchants, bankers and even white segregationists ought also, by the same logic, to be relieved of their burden of personal guilt: they too, in their own manner, are merely unfortunate products of the bad conditions into which they were born and the inadequate education they received. But liberal rhetoric has a difficult time adjusting to this even balance, and does tend to scold bankers, professional soldiers, corporation heads, oil millionaires, Southern governors, Nazis and British diplomats rather more sternly than Negro delinquents, strikers who beat up violators of a picket line, anti-H-bomb rioters, communists,

---

1. This echo of one of Franklin Roosevelt's Four Freedoms—in one form or another, of course, a liberal commonplace—is the message of a book published by Americans for Democratic Action in 1951 and thereafter heavily promoted: *The Only War We Seek*, by Arthur Goodfriend, with an Introduction by Chester Bowles. This book provided in a popular form a good deal of the ideological underpinning for foreign aid, Point 4, and even such subsequent programs as the Peace Corps.

or natives of a new nation smashing the windows of a British or American consulate. The divergence here is a rather crucial one, to which I shall return at greater length.

9. How is society to carry on the educational process that is to overcome ignorance and thereby assure progress, peace, justice and well-being? Education must be, in Mr. Hutchins' words, a "universal dialogue," and in a double sense. Not only must everyone be educated. There must also be a universal and absolute freedom of opinion in the schoolroom above a certain academic level, and considerable freedom at all levels; there must be "academic freedom," as we usually refer to it. The claims of reason will permit nothing less; and nothing else than reason has any claim in the premises. Every teacher, or at any rate every university teacher—and in the last analysis, every pupil—has the right to put forward *his* point of view, which after all may be the true one, however unpopular at the moment; in the "free forum of ideas" reason will freely pick and choose. Any interference with academic freedom is reactionary, and a brake on the continuous process of dispelling the ignorance that blocks progress.

In the United States this principle is the special province of the American Association of University Professors, the trade association charged not only with refining the theoretical content of academic freedom but with applying it to the disputes that from time to time arise in the colleges, as well as to such public matters as McCarthyism, the Fifth Amendment, loyalty oaths and censorship.

10. But politics, as defined by the categories of liberalism, is simply education generalized: a school in which all voters and indeed all of mankind are the pupils. Politics too must be thought of as a universal dialogue. Academic freedom in the schools is

merely a special application of the more general principles of freedom of opinion and free speech in society at large. The ideal of "the faith in which I was brought up," Mr. Hutchins reports in the address from which I have quoted, "was the civilization of the dialogue, where everybody talked with everybody else about everything, where everybody was content to abide by the decision of the majority as long as the dialogue could continue....In this view the great crime is to prevent other people from speaking up, or to say that there are certain things you won't talk about, or certain people you won't talk to, either at home or abroad."

This is the conception of absolute, or nearly absolute,[2] free speech, presaged though not quite driven to totality by John Stuart Mill, that is upheld in current theory by writers like Zechariah Chafee and Henry S. Commager, and almost all the sharper critics of the House Committee on Un-American Activities—that is to say, among others, most university professors. It is defended in practice by the American Civil Liberties Union and, in recent years, by the Supreme Court—in particular by the Chief Justice and Justices Hugo Black and William O. Douglas. Justice Black, indeed, extended the doctrine to entirely new ground as late as 1962 when, in a speech widely reported in the press, he stated his personal wish for the abolition of all legal restraints not only on any sort of political, religious, moral and sexual utterance, which is a routine position, but on slander, libel and misrepresentation.

"Of all civil liberties," Professor Schapiro notes in a comparative estimate that perhaps holds more generally for his own

---

2. Some qualification is usually made, even by the most intransigent free speech defenders, in terms of the "clear and present danger" doctrine. Nearly everyone, though not quite everyone, will agree with the Supreme Court that one may not shout "Fire!" falsely, in a crowded theater.

older than for the newer, liberal generation, "the most prized has been liberty of thought and expression. Liberals came to the deep conviction that all opinions, even erroneous ones, should have freedom of expression."[3] The point could not be made much more strongly than by John Stuart Mill's famous dictum: "If all mankind minus one, were of one opinion, mankind would be no more justified in silencing that one person, than he, if he had the power, would be justified in silencing mankind."[4]

11. If we know the truth, we might reasonably ask, why waste society's time, space and money giving an equal forum, under the free speech rule, to error? The only consistent answer is: we cannot be certain that we know the truth—if, indeed, there is any such thing as objective truth. Liberalism is logically committed to the doctrine that philosophers know under the forbidding title of "epistemological relativism." This comes out clearly both in theoretical discussion by philosophers of liberalism and in liberal practice.

We confront here a principle that would seem strangely paradoxical if it had not become so familiar in the thought and writings of our time. Liberalism is committed to the truth and to the belief that truth is what is discovered by reason and the sciences; and committed against the falsehoods and errors that are handed down by superstition, prejudice, custom and authority. But every man, according to liberalism, is entitled to his

---

3. J. Salwyn Schapiro, *Liberalism: Its Meaning and History* (Princeton: D. Van Nostrand, 1958), p. 11.

4. John Stuart Mill, "On Liberty." Quoted from Bantam Books edition of *Essential Works of John Stuart Mill,* edited and with an Introduction by Max Lerner (New York, 1961), p. 269. A perfect example of a purely ideological statement that makes no sense at all in relation to the real world.

own opinion, and has the right to express it (and to advocate its acceptance). In motivating the theory and practice of free speech, liberalism must either abandon its belief in the superior social utility of truth, or maintain that we cannot be sure we know the truth. The first alternative—which would imply that error is sometimes more useful for society than the truth—is by no means self-evidently false, but is ruled out, or rather not even considered seriously, by liberalism. Therefore liberalism must accept the second alternative.

We thus face the following situation. Truth is our goal; but objective truth, if it exists at all, is unattainable; we cannot be sure even whether we are getting closer to it, because that estimate could not be made without an objective standard against which to measure the gap. Thus the goal we have postulated becomes meaningless, evaporates. Our original commitment to truth undergoes a subtle transformation, and becomes a commitment to the rational and scientific process itself: to—in John Dewey's terminology—the "method of inquiry."

But this process or method of inquiry is nothing other than the universal dialogue made possible by universal education and universal suffrage under the rules of freedom of opinion, speech, press and assembly. Throughout his long life, the commitment to the method of inquiry that is at once "the scientific method" and "the democratic method" was perhaps the major theme of Dewey's teaching. Let us add that truth thus becomes in practice relative to the method of inquiry. For all practical purposes, truth in any specific scientific field is simply the present consensus of scientific opinion within that same field; and political and social truth is what is voted by a democratic majority.

It is not clear in advance how wide the field of political and social truth should be understood to be; presumably that question too can be answered only by the democratic method, so that the field is as wide as the democratic majority chooses to make it. The plainest summary of the net conclusion of the liberal doctrine of truth is that given in Justice Oliver Wendell Holmes' aphorism. He conjoins the two key propositions, though I place them here in a sequence the reverse of the original: 1) "truth is the only ground upon which [men's] wishes safely can be carried out"; 2) "the best test of truth is the power of thought to get itself accepted in the competition of the market."

Another of the prominent American philosophers of liberalism, Professor T.V. Smith of the University of Chicago—whose influence has been spread much beyond the academies by virtue of his mellifluous prose style and his popularity as an after-dinner speaker—has made the idea of relativity the core of his essay on "Philosophy and Democracy." "This inability finally to distinguish [truth from falsity, good from evil, beauty from ugliness] is the propaedeutic for promotion from animal impetuosity to civilized forbearance. It marks the firmest foundation"—again the paradox is near the surface—"for the tolerance which is characteristic of democracy alone."

Professor Smith very rightly cites Justice Holmes as a major source of the influence of this doctrine of relativism among us. "As Holmes put it, we lack a knowledge of the 'truth' of 'truth.'" Professor Smith attacks all of the classical theories of objective truth, and declares: "No one of these theories can adequately test itself, much less anything else." The idea of objective truth is only the rationalization of private, subjective "feelings of certitude...; and certitude is not enough. It more easily marks the beginning of coercion than the end of demonstration.... The only insurance the modern world has against the recurrence of the age-old debacle of persecution for opinion is the presence in

it of a sufficient number of men of such character as will molli-
fy assertions of truth with the restraints of tolerance."

Since final truth cannot be known, we must keep the dialogue eternally going, and, where action is required, be "content"—Mr. Hutchins echoes Justice Holmes—"to abide by the
decision of the majority."

FIVE

Equality and Welfare

I

OVERCOMING IGNORANCE THROUGH the universal dialogue, and reforming the faulty institutions inherited from the past, men will be in a position to move toward peace, freedom, justice and well-being. Let us now see how liberalism imagines the structure of the good society within which those values will be realized.

12. It is implicit in the principles already examined that liberalism holds a democratic theory of government. "The great contribution of Rousseau to the making of the liberal state," writes Professor Schapiro, and he is probably correct to single out Rousseau from the many others who were more or less simultaneously thinking toward similar conclusions, "was the doctrine of popular sovereignty as expressed in universal suffrage."[1] Let us add that the strict liberal rule for the exercise of the suffrage must be: one man, one vote—"man" in the generic sense, of

---

1. J. Salwyn Schapiro, *Liberalism: Its Meaning and History* (Princeton: D. Van Nostrand, 1958), p. 25.

course, male or female. All other suggested grounds for sovereignty are prejudices or superstitions inherited from the obsolescent past: divine right, patrician blood, race, property, priesthood, wisdom. Government is legitimately based on, and only on, the general will, the will of the people (and of all the people, or at any rate all adults other than the insane and criminal), expressed through the arithmetic of the electoral process.

This democratic theory of sovereignty, like most of the other symptoms I am describing, is included in the Universal Declaration of Human Rights as proclaimed by the General Assembly of the United Nations. Article 21, paragraph (3) reads: "The will of the people shall be the basis of the authority of government; this will shall be expressed in periodic and genuine elections which shall be by universal and equal suffrage and shall be held by secret vote or by equivalent free voting procedures." (This clause along with the rest of the Universal Declaration, which reads almost like a clinical summary of the liberal syndrome, won for its adoption in 1948 the affirmative votes of the representatives of Juan Perón, King Saud, the Imam of Yemen, the Emperor of Ethiopia, the Shah of Persia and Fulgencio Batista.)

Liberalism tends toward a plebiscitary interpretation of democracy. Government ought to reflect the will of the democratic majority as immediately, sensitively and accurately as possible. Liberals thus distrust those political institutions and processes that mediate, deflect, distort or otherwise interfere with the direct expression of the popular will: such as, for example, the electoral college method of electing chief magistrates; the non-proportional basis for electing the United States Senate and other "upper chambers"; and, as we have noted, the non-democratic procedural rules that characterize American and many other legislative assemblies.

Liberal fundamentalists usually favor the election of the head of government by a "direct consultation" of the electorate as a whole; that is, by a plebiscite or something approximating a plebiscite. Their distrust of intermediate political institutions also leads modern liberals—in this respect very different from their namesakes of a century ago—to favor centralization of governmental power. Decentralization, such as persists in the American federal structure in spite of a century's erosion, and the whole tradition of States' Rights—whether in the United States, the Congo, India or Kenya—become in practice, as the liberal sees it, instruments of reactionary minorities that break up and often thwart the democratic will of the majority.

13. From the theoretical point of view there is no reason why democratic centralization should stop with the single nation. Modern liberal doctrine tends naturally toward internationalist conceptions and the ideal of a democratic world order based through one mode or another on the majority will of all mankind. The logic of liberal principle unites with the normal bias of liberal temperament to incline modern liberals favorably toward ideas, movements and organizations that can be thought of as steps toward world cooperation, federalism, unification and government: world courts, world leagues of nations; worldwide cultural exchanges; world congresses and parliaments; world conventions and committees. To the liberal it has become self-evident that "national sovereignty is an outworn concept" that must be drastically modified if not altogether abandoned.

Experience since the Second World War should have made it clear that a liberal foreign policy must assume that liberalism and democracy can only flourish or indeed survive

79

in a suitable environment, that such an environment under present conditions can be no less extensive than the entire world, and that, therefore, liberal foreign policy must look at the world as a whole. Any form of isolationism and regionalism is obsolete. The nation that would save itself must subordinate its immediate interests to the maintenance of a peaceful, stable, and just world. That is the assumption that the United States and other nations made in establishing the United Nations.[2]

In this passage, Professor Wright's initial appeal to "experience since the Second World War" is altogether unnecessary—and certainly incapable of proving the extreme and unqualified assertions that follow. What makes them persuasive to Professor Wright, and to liberal readers, has nothing to do with experience; it is, rather, their intellectual and emotional cohesion with the corpus of the liberal ideology.

The Platform of Americans for Democratic Action has declared year after year that "support of the principles of the United Nations"—no reference is made to the national interests of the United States—"is [i.e., ought to be from the standpoint of liberalism] the cornerstone of our foreign policy." In its official Program, ADA describes itself as "dedicated to the achievement of freedom and economic security for all people everywhere," not just for fellow nationals. ADA's founding Charter (1947) declared unequivocally: "The establishment of a world government with powers adequate to prevent war must be an objective

---

2. "Policies for Strengthening the United Nations," by Quincy Wright, included in *The Liberal Papers*, edited by James Roosevelt (Garden City: Anchor Books, Doubleday & Co., 1962), p. 313.

of the United States foreign policy to be achieved at the earliest possible date."[3] These forthright statements push things further than many liberals are prepared to do at present; but in making them, ADA has been loyal to the spirit and logic of liberalism.

Liberalism's internationalist tendency has been traced at this point to its doctrine of democratic sovereignty, which in turn is linked to the beliefs about human nature, social reform and the universal dialogue. As we shall see, an internationalist attitude is also promoted, in fact required, by the liberal concepts of equality.

14. In liberalism's relativist theory of truth and democratic political doctrine, as in its account of human nature, there is no room for qualitative distinctions among men. In their essential attributes of plasticity and rationality, which are the attributes relevant to political and social affairs, men do not differ qualitatively; their differences are only quantitative; each man counts for one and one only. The right man to govern and the right policy to pursue—like, in the last analysis, the good and the true and even the beautiful—are known by counting the votes, each man counting for one, in the ballot box. This man, that man, this or that woman are all alike Common Men, all are Humanity or Mankind. Former Vice President Henry Wallace was correctly expressing the liberal aspiration in naming ours the Century of the Common Man.

Thus liberalism tends to be egalitarian. Professor Oakeshott brings this out along a somewhat different perspective:

---

3. It should perhaps be recalled that the founding ADA members included Chester Bowles, Hubert Humphrey, James Loeb, Jr., Arthur M. Schlesinger, Jr., Franklin D. Roosevelt, Jr., Wilson W. Wyatt and others prominent in the Kennedy-Johnson administration.

From this politics of perfection springs the politics of uniformity; a scheme which does not recognize circumstance can have no place for variety. "There must in the nature of things be one best form of government which all intellects, sufficiently roused from the slumber of savage ignorance, will be irresistibly incited to approve," writes Godwin. This intrepid Rationalist states in general what a more modest believer might prefer to assert only in detail; but the principle holds—there may not be one universal remedy for all political ills, but the remedy for any particular ill is as universal in its application as it is rational in its conception. If the rational solution for one of the problems of a society [segregation in school classrooms, let us cite as an example] has been determined, to permit any relevant part of the society to escape from the solution is, *ex hypothesi*, to countenance irrationality.[4]

The egalitarianism that lurks in the ideology found its first practical expression in the political field, with the liberal program for universal and equal suffrage unrestricted by property, sex, race, color, religion or ancestry. It then spread to the economic and social fields, where the egalitarianism takes the practical form of progressive income and inheritance taxes (or direct expropriation when impatience spurs a more rapid approach to the ideal); subsidies under one or another formula to the poorer strata of the population; and movements for universal equality in arrangements for education, residence, jobs, recreation and transportation ("employment, housing, education, transportation, suffrage, and all other aspects of public and community life," is the inclusive coverage given by the ADA Program).

---

4. Michael Oakeshott, *Rationalism and Politics* (New York: Basic Books, 1962), pp. 5-6.

Liberals differ among themselves in the totality of their commitment to egalitarianism. For most liberals, the egalitarian
tendency is not extended to every conceivable field, and it is
carried further in some fields than in others. Just where limits
are to be drawn is a problem rather for intuition, even if unac-
knowledged, than for logic; since from a purely logical point
of view there seems to be no particular reason to draw the line
short of the extremest limit. In economic matters, for example,
all liberals favor taxation, subsidy, welfare and relief policies
that have the effect, or are intended to have the effect, of cut-
ting down the differential between wealthy and poor: that is,
have an egalitarian effect, so far as they go. But few liberals
insist on an absolute even-Stephen quantitative sharing of the
wealth—though the slogan proves attractive to the liberal rank
and file, not surprisingly, since it expresses basic liberal ideology
and impulse.

It is observable that liberals aim sharper polemics against capital
than against income. Capital, especially in the form of real property but in some degree all large accumulations of capital, usually
is bound up with the past, with the family, even with local do-
micile and tradition. Thus capital, from the standpoint of liberal principles, seems more irrational and backward-looking than
income, which may be thought to be the product of intellectual
talents similar to those that enable a bright student to score well
in examinations, therefore qualifying as rational—up to a point.
It may have some significance that a good many thorough liberals possess talents of this sort, and make successful use of them.

5. Looked at somewhat differently, liberalism's egalitarianism is
equivalent to a tendency—and we must continue to speak here
of "tendencies" rather than of anything absolute—against social

hierarchies and distinctions, against those factors in human life that mark off one group of men from the rest of mankind. In accord with the general principles of the liberal ideology, this anti-hierarchical or anti-discriminatory tendency is especially pronounced when the operative distinction marking off the group is based—as most social distinctions are in fact based—on factors of tradition, custom, prejudice, superstition or sentiment that liberalism regards as non-rational.

Thus liberals are anti-aristocratic, and are opposed to political, economic or social distinctions based on family, religion or property, especially landed property, and perhaps most passionately of all to distinctions based on race or color. Not only do liberals want schools[5] to be integrated with respect to all such attributes; they also reject "quota systems," especially systems related to race, color or religion, in admitting students to universities and professional institutions. A quota system could satisfy the ideal of arithmetic equality, but would imply qualitative discriminations. In setting admission priorities, liberals usually object to any preference shown to athletic prowess, appearance, "character" or "exemplification of American (or British or French as the case may be) ideals," all of which are judged to be irrational factors. Liberals object also to a selection based on money, which follows, unless counterbalanced, from the fact that some families have the money to pay the fees and others don't. This objection has led in recent years to the general current practice of awarding scholarship funds primarily in terms of financial need: need, evidently, does not seem an irrational criterion from a liberal standpoint, though it is not al-

---

5. Housing, employment, accommodations or services could be substituted as the example.

together easy for a non-liberal to see just where the difference is. The priority scale actually in force in the major universities, based on certain rather specialized intellectual skills and attainments, likewise qualifies, it would seem, as rational.

From the standpoint of the liberal ideology, it is difficult to justify the strong attachments so often found in the past to such non-rational human groupings as the family or the nation, or indeed to any groupings more parochial than Mankind. Not surprisingly, we find that most liberals favor easy divorce laws—indeed, these are ordinarily called "liberal" divorce laws. Liberals and their forebears have carried the brunt of the campaigns that over the past hundred and fifty years have so greatly loosened the bonds of matrimony.

Liberals, unless they are professional politicians needing votes in the hinterland, are not subject to strong feelings of national patriotism and are likely to feel uneasy at patriotic ceremonies. These, like the organizations in whose conduct they are still manifest, are dismissed by liberals rather scornfully as "flag-waving" and "100 percent Americanism." The national anthem is not customarily sung or the flag shown, unless prescribed by law, at meetings of liberal associations. When a liberal journalist uses the phrase "patriotic organization," the adjective is equivalent in meaning to "stupid, reactionary and rather ludicrous." The rise of liberalism to predominance in the controlling sectors of American opinion is in almost exact correlation with the decline in the ceremonial celebration of the Fourth of July, traditionally regarded as the nation's major holiday. To the liberal mind, the patriotic oratory is not only banal but subversive of rational ideals; and judged by liberalism's humanitarian morality, the enthusiasm and pleasures that simple souls might have got from the fireworks could not compensate the occasional damage to the eye or finger of an unwary youngster.[6] The purer liberals of the Norman Cousins strain, in the tradition of Eleanor Roosevelt, are more likely to celebrate UN Day than the Fourth of July.

This cooling off of patriotic feeling, which reinforces the liberal tendency toward internationalism that we have already remarked, is not at all an arbitrary quirk of liberal sentiment. Modern liberals, in their emotional shift, are true to their principles. They are, in effect, bringing the older liberalism—which was nationalistic, sometimes very fiercely so, in its day, when the logic of liberalism was only half spun out—up-to-date.[7] Patriotism and nationalism, too, are non-rational and discriminatory. They invidiously divide, segregate, one group of men ("my group") from humanity, and do so not in accord with objective merits determined by deliberate reason but as the result of habits, customs, traditions and feelings inherited from the past. Patriotism and patriotic nationalism thus come under liberalism's logical taboo. The duty of the fully enlightened liberal, as the Committee for a Sane Nuclear Policy reminds us in frequent public declarations, is to nothing less than mankind.

16. Liberalism's democratic, egalitarian and universalist beliefs

---

6. In 1962 William I. Nichols, editor of *This Week*, conducted a survey and analysis of American history textbooks used in American public schools: fourteen of them written several decades ago and for the most part retired from active service; forty-five, recently written and widely used at present; the two groups selected at random. The results of the survey confirm statistically a change that everyone knows to have taken place: the virtual disappearance of the patriotic stories and references that were always present and often prominent in the older textbooks. For example: Patrick Henry's "Give me liberty or give me death!" was cited in twelve of the fourteen older books, and in two of the forty-five newer; Nathan Hale's reputed last words at the gallows ("I only regret that I have but one life to lose for my country") was in eleven

seem to entail a principle that might be put as follows: Sub-groups of humanity defined by color, race, sex or other physical or physiological attributes do not differ in civilizing potential. Individuals obviously do differ in this respect, either congenitally or from variations in education and environmental influence; and even the most orthodox liberal is willing to put those individuals whose negative differences are extreme into jail or asylum. But these individual differences, liberal doctrine would seem to hold, are random in humanity at large, and not correlated with any generalized physical or physiological differences.

Perhaps in pure logic this principle is not a necessary presupposition of the democratic, egalitarian and universalist beliefs; but in any event I have never known or known of a liberal who denied it publicly. It is not hard to see why this should be so. Suppose I believe that men of a certain color, size or shape, or in some other way physically marked off as a group, are in point of fact distinctly inferior, on average, to other men in their ability to create and maintain a civilized society. I might still think that this inferior group and its members should be equal in certain respects to all other men: equal as moral beings and equal before the law, let us say. And I might still judge it proper that exceptional members of the inferior group should be free to rise to whatever social level might be consonant with their talents. But it would be imprudent, and manifestly dangerous both for society and for the inferior group itself, if *as a group*—no matter how large, no matter if it

---

of the fourteen older books, and in only one of the forty-five newer; John Paul Jones' "I have not yet begun to fight," in nine of the older, none of the newer.

7. Later on, in the discussion of the "dialectic of liberalism," we shall consider the seeming paradox that in and in relation to the Afro-Asian "third world" of ex-colonial and colonial regions, those who profess themselves liberal are still very fiercely nationalistic.

were a sizable majority of mankind—it were granted the same share as superior groups in running things: if, in other words, the inferior group were granted political equality. By the hypothesis of its inferiority, it could not be expected to run things as well, and it might run them very badly indeed.

Of course, even if I share the liberal belief that in objective fact all groups are equal in civilizing potential, it still does not follow that I must accept liberalism's political conclusion. I might continue to want my group to have more than its arithmetic share in running things, simply because it is my group, or because that's the way it's been for a long time and things might get worse if big changes were made; but then I would no longer be reasoning like a liberal, or feeling as a sincere liberal ought to feel.

17. Liberalism, with its optimism about human nature and social progress, its confidence in science, its rejection of nonrational modes of knowledge and its democratic egalitarianism, is *secularist* in outlook and goal. It is secularist philosophically, in the definition of its ideal as something to be realized in this world, not the next; its paradise is earthly; the purpose of society and government is the improvement of the material life of mankind through the elimination of poverty, hunger, slums, oppression, physical suffering and war. And liberalism is secularist in the practical political sense of opposing the "theological state" and, more generally, the intrusion of the church into government.

The forebears of modern liberalism often supported this secularism in social outlook by an all-sided attack on organized religion. "In its militant aspect," Professor Schapiro summarizes, "the secularism of the Enlightenment warred against all revealed religions as having their origin in the fears and superstitions of primitive life.... According to secularism, man's supreme aim was to attain happiness in this world through mundane ideas and scientific method. Most of the thinkers of the Enlightment believed in deism, or natural religion, according to which God created the world and the natural laws that governed it. But they disbelieved in theological dogmas, flouted rituals, and repudiated churches."[8]

In the second half of the nineteenth century the deism gave way in the case of some of the pre-liberals to proclaimed atheism or agnosticism—as is true of some of the older generation still living: Bertrand Russell, for example, or Max Eastman, who has dropped his liberalism but kept his atheism. Avowed atheism and agnosticism are no longer fashionable, but most modern liberals maintain strict views about separation of church and state (though this is an issue on which Catholic converts to liberalism continue to be troubled). According to liberal doctrine, religion, separated by a "solid wall" from the state, is a private affair, a question of individual belief and private, voluntary association.

18. Because coercion and force are felt to be intrinsically irrational, and because they undoubtedly interrupt the universal dialogue of the democratic process, liberals tend—here again it is a "tendency" that is in question—to be against both war and warriors. Some liberals, and an increasing number since the advent of nuclear weapons, go all the way to strict pacifism; others, to the myriad sorts of modified or conditional pacifism like the movements for partial or total disarmament, against nuclear weapons or nuclear weapons tests, and so on.

There are some pacifists who reach their position through special sorts of anarchism (of both Left and Right varieties) and more who derive it from religious belief; and some seeming pac-

---

8. Schapiro, *op. cit.*, pp. 18-20.

ifists are communists in pacifist clothing. But most present-day pacifists of all shades, including most of the religious pacifists, are liberals, as can quickly be confirmed by checking the membership of any of the pacifist, anti-bomb or disarmament organizations.[9]

The veteran liberal, Walter Millis, now a prominent associate of Mr. Hutchins' Center for the Study of Democratic Institutions, sets down what he evidently takes as an axiom in his analysis of "A Liberal Military-Defense Policy": "It is difficult to see how a liberal statesmanship in the modern era can take as its ultimate goal anything less than the abolition of the war system itself. The abolition of war appears to demand, as its minimum requirement (and its minimum consequence) a universal and total disarmament, down to police-force levels, by all the nations of the world."[10] Some liberals, especially among those currently charged with the practical conduct of military-defense policy, will doubtless feel that Mr. Millis' formulation is too unqualified; but it may be recalled that, following an initiative taken by Nikita Khrushchev, all member nations of the United Nations are on formal record as favoring "a universal and total disarmament, down to police-force levels." No liberal would declare himself flatly *against* disarmament; every liberal approves some sort of disarmament, at least "in principle." All liberals, by the nature of liberalism, always favor discussion, negotiation and compromise—the normal liberal procedures—as the methods for settling all disputes. "We must go on negotiating," declared Senator Hubert Humphrey on his return in 1960 from his

9. In 1962 the National Director of Americans for Democratic Action, Mrs. Violet M. Gunther, told me she believed that most ADA members had joined the limited-pacifist Committee for a Sane Nuclear Policy and that all ADA members supported its aims.

10. Included in *The Liberal Papers*, p. 98.

seven-hour dialogue with Khrushchev. "We must be willing to talk to the Russians [and whomever] wherever and whenever there seems to be the faintest hope."

19. One rather drastic and very important change that modern liberalism has made in the ideology that was called "liberalism" in the nineteenth century is well known and often commented on. The liberal economists, moralists and philosophers of the nineteenth century tended toward a doctrine of laissez faire that set strict boundaries to the field of government. John Stuart Mill, still hailed by his most recent editor, Max Lerner, as High Priest of Reason, gave insistent and repeated utterance to his distrust of governmental operations that reached out beyond narrowly circumscribed limits. Mill opposed out of hand, of course, government interference with a citizen's liberty of thought, speech and action, except where this interference might be necessary to prevent that citizen from injuring the liberties of another. But beyond this Mill is at repeated pains to make explicit "the objections to government interference, when it is not such as to involve infringement of liberty"—that is, to government interference in general. These objections he summarizes near the close of "On Liberty" as follows:

> The first is, when the thing to be done is likely to be better done by individuals than by the government....
>
> The second objection is [that] in many cases, though individuals may not do the particular thing so well, on the average, as the officers of government, it is nevertheless desirable that it should be done by them, rather than by the government, as a means to their own mental education....
>
> The third, and most cogent reason for restricting the inter-

ference of government, is the great evil of adding unnecessarily to its power. Every function superadded to those already exercised by the government causes its influence over hopes and fears to be more widely diffused, and converts, more and more, the active and ambitious part of the public into hangers-on of the government, or of some part which aims at becoming the government. If the roads, the railways, the banks, the insurance offices, the great joint-stock companies, the universities, and the public charities were all of them branches of the government; if, in addition, the municipal corporations and local boards, with all that now devolves on them, became departments of the central administration; if the employees of all these different enterprises were appointed and paid by the government, and looked to the government for every rise in life; not all the freedom of the press and popular constitution of the legislature would make this or any other country free otherwise than in name.[11]

This reads like pure Barry Goldwater; it would surely get an applicant blackballed by Americans for Democratic Action, and most probably exiled from the New Frontier.

Mr. Hutchins, in the address from which I have several times drawn, expresses the point of view of present-day liberalism: "The notion that the sole concern of a free society is the limitation of governmental authority and that that government is best which governs least is certainly archaic. Our object today should not be to weaken government in competition with other centers of power, but rather to strengthen it as the agency charged with the responsibility for the common good."

11. Mill, *op. cit.*, pp. 364-66.

The older liberalism believed, thus, in a *limited state*. In particular, the positive or "substantive" tasks assigned to government were very few: besides defense against foreign aggression and domestic violence, perhaps the provision of a small number of essential public services. For the rest, the government's duties as defined by the older liberalism were largely negative: to prevent the kind of fraud, coercion or monopoly practices that blocked the exercise of civil liberties and the processes of the free market. Even with respect to civil rights and liberties, the function of government was thought of as negative: not to bring about or compel the substantive enjoyment of the liberties, much less to create them, but merely to prevent coercive interference with their enjoyment by citizens who might choose to exercise them.

Modern liberalism has shifted to a belief in one or another degree of what may properly be called in a general sense, *statism*. It has an always critical and sometimes wholly negative attitude toward private economic enterprise. (It was the liberals and pre-liberals who popularized the conception of the major individualist entrepreneurs as "robber barons," of the companies that furnish armament as "merchants of death.") Liberals accept and advocate a multiplication of the substantive activities of government in nearly all social dimensions, extensive government controls over the economy, and at least some measure of government ownership and operation. Modern liberalism insists that the entry of government into nearly every phase of social life except religion aids rather than hinders the attainment of the good life and the good society.

It is evident that in thus changing, in fact very nearly reversing, the inherited doctrine of the relation between state and society, modern liberalism has absorbed an important segment of the ideology of socialism. Liberalism does not, it is true, share the total demand of orthodox Marxian socialism: for nationalization of all major means of production, transport and distribution; and we have noted that the non-communist socialist parties in most Western nations have also dropped this extreme position during the course of the past decade or so. The ideological movement has gone both ways: just as liberalism shifted toward socialism in its doctrine of the state and its economics, so has the reformist or democratic wing of traditional socialism shifted toward liberalism. The two have come close to meeting in the concept of what has come to be called "the Welfare State"; and there they meet up also with still other currents from radicalism, Christian socialism and even "modern," as it is sometimes designated, conservatism.

Undoubtedly liberals differ a good deal among themselves in the degree of their statism. Some incline more toward Marx, some toward John Maynard Keynes, and there are still perhaps a few who have an occasional hankering after John Stuart Mill. But all modern liberals agree that government has a positive duty to make sure that the citizens have jobs, food, clothing, housing, education, medical care, security against sickness, unemployment and old age; and that these should be ever more abundantly provided. In fact, a government's duty in these respects, if sufficient resources are at its disposition, is not only to its own citizens but to all humanity. Contemporary American liberals are probably unanimous, for example, in accepting an obligation—to be implemented at least in part through government—to help feed and succor the hungry of the underdeveloped regions, and to aid them in improving their material condition.

Whatever the measure of a liberal's theoretical statism, liberals almost always support the side of government control, planning, financing or take-over when this is posed as a specific issue. In Congress, for example, the record of the liberal bloc on such issues shows few exceptions over the past generation. Since its founding in 1947, the liberal collegium, Americans for Democratic Action, has published an annual Scoresheet after each session of Congress. Every Congressman gets a rating according to his votes on fifteen or twenty measures that are selected as the most significant of the session: a *plus* if he has voted the ADA, that is the liberal, line; a *minus* if he has voted anti-liberal. Hundreds of bills have thus appeared on the Scoresheets over the years. The ADA has invariably assigned a *plus* to a vote for a measure that entails an increase in the power of the Federal (that is, national) executive or that authorizes more spending, control, planning or activity by any branch of the Federal Government— with the sole exception of control over free speech, assembly and subversion. Conversely, a vote for any of the infrequent measures that call for a reduction in the power or purse of the Federal Government is invariably rated *minus*.

The platforms and programs of Americans for Democratic Action are studded with statements that motivate these ratings by appeal to the principles and rhetoric of the liberal ideology. "The leadership role of the Federal Government is central to the achievement of growth and full employment." "The Government must undertake to build firm foundations for enduring prosperity by bold long-range programs for the development of our resources, the rebuilding of our cities, the elimination of our slums, and the provision of full and equal opportunities for health, education and security for all our people." "Government subsidies and financing and, if necessary, government plants must be used to provide more power, more steel and other vitally necessary raw materials." (That last is from a vintage platform of the late 1940's, before it became clear to everyone that more steel plants besides what private industry built on its own account were far from a burning economic need.) "The Government needs increased authority over the amount of bank credit and bank resources." "Housing goals must be set by the Federal Government." In January 1962, ADA's official organ, *ADA World*, demanded, along with full government medicare and care of the aged, "a broad and comprehensive Federal program…for schools, hospitals, cultural and recreational centers, mass transit and water supply systems." In the 1962 session of Congress, the Senate's liberal bloc under the leadership of ADA members fought *for* a government-owned, as against industry-owned, high-voltage power-transmission grid just as it fought *against* assigning the operation of communication satellites to a group of private corporations. Gazing out into space, the liberals, unappeased by the progress toward the Welfare State on earth, see new worlds to plan for. Both those 1962 battles were lost, as it happened; the liberal fundamentalists had jumped beyond the President as well as their more moderate brethren.[12]

The leap from the concept of the limited state to that of the Welfare State is a wide one. In affective terms, it means a reversal of emotive priorities, with the impulse toward social reform, always present in liberalism but formerly in second rank, taking precedence over the libertarian impulse. Logically, the leap has not been achieved without a good deal of doctrinal acrobatics, even, perhaps, some signs of a strained backbone. The gap has been bridged, if precariously, with the help of the theory and practice of political democracy.

---

12. Studies made by ADA researchers show that in Congressional voting during the postwar period liberal proposals (as ADA defines them) have been much more successful in foreign than in domestic policy disputes. *Cf.* Clifton Brock, *Americans for Democratic Action* (Washington: Public Affairs Press, 1962), pp. 177, 185. It should be kept in mind that by liberal criteria Congress is the most reactionary of the nation's political institutions.

If we consider the problem historically, we will recall that for the eighteenth- and nineteenth-century liberal ancestors, "the state" meant a non-democratic regime in which such conservative and reactionary forces (according to their listing in the liberal lexicon) as landlords, a hereditary aristocracy, a hereditary monarch, the army and the church had weight much beyond their numerical proportion. This was true of the regime as a whole, and to a large extent even of the parliaments within the regime, which were elected on a limited, manipulated franchise, and wielded in any case only portions of the power. Such a "state" was obviously not a very promising instrument for bringing about the liberties, reforms and general prosperity which the pre-liberals sought; in fact, the active intervention of government could be expected to push, much of the time, in the opposite direction.

With the gradual extension of the franchise toward universality and the transfer of sovereignty more and more fully into the hands of elective assemblies and officials, the state could be thought of as changing its character from Bad to Good or at least promising Angel. The "state" came to seem to express more and more, at least more than other institutions, the popular or general will. It was no longer outlandish for liberals to expect their democratic state to do liberalism's work.

John Dewey probably did as much as any man to engineer this dialectical shift. The older liberalism, with its belief in laissez faire and the limited state, he concluded, "is in effect simply a justification of the brutalities and inequities of the existing order.... Gradually a change came over the spirit and meaning of liberalism. It came surely, if gradually, to be disassociated from the laissez faire creed and to be associated with the use of governmental action for aid to those at economic disadvantage and for alleviation of these conditions.... The majority of those who call themselves liberals today are committed to the principle that organized society must use its powers to establish the conditions under which the mass of individuals can possess actual as distinct from merely legal liberty." He completes the turn with a triumphant Hegelian synthesis:

> Since liberation of the capacities of individuals for free, self-initiated expression is an essential part of the creed of liberalism, liberalism that is sincere must will the means that condition the achieving of its ends. Regimentation of material and mechanical forces is the only way by which the mass of individuals can be released from regimentation.... The notion [still held by some people in 1935] that organized social control [a Dewey-ite expression for state control] of economic forces lies outside the historic path of liberalism shows that liberalism is still impeded by remnants of its earlier laissez faire phase.... Earlier liberalism regarded the separate and competing economic action of individuals as the means to social well-being as the end. We must reverse the perspective and see that socialized economy is the means of free individual development as the end.[13]

Arthur Schlesinger, Jr., sticking to his last, very naturally calls first on American history rather than Germanic metaphysics for a helping hand across the gap. "American democracy emerged in an age which had conquered freedom by limiting the power of government," he wrote in *The Vital Center.* "This experience had a traumatic effect on the early radicals. The state had given them, so to speak, a prenatal fright." But Mr. Schlesinger finds it possible

---

13. John Dewey, *Liberalism and Social Action* (New York: G.P. Putnam's Sons, 1935), pp. 21, 27, 90. The three lectures that comprise this volume are a primary source for the understanding of modern liberalism.

to date the beginning of their recovering from this infantile sickness of liberalism (as we might call it, borrowing from Lenin) all the way back to Andrew Jackson, the subject of Mr. Schlesinger's first Pulitzer Prize and book club selection. "The administration of Andrew Jackson was the first one to govern energetically in the interests of the people." (Mr. Schlesinger does not specify whose interests Washington, Jefferson and Jackson's other predecessors governed in, but in any case it was not the people's.) "But, in order to combat the power of concentrated wealth, Jackson was obliged to enlarge the power of the state....Under the banner of anti-statism, Jackson made the state stronger than ever before." It turns out that Germanic metaphysics cannot be dispensed with after all: the contradictories, statism and anti-statism, fuse into the synthesis of popular, democratic government.

The next boost comes from Theodore Roosevelt, who "was the first modern statesman to note the spirit of irresponsibility which was suffusing industrial society and to call upon positive government to redress the balance. In so doing, he invoked the dream of the benevolent state [i.e., what came to be known as the Welfare State]." Under the next Roosevelt and the New Deal (occasion, in Mr. Schlesinger's rendering, of subsequent prizes and book club choices), the dream begins its translation into reality. "The New Deal completed the exorcism of Jeffersonian inhibitions about strong government, committing liberals ever after to the Hamilton-T.R. faith in the state as a necessary instrument of social welfare."[14]

In recent years the revised doctrine has become ever more

14. Arthur M. Schlesinger, Jr., *The Vital Center* (Boston: Houghton Mifflin Co., 1949); quoted from 1962 Sentry edition, pp. 175, 176, 177, 181 *passim*.

persuasive as the liberals themselves have moved into commanding posts within the governmental structure, particularly in the executive and the permanent bureaucracy. Surely it would be quixotic for liberals to distrust unduly or to strive to limit strictly a state that they are themselves running.

THESE NINETEEN IDEAS, principles and beliefs comprise the primary elements of the liberal ideology, the symptoms of the liberal syndrome. Although I have used American references, for the most part, in displaying them, they are not peculiar to American liberalism, but common to liberalism everywhere in the world— though we should keep in mind that in other countries liberals in the American sense may be called, as we have noted, by different names: progressives, radicals, social democrats, democratic socialists, Christian democrats, *La Gauche*, *il sinistrismo*, Fabians, the Left, leftists, *progressistes* laborites, and so on. (In some instances the groups that would be so designated overlap rather than coincide with "liberals" in the American sense.) Indeed, the logic of the liberal doctrine necessarily yields principles that are internationalist and universal rather than local or national.

Because of their prominence and practical importance, I add, without comment or analysis, three corollaries of the basic doctrine that the American form of liberalism applies in its particular context.

A. American liberalism tends to a thoroughly instrumentalist interpretation of the Constitution, and holds that the meaning of the Constitution should be understood as wholly dependent on time and circumstance. Actually, liberalism is logically committed to such an interpretation of any constitution, written or unwritten.

B. Modern American liberalism, in theory and even more

consistently in practice, has only a minor concern for, or even a definite opposition to, States' Rights. Both on doctrinal grounds and because of the non-liberal social forces that often find expression in the institutions of the several States, liberalism sees the Federal (central, national) Government as the more promising instrument of progress, and the State structures as obstacles.

C. Since the executive (along with the bureaucracy) is naturally the coordinating and dynamic branch of the American form of government, through which progress can most readily be assured and the Welfare State developed, American liberalism has a strong presumption in favor of the executive as against the legislature, that is, Congress. Its attitude, like that of non-liberals, toward the judiciary tends to be opportunist: determined by the current ideological makeup of the bench, in particular of the controlling Supreme Court. The liberals are pro-Court when it is handing down liberal decisions, and anti-Court when it is on an anti-liberal swing. But the preference for the executive (and bureaucracy) is much more stable, a matter "of principle" rather than of immediate tactics.

In his history of Americans for Democratic Action, to which I have made reference, Professor Brock both discusses and illustrates this liberal predilection for the executive. "Since the First Hundred Days of the New Deal," he summarizes, "if not since the time of Woodrow Wilson's New Freedom, American liberals [have] looked to the executive branch to supply the political power for the great changes which slowly transformed the nation from a laissez faire to a welfare state. Except for a brief period in the late Twenties..., liberals [have] carried on a long love affair with the Presidency."[15]

---

15. Brock, *op. cit.*, p. 153.

SIX

Ideological Thinking

I

THE PRECEDING THREE CHAPTERS have put before us, lighted and focused under an analytic microscope, the ideology of liberalism exhibited as a set of nineteen primary ideas and beliefs—twenty-two, if we include the three corollaries. Just as in the case of the thirty-nine sentences listed in Chapter II, I think most Americans and Europeans will find that they agree with all or almost all of the nineteen, or disagree with many or most of them. That is to say, Americans and Europeans are either infected with the liberal ideology and therefore manifest many of the symptoms of the liberal syndrome; or they are not, and don't.

To liberals, many of these nineteen ideas are likely to seem so obviously true that they have never bothered to put them into words; too obvious for fruitful discussion; not so much the private chattels of liberalism as the common ideas that all enlightened, educated, rational and decent men of the present age share, to the exclusion only of archaic types like U.S. senators from the Deep South, along with extremists, fascists and crackpots. To most liberals, these ideas and beliefs do not seem to require proof or even careful examination; and in fact they have seldom been submitted to careful and systematic examination. They are not part of the content but of the form of current discussion, of Mr. Hutchins' universal dialogue; rational discussion of moot problems tends to assume them as a framework.

This is perfectly illustrated by an official memorandum that was issued to the teachers and pupils of the Washington, D.C., school system late in 1962 in connection with an anti-Nazi, anti-racist project. The pupils—85 percent of whom were Negroes—were to read accounts of the Nazi massacres of Jews and then tell in class their own experiences with racial discrimination. "In a democracy,"the memorandum explained, "everyone has the right to his own convictions and attitudes toward others, but...all attitudes and convictions must be based on truth and reason." Attitudes and convictions based on truth and reason are those, it is needless to add, that are consistent with the liberal ideology.

When we discover that certain ideas about man, history and society seem, to those who believe in them, to be either self-evident or so manifestly correct that opposing them is a mark of stupidity or malice, then we may be fairly sure we are dealing with an *ideology* and *ideological thinking*. The fact that most liberals, though prepared to debate about concrete application and specific program, feel that sort of certainty about the basic ideas of liberalism is a strong indication of what is indeed the case: that liberalism is an ideology.

Before continuing with the analysis of the content of liberalism, let us examine somewhat more closely the nature of ideologies and ideological thinking.

II

A CONVINCED BELIEVER IN the anti-Semitic ideology tells me that the Bolshevik revolution is a Jewish plot. I point out to him that the revolution was led to its first major victory by a non-Jew, Lenin. He then explains that Lenin was the pawn of Trotsky, Radek, Kamenev, Zinoviev and other Jews who were in the Bolshevik High Command. I remind him that Lenin's successor as leader of the revolution, the non-Jew Stalin, killed off all those Jews; and that Stalin has been followed by the non-Jew Khrushchev, under whose rule there have been notable revivals of anti-Semitic attitudes and conduct. He then informs me that the seeming Soviet anti-Semitism is only a fraud invented by the Jewish press, and that Stalin and Khrushchev are really Jews whose names have been changed, with a total substitution of forged records. Suppose I am able to present documents that even he will have to admit show this to be impossible. He is still unmoved. He tells me that the real Jewish center that controls the revolution and the entire world conspiracy is not in Russia anyway, but in Antwerp, Tel Aviv, Lhasa, New York or somewhere, and that it has deliberately eliminated the Jews from the public officialdom of the Bolshevik countries in order to conceal its hand and deceive the world about what is going on. Q.E.D.

A believer in dialectical materialism—the communist ideology—states that the Communist Party represents the interests of the proletariat, that is, of the workers. I show that in this, that and the other country, most of the workers do not support the Communist Party, even where a democratic political order would permit them to do so without hindrance. He explains that the opinions of the workers have been corrupted by capitalist social conditions and pro-capitalist indoctrination. I note, with adequate documentation, that in countries run by the Communist Party the workers are worse off and have still less influence on the government than in many non-communist countries. He tells me that this reflects the survival of capitalist remnants, the backwardness of the economy taken over from capitalism and the hostile pressure of the surrounding impe- rialist environment; and that, in any case, what the Commu- nist Party represents is not the "present consciousness" of the workers, blinded by ignorance and illusion, but their "objective historical interest." Q.E.D.

A liberal informs me that the races of mankind do not differ in intellectual or moral capacity, in "civilization-building" talent, or in any other attribute fitting them to exercise full and equal political rights. I mention that most scholars in the field, what- ever their philosophical views, seem to agree that at any rate the Australian bushmen and African pigmies are somewhat defec- tive in these respects, however admirable in others. These two instances he dismisses as no more than living fossils, evolution- ary accidents that have no practical significance. I recall studies proving that the various races show considerable differences, not traceable to social environment, in susceptibility to certain dis- eases, in physiological reactions and physical measurements, etc. He answers (even when, as is not seldom the case, his theoretical philosophy commits him to a view that denies the independent reality of "mind") that these physical differences have no bearing on the question of mental differences. I point out to him that Ne- groes in the United States have not attained levels of intellectual eminence in as high a proportion to their numbers as have whites. He explains that this is obviously due to their lack of equal edu- cation. I restrict the comparison to the members of the two races who have received the same amount of schooling. He says the schooling provided for Negroes is inferior in facilities and quality to that provided for whites, even when equal in amount. I accept the further restriction, and still note a disparity in attainments. He then explains that there cannot be equality in racially separate schools no matter if they are equal in all other respects, because the separateness itself causes traumatic disturbances that have a negative effect on the educative process. I offer the comparative records of graduates of schools in which the two races sit together. He assimilates these by pointing to the less favorable economic, social and cultural condition of the Negro sample outside of school. I ask about the results of tests that have been alleged to rate intellectual abilities independently of environment and education. When these are found to rate Negroes at levels substantially below whites of the same age, he concludes that the tests do not really do what is claimed, that they have been devised in a white-controlled culture and reflect not innate but in part acquired traits unconsciously introduced. And so on. Q.E.D.

The militant segregationist will have equivalent answers, in reverse, to all possible queries. I mention, after hearing him assert the innate inferiority of the Negro race, the fact that in baseball, boxing, track and field sports, Negroes are the champions. These purely physical achievements, he explains, are proof how close Negroes remain to animals in the evolutionary scale. I add the names of Negro musicians, singers, actors and writers of the first rank. Naturally, he comments, they carry over a sense of rhythm from the tribal dance and tom-tom ceremonies. I ask how many law graduates of his State university could stand up against Judge Thurgood Marshall; how many sociologists, against Professor C. Eric Lincoln; how many psychologists, against Professor Kenneth Clark? Doubtless all such have plenty of white blood, he answers, but in any case they are only exceptions to prove the general rule of inferiority; that is confirmed by the low intellectual attainments of the average Negro. I observe that the average Negro has been educated in worse schools, and for fewer years, than the average white. Of course, he agrees: no use wasting good education on low-grade material.... Q.E.D.[1]

An ideologue—one who thinks ideologically—can't lose. He can't lose because his answer, his interpretation and his attitude have been determined in advance of the particular experience or observation. They are derived from the ideology, and are not subject to the facts. There is no possible argument, observation or experiment that could disprove a firm ideological belief for the very simple reason that an ideologue will not accept any argument, observation or experiment as constituting disproof. This we saw candidly proclaimed in Mr. Hutchins' speech: "One advantage of this faith [in liberalism] is that it is practically [there is no reason for even that modest qualification] shock-proof."

An ideology is a more or less systematic and self-contained set of ideas supposedly dealing with the nature of reality (usually social reality), or some segment of reality, and of man's relation (attitude, conduct) toward it; and calling for a commitment independent of specific experience or events. In some instances, among which dialectical materialism is currently conspicuous, the commitment is total and the system both rigorous and inclusive. Liberalism, for most of its adherents, is looser in logic, more limited in range, and less wholly demanding in its spiritual claim. But it shares with dialectical materialism and many

---

1. My interest in this section is solely in the method of reasoning, and has nothing to do with the merits of the positions defended or questioned in these hypothetical instances: anti-Semitism, communism, the belief in the innate equality of races, and the other instances that will follow.

another modern doctrine the distinctive traits of an ideology, which Professor Oakeshott describes as follows:

> As I understand it, a political ideology purports to be an abstract principle, or set of related abstract principles, which has been independently premeditated. It supplies in advance of the activity of attending to the arrangements of a society a formulated end to be pursued, and in so doing it provides a means of distinguishing between those desires which ought to be encouraged and those which ought to be suppressed or redirected.
>
> The simplest sort of political ideology is a single abstract idea, such as Freedom, Equality, Maximum Productivity, Racial Purity, or Happiness. And in that case political activity is understood as the enterprise of seeing that the arrangements of a society conform to or reflect the chosen abstract idea. It is usual, however, to recognize the need for a complex scheme of related ideas, rather than a single idea, [as in] such systems of ideas as: "the principles of 1789," "Liberalism," "Democracy," "Marxism," or the Atlantic Charter. These principles need not be considered absolute or immune from change (though they are frequently so considered), but their value lies in their having been premeditated.... A political ideology purports to supply in advance knowledge of what "Freedom" or "Democracy" or "Justice" is.[2]

The liberal opposition to seniority and similar rules in the legislature is a typical example of ideological thinking. This opposition is derived from, or perhaps, more exactly, justified

---

2. Michael Oakeshott, *Rationalism and Politics* (New York: Basic Books, 1962), p. 116.

by, certain "principles": from, specifically, the abstract doctrine of popular sovereignty and democracy as this is developed in the liberal ideology. The liberals are certainly correct in finding that the seniority rules are inconsistent with their abstract doctrine. But to accept that finding as conclusive and as dictating the abolition of the seniority rules, we must assume not only that our particular doctrine (liberalism) is true, but also that abstract reasoning takes precedence over "practical experience." Practical experience undoubtedly supports the seniority rules; in fact, the rules are merely the formalization of long practical experience.

III

LET US CONSIDER VARIED additional examples, some rather more sophisticated than those already given, of ideological thinking based on liberal doctrine.[3]

1. Some years ago liberals concerned with social reform and urban renewal, as it has come to be called, turned their attention to Skid Row. In accord with the canons of ideological thinking, Skid Row was understood as a "problem"; and, since it was a problem, liberals had a duty to "solve" it. During the past decade they have attempted a direct and, it would seem, sufficiently drastic solution: in a number of American cities, including some of the largest (New York, Boston, St. Louis, San Francisco) they have been simply destroying the local embodiments of Skid Row and replacing these with boulevards, parks, garden apartments, new shopping areas, etc.

---

3. I stress again that my concern here is not with the correctness of the "positions" taken, but only with the method of reasoning.

But what exactly *is* Skid Row? In reality it is not, other than incidentally, a spatial concept at all, but a functional concept; and not so much a special "problem" as merely a natural, indeed inevitable, condition of every articulated community of any size, except perhaps for some artificial communities like zoned bedroom suburbs or carefully controlled company towns—and even these are not usually exceptions for long.

Skid Row is the end of the line; and there must be an end of the line somewhere. It is the state of those individuals who by destiny or choice drop out of normal society, even out of criminal society, which is after all part of the normal order of things. Most of these individuals are alcoholics and some are drug addicts. Where they are is Skid Row; and Skid Row exists in every city, and always has.

In the natural course of events, when the process is not interfered with by ideologues relentlessly determined to solve problems, the citizens of Skid Row usually gather together in one particular district of each town and city: in New York it was the Bowery, as everyone knew, the most famous of America's Skid Rows. That district is always frightfully run-down. It has cheap bars selling rotten liquor, and cheap stores selling even rottener liquor substitutes; flophouses offering flea-bitten cots for a few cents a night; greasy hamburger joints; vacant lots where bonfires can be made of old boards and packing boxes; a tenth-rate pawnshop or two; sagging doorways where the cops won't bother a man while he sleeps off his drunk; a commercial blood bank where you can sell a pint of blood every month or so if you don't have an active disease; a dreary Catholic church and two or three evangelical chapels in old loft buildings; a Salvation Army station where you can get some soup or stew in exchange for singing a hymn; a city-run flophouse where you can have, when the mood strikes you now and then, a delousing and shower along with a plate of food and a bed for the night. This district is where the Skid Rowers stay when they are in town; and where they head for when they arrive, since every certified Skid Rower is equipped with a built-in homing compass.

To the respectable citizen Skid Row seems a macabre place, but in its own way Skid Row is an ingenious product of the long and wonderfully intricate natural evolution of the City. In society as it really is—hierarchical and differentiating, not equalized or regimented—there has to be an end of the line. The localization of Skid Row and the growth of its distinctive institutions and customs are gradual developments serving to take care of those at the end of the line in a way that recognizes the reality of the condition, makes appropriate exceptions to the usual social rules, adds a certain warmth and humaneness along with exits left open for those—they are not many—who wish to take one, and shields the rest of society from Skid Row's potentially destructive effects.

But this cannot be the way liberalism understands Skid Row. For liberalism, Skid Row is not a natural and inevitable social condition but a definite place—the Bowery, the Embarcadero, South State Street, wherever—that constitutes, as I began by noting, a problem: a "blighted area." The people in it are—they must be, by the principles of liberalism—the exploited victims of the area's blight, of inadequate education and bad institutions. Therefore the area must be renewed and the victims reformed. This is the reasoning that has produced the recent movement to abolish Skid Row, as a result of which New York's Bowery and a number of its equivalents in other cities have in fact been in varying degrees cleaned up. The law clamped down on the flophouses, bars and sleeping drunks—they were always illegal, of course, but before the renewers struck, the cops, knowing the condition with which they were dealing, looked the other way. The rotted buildings were bulldozed aside, and the exiled inhabitants invited to the joys of rehabilitation.

The whole operation has proved to be, inevitably, an ideological illusion. Since Skid Row is not in reality a static thing or a place, it cannot be abolished or rubbed out. The most noticeable consequence of this anti–Skid Row campaign has merely been to diffuse Skid Row, for a while, throughout the City. The displaced alcoholics, hoboes and junkies, who had their own localized and more or less self-sufficient society along the Bowery or South State Street, have been lurching all over New York, Chicago, Boston and St. Louis, trying to cadge money for drinks or dope, knocking into the respectable citizens, making scenes in decent bars, and in general acting, with more than a little justification, like resentful aliens. But of course the liberal reformers can drive you through the old locales and show you triumphantly that Skid Row has vanished. There are not a few who hope that it will be refounded; and it will be.

2. A second homely example: I often walk back from work, when I am working in New York, along some blocks where there are many small grocery and fruit stores. One afternoon I stopped to look rather idly at a truck I had noticed before in the neighborhood. It was such a piece of tied-together junk that one wondered how it kept going, but it managed to. It was operated by two Negroes. They were pulled up at one of the stores, and were carrying out big piles of old paperboard boxes. After folding each box flat—a considerable job, as those know who have tried it—they would tie a score of them together and pack the bundle in their wobbly truck.

The two Negroes were cheerful, pleasant fellows. They worked amicably together. I got to know them a little that day and thereafter, and it was plain that they had IQ's down almost out of sight; but they could handle the work they were doing, and they took pride in doing it well. One reason I became interested in this little vignette of city life at that time was because just then the Mayor, Robert Wagner, a leading liberal politician, backed by all liberal opinion in the city, was demanding that the State government lift the minimum wage floor to $1.50 or $2.00 or $1.75 or whatever it was an hour. And what struck me as I watched my two friends, and what I verified by a little inquiry, was that a rise in minimum wage, if enforced, would most certainly throw those two chaps out of their jobs. The truck was owned by some dim exploiter in the background; he made the deals with the little shops, and with whatever mysterious party wanted those bundles of discarded boxes; and the whole operation could be carried on only because he could get these two men at a small wage, which by chiseling he made even smaller. A terrible thing, no doubt, such sordid exploitation; and no one, or hardly anyone, it would seem, could live in our affluent society on so little money as those wages provided. Yet here these two were, working hard, liking their job—which was, to tell the truth, as much of a challenge as they could have met successfully; proud to be self-reliant, standing on their own feet. And with their wives going out some as part-time maids and the older children running a few policy tickets, they and their families managed to eat and to keep the households going. When the Mayor gets his new minimum wage—he failed that round, but he, or the next Mayor, will surely return—those boxes will be thrown into one of the big grinder trucks for dumping at sea; my friends will go on relief and soon, quite probably, become bums and delinquents; but an ideological abstraction will have been satisfied.

3. Another item, much too small to be noticed in a world dominated by glittering abstractions and their dark opposites. My wife and I (our children being no longer at home) live in a rather primitive area of the northwest Connecticut hills; and we have a large police dog who is very unfriendly, as he is supposed to be, to nearly everyone except members of our family. Because we are often away and he too big to take traveling, we must leave him periodically at a kennel; and this has been a difficulty, because he does not like to leave us, or to go to kennels, and he does not like most kennel owners. Moreover, many kennels out in the country are not clean and pleasant enough, we think, for this dog.

But we found one, a while ago, that is perfect for all parties concerned. It is run for police dogs only by a family of German origin: the husband, as Germans often do, teaches minor musical instruments, and the kennel is run as an auxiliary operation. The kennel, or kennels, are well built, very clean and very well taken care of. They and the dogs are handled, physically speaking, by a serf named Ralph—that seems to be his only name. Ralph has no fixed hours and no days off. His master would never think of leading a newly arrived dog up the hundred feet to the kennel; he summons Ralph in the German manner, without saying please, even when Ralph is in the middle of supper or sleep. But Ralph never complains and is indeed an exceptionally cheerful man. He seems content to live at the same intellectual level as the police dogs; and he and the dogs, including our normally unfriendly dog, love each other. Ralph cannot say much, or does not—thank you, when you give him a pair of gloves for Christmas, or hello, or a word about how well your dog ate—but he smiles well. And he is proud, too; and his spick-and-span half-acre, with the decorations he has carved to go with his trim kennels, prove he has a right to his pride.

There are no minimum wages yet in the hills of northwestern

Connecticut, or even unions. So for a while longer Ralph can stay out of an institution and continue his busy medieval role of man to master. But the ideologists will probably get him soon. A neighbor of ours, who is an immaculate and uncompromising liberal, indignantly withdrew her dog from boarding there when she learned what the setup is—even Russia abolished serfdom a century ago, she declared; and she is complaining to the proper authorities.

NOW IT IS LIKELY THAT some liberals will say about one of these little case histories, or even all of them: in such circumstances a good liberal is not necessarily doctrinaire; he might quite possibly agree to an easier, more flexible attitude, letting well enough alone, and permitting people to work out such marginal cases as best they can. Some liberals will feel so, because they are humane, and because they see on reflection that in the real circumstances, the doctrinaire liberal "solution to the problem" is inhumane in its almost certain consequences. Nevertheless, as soon as those same liberals turn their eyes away from specific realities—as soon, that is, as they return to the world of their ideology—they will again declare for the prescribed solutions. And this will be proved by the spontaneity with which they join the criticism of some Congressman, say, who "wants to turn the clock back," and votes against minimum wage laws or attacks grandiose urban-renewal projects. As for anyone who would say a kind word for serfdom in our day, the only thing for him is to have his head examined.

4. The proposition that "for the first time in history we are in a position to provide all men with enough to eat" is so much a commonplace of current thinking that we are likely not to recognize its integral relation to liberal ideology. In an address to a

World Food Congress, the late President John F. Kennedy gave it orthodox expression in these words: "We have the ability, we have the means, and we have the capacity to eliminate hunger from the face of the earth."[4]

This belief was first formulated by the early socialists. It was a favorite subject for those whom Marx called the Utopian Socialists—Fourier, Saint-Simon, Robert Owen—as well as for Auguste Comte and the nineteenth-century enthusiasts of science. It has been a stock in trade, also, of Marxism. In my own Trotskyite days in the 1930's I used to expatiate on it frequently in articles for the official paper or when carrying the word to the meager but earnest audiences that my comrades were able to round up for a lecture. To many persons today, liberals and non-liberals, it seems to be, indeed, a truism.

It is just that seemingly self-evident certainty that should make us suspect that this proposition is empty of empirical, existential content, is merely an ideological cliché—an abstract deduction from ideological principles that has little if any relation to the real world of space and time. In order to delve further into the nature of ideological and therefore of liberal thinking, let me suggest a few considerations that lead to this conclusion.

A. It would have made just as much sense, or as little, to have stated this proposition in many past ages as to state it today. True, the past ages did not have modern science and technology. But they also had only a tenth or a twentieth as many people, and the people occupied much less of the earth's surface. They were capable of a much greater local self-sufficiency—if the inhabitants of the locality were prepared to work hard enough. In a bad season they might run out of food, and did. But Joseph

---

4. *New York Times*, June 5, 1963.

showed how that difficulty could be solved by storing up the surpluses from good seasons. Food got low in winter? Naturally, if people preferred to guzzle when they had it in the summer, and didn't bother to preserve it by drying, salting, storing in caves or whatever. And as a matter of fact, a number of communities did have enough food most of the time.

B. Most people who talk about our present potential for giving everyone enough food have not studied even the technical side of the problem. The fact is that there is not much good unused arable land remaining on earth. From the small reserve, 100 million acres were added to agriculture in the years 1935-60; and of course people, houses, not to speak of roads, are using up the land surface at a tremendous rate. In the past fifteen years the average per capita food consumption has been going down, not up. An increase of food sufficient to have some significance—even though at best it couldn't amount to very much on average—would have to come primarily from more intensive cultivation of land already being farmed in the large, heavily populated nations. This in turn would require as first premise an enormous increase in the use of artificial fertilizers. That is the way—along with very hard work, which is still more unusual—that Japan manages to keep all her population fed, though at a level much below what Americans would regard as a minimum. But Japan manufactures and uses much more fertilizer than all the rest of Asia combined, with Africa thrown in. How are those huge and multitudinous fertilizer plants going to appear in India, China, Pakistan? Fertilizer plants require a big electrical industry, a machine industry, adequate transport, trained technicians and workers.[5]

---

5. After writing this section, I chanced to receive from Mr. Ira B. Joralemon, an engineer and geologist with fifty years of international experience, the text

C. In affirming that we can now provide everyone with enough to eat, even the most optimistic of liberals are nowadays constrained to add the condition: *if* we can dampen the population explosion. It is certainly the case that many, and an increasing number of, human beings will continue to go hungry if the population does go on expanding at anything like the current rate. But it does not at all follow that everyone will be fed if only the rate drops: there are many other interfering facts, material, technical, psychological and cultural. These apart, what evidence is there to suggest that humanity in the world at large will oblige the food planners by the prescribed restraint in their breeding habits?

In keeping with their doctrine, liberals explain the baby boom as due to ignorance (the mothers not knowing how to prevent conception) and poverty (the society not being technologically equipped to supply the contraceptive mechanisms or pills). The "solution" of the "problem" is therefore standard and simple: on the matter of having babies, the parents of the world will take the advice of the liberals and the mechanisms or pills supplied by the technologically advanced nations.

And if, in spite of the advice and the available mechanisms, people just want to have a lot of babies? Or if the rulers of

---

of a study he made during 1962-63. He calculates in detail the quantity of basic materials that the poorer countries would require to bring their food supply up to a minimum of health. The notion that this quantity could in fact be realized is utterly unrealistic. The 1961 per capita use of chemical fertilizers, for example, in Latin America, Africa and Asia (excluding Japan and Siberia) is about one-twentieth that of North America, Western Europe, Australia and New Zealand. "Even with their present population," Mr. Joralemon demonstrates, "if [the poorer countries] are to acquire all the raw materials and manufactured goods that must precede freedom from hunger, they must increase their income by more than a thousand billion dollars a year."

nations or churches or races want their subjects to go on having more babies than the subjects of the next nation, church or race, hunger or no hunger? About some things, human beings may not be quite so ignorant as liberals are compelled to assume in order to explain why the world fails so conspicuously to conform to the liberal recipes for the good society. The history of many tribes and nations proves that there are many ways by which parents have reduced the number of babies without benefit of modern technology. And the history of many others proves that the rational certainty of poverty and hunger is not always enough to make parents want to limit the size of their broods.

One day, very much against advice received, my wife and I made our way to a remote sector of Calcutta where, in a large temple enclosure, the chief annual rite of the dread goddess Kali was being celebrated. The neighboring streets, like the enclosure itself, were filled with disorderly, noisy processions, deformed beggars, crowds dancing wildly around wailing musical instruments, hideous naked holy men and fakirs, stunted children and the miscellaneous poor. The air was reeking with smells, dominated by the oily smoke from the fleshy offerings that were being burned by scores of little groups of worshipers squatting in the open spaces inside the enclosure. To one side, about fifty feet from a corner of the main temple, which was surrounded by a covered porch, was a curious, many-branched tree. An endless line of wretched, half-starved women was moving around the tree and onto the temple porch. Each woman, as she passed the tree, hung a small piece of colored wool or cloth on one of the branches. By doing so, we learned, and by then completing the circumambulation of the temple, she would be granted more babies by Kali, who is goddess of Fertility as well as of Destruction.

D. The proposition says that "we" are in a position to provide all men with enough to eat. Who is "we"? No single nation could do it; in fact, no outside combination could do it for the three great hungry nations, China, India and Pakistan: they would have to do it largely by and for themselves, and for the foreseeable future this is excluded on technical grounds even if all other conditions were realized. "We" is mankind? But mankind is not articulated into any sort of coherent entity that can "do" anything at all; mankind has no mind nor any decision-making institution; it has no way of working together on a chosen project or toward a deliberate goal.

E. Actually, this belief that we are now in a position to provide all men with enough to eat is an element of a purely abstract model. *If* all men would act rationally, and *if* they would make the getting of enough food for all their goal of highest priority, and *if* they would follow the advice of the best scientists and technicians in allocating resources and energy, etc., etc., *then* there would be, or could be, enough to eat. But every one of these hypothetical premises is manifestly so contrary to fact as to be absurd. Of course men do not act rationally, generally speaking. They don't even consider food the matter of highest priority, whatever ideologues may imagine.

India could quickly give a big boost to her food supply merely by getting rid of the sicker and uniformly useless two-thirds of her cows—eating them while doing so, and continuing to eat all the grain the cows now get and to farm the land their overcropping ruins; and for good measure shooting a few scores of millions of monkeys that gobble up fruit, grains and vegetables. But the Indians prefer honoring the divinity of the cows and monkeys to eating more food. (I happened to mention the cows briefly, in connection with problems of economic development, in a lecture I gave some years ago in Bombay. The leading paper the next morning carried an across-the-page headline: BURNHAM ATTACKS OUR COWS!) Among the trams, cars and buses of Calcutta and Madras as well as in the smaller towns there are still to be seen cows wandering up to the food stalls to take their pick of delicacies; and starving workers will buy food not for themselves but to place on the public altars available to their bovine divinities. In Indian villages it is not at all uncommon to see a peasant, shrunk with hunger to little more than a skeleton, feeding stalks of grain to an abscessed, limping cow incapable of doing any work or giving an ounce of milk—the condition of most of them.

Nor is it only cows that take priority over food. Indonesia had had enough food for centuries, before the Dutch as well as under them, until Sukarno took over. Now its people are barely getting fed with the help of massive international handouts. Sukarno's regime is more interested in arms, warships, monuments, glory and conquest than in food. Rumania, Hungary, Poland, Czechoslovakia, and in many periods Russia itself, were all food surplus countries before communism moved in. But communism wants power more than food, and power dictates policies that conflict with those that might induce peasants to grow more food.

Or take the famous White Highlands of Kenya that liberal publicists are fond of citing as an example of colonial and racist exploitation. The Highlands[6] are the part of Kenya that, by its temperature, rainfall and soil, makes successful farming *possible*. They comprise in all about 45,000 square miles. Of these, 37,000 square miles are, as they have been in the past, farmed by

---

6. In 1962 the International Bank for Reconstruction and Development published a report on Kenya's economy that includes a detailed discussion of the Highlands.

African Negroes. The Europeans have been farming about 4,500 square miles, one-tenth of the lot: virtually all developed from scratch in the course of the past sixty years. From these 4,500 square miles the Europeans have been raising sufficient commercial crops to make up 80 percent in value of Kenya's export total of all goods and products—the factor on which Kenya's long-run economic development inevitably depends.

But this is because the Europeans have the best land, the capital and so on, ideology at once protests. The facts teach otherwise. Much of the Highlands land—considerably more than the 4,500 square miles that were the European maximum—is at least as good; all of it is of the same basic character. Comparative studies have been made of African and European farming operations that are closely comparable in all respects, including available capital. They show that the European-farmed land produces approximately four times as much per square mile as the African-farmed land: approximately £4,300 in annual value as against £1,100. It is certain that the economic condition of the Highlands, and thus of Kenya as a whole, will continue in the next period the worsening that began several years ago, and that there will be less food for Kenya's inhabitants. As the Europeans continue to leave, their highly productive, technically advanced and efficiently managed farms are being broken up into subsistence plots or small uneconomic units, both types largely in the hands of incompetent Negroes. Very probably thousands of acres of the Highlands will revert rather soon to the sterility in which the Europeans found them sixty years ago, cropped down to sour bare soil, perhaps, by cattle and horses kept to expand a tribe's prestige and status rather than its food supply. It may not be long before the rising young nation of Kenya is added to the list of those living by the surplus food of the citadel of world imperialism. There is no mystery here.

It is simply that the native leaders of Kenya's African inhabitants want other things more than they want food.

But if men don't even *want* food exceedingly, if they are willing to sacrifice food for the sake of power, glory, piety, laziness, resentments and large families, there is no practical point to insisting that in what can only be some purely abstract and theoretical sense, "We have the ability, we have the means, and we have the capacity to eliminate hunger from the face of the earth." This proposition amounts in substance merely to the old familiar theorem that reappears in so many forms over the centuries: If men were angels, then the earth might be a little bit of heaven.

Does it then follow that many human beings are destined to go hungry over the years to come? Yes, even so. But the liberal ideology—which, by clinging to an optimistic theory of human nature and history, by denying the objective reality of evil and affirming that all social problems can be solved, excludes genuine tragedy—cannot face this tragic fact. That is the real reason why the liberal repeats the proposition, derived not from fact but from doctrine, that we have the ability to provide all men with enough food. When the fact is tragic, his ideology offers him refuge from fact.

5. On January 13, 1963, Ralph McGill, an intransigent and orthodox liberal, commented in his syndicated column, "Behind the Headlines," on what he described as "a small item in the paper, two paragraphs long." He began by reproducing the item in its entirety:

> "Lima, Peru—Five persons died early Wednesday in clashes between police and striking peasants at two sugar mills near Chiclayo, in northern Peru.

"The clashes occurred after strikers attacked and sought to burn down the Patapo and Pucala mills, inflicting heavy damage."

Mr. McGill continued with an excoriation of "news reporting in our time," as illustrated by this item, because it only tells us what happens and not "why something happens.... This did not give us a picture of what conditions are in Chiclayo in northern Peru."

He then fulfilled his liberal duty to enlighten us:

> Drawing on our general knowledge of South American conditions, we can assume, with some confidence, that feudal conditions obtain in Chiclayo. We may be rather certain that low wages, long hours, and poor working conditions prevail. Agriculture in Latin America is almost everywhere depressed. Its workers live in poverty and wretchedness. Their political status is prejudiced. Illiteracy is the rule. Health conditions are primitive. The story is an old one.
>
> It is, however, no older than the familiar one of police *vs.* strikers in an area where labor has no bargaining rights.
>
> The two paragraphs out of Chiclayo would, if amplified, help us to understand why President Kennedy's intelligent plan for assistance to Latin America is inoperative. It depends, for a beginning, on reform by land-holders and industrialists in Latin America. Killing hungry and desperate men is hardly a reform.

Where in the world did all this stuffing come from?—this confident description of Chiclayo's feudal conditions, low wages, long hours, absence of bargaining rights, etc.? There is nothing about all that in the news item. Mr. McGill did not get his data from observation: he has never been in Chiclayo nor anywhere in northern Peru nor, so far as I gather, anywhere else in Peru. He has never read anything about Chiclayo except, as he mentions in this column, a line or two in "a book" he looked up after reading the item, which told him: "It is an agricultural coastal city of about 40,000 population. It is in a rice and sugar district. Sugar is the more important export." He did not consult anyone who had any firsthand knowledge either of Chiclayo in general or of the events reported to have transpired there.

Mr. McGill's entire commentary was derived solely from ideology, untainted by even the most indirect touch of a single fact.

This column appeared during the New York newspaper strike, and I happened to read it in the *Waterbury Republican* in the course of my search for substitutes for the fodder normally provided by the New York press. It was such a pure and classic example of ideological thinking that I decided to try to find out something more about Chiclayo and what had actually happened there, just for the fun of it. Undoubtedly it was not unlikely, from a statistical point of view, that what McGill had written was roughly accurate, discounting the emotive slop in which his prose is bathed, since it would hold for many, perhaps most, South American towns taken at random. Still I had somehow got curious about Chiclayo.

The first thing I learned was that Chiclayo is the modern offshoot of a colony from Cuzco, capital of the Inca Empire; and the second, that McGill had apparently not even been firsthand in his ideological derivations. The *New York Times*, ideological fountainhead for right-thinking citizens, had picked up the report two days before and ideologized it into a ponderous editorial along exactly the same lines ("Indian peasants...expressing a protest, the specific motivation of which was less important than the general discontent....Now, for the first time, the people are learning that their poverty, illiteracy and disease are based on social injustice..." etc.). The *Times'* apodictic rhetoric had been mostly squandered on the desert air served by the Western and European editions, but possibly it had wafted its way onto McGill's desk.

I next talked to a friend of mine who had lived in Peru, spent some while studying conditions there, and visited the scene of the episode. He informed me that this area, which has mines and some industry as well as agriculture, was one of the relatively more advanced parts of Peru; that the sugar mills were technically excellent, and their workers and those on the plantations supplying the mills relatively well paid; that they were mostly unionized and had many fringe benefits, such as medical care and help with housing, that are uncommon in South America. He said he had heard that communist agents, reinforced by operatives newly trained in Cuba, were active in the region and in the high mountains not far away, where the Indians were badly off.

This evidence was confirmed by several other persons with firsthand knowledge, and with it McGill's ideological bubble shrank to droplet size. But I had not yet succeeded in getting direct knowledge about the particular incident mentioned in the news item; or, more exactly, the only direct report I had so far got was from a man with business interests in the area that might have prejudiced his account.

I closed my own dossier on the McGill-Chiclayo case when I read the testimony that Edwin M. Martin, Assistant Secretary of State for Latin-American Affairs—and thus in charge of "President Kennedy's intelligent plan for assistance to Latin America" on which both McGill and the *Times* bestowed their blessing—gave on February 18, 1963 to the House Committee on Foreign Affairs:

In Peru we have another dramatic example of the increasing tempo of communist-inspired subversion and violence. For the past several months, in an agricultural area of the Andean Department of Cuzco, communist agitators, many of whom were trained in Cuba, have been responsible for the forceful seizure of lands, armed attacks, and considerable bloodshed. Last December, Castro-communist agitators subverted a strike at the smelter of the American-owned Cerro Corp. at La Oroya in the central Andes, seized control of the installation and caused about $4 million worth of damage.

Early in January, following a strike that had been settled between the management and the legitimate trade union leaders, communist agitators persuaded workers on two Peruvian-owned sugar plantations near Chiclayo on the north coast, to damage installations and fire canefields—about a million dollars of damage in all.

IV

THERE IS A TEST FAIRLY SIMPLE in theory, though not always easy to carry out, that will show whether we are dealing with an ideology. Suppose we ask a man who believes so-and-so: "What specific evidence, what observations, happenings, experiments, might *conceivably* prove you wrong?" He is, let us say, an all-out anti-Semite. Will he admit—and stand by the admission—that if such-and-such happens, then that will prove his anti-Semitic beliefs to be wrong? Of course not. No matter what happens he will regard it as either irrelevant or one more proof of his doctrine. If there is any seeming conflict between doctrine and reality, then reality, not the doctrine, must give way. This is exactly what proves that his system of belief is not a meaningful assertion about what is or is not the case in the real world, but an ideology, the primary function of which is not to state truths but to adjust attitudes.

The rules for a meaningful assertion about the real world are entirely different. If I say that it is seventy-five feet from here to the driveway, my statement may in fact be a hundred percent true; but it would be proved false, and everyone would recognize that it would be proved false, if we measured the distance with a tape or other suitable instrument and got as the result something other than seventy-five feet. If I say that at a given temperature the volume and pressure of a gas vary inversely, then there is no difficulty in *conceiving* how I might be proved wrong (though in fact I am right): namely, if I measure the two quantities and find that they do *not* vary inversely.

But how will I ever prove to a strict classical economist that his laissez faire equations do not always hold? No matter how many examples of apparent exception I point to, he will always explain that there has been an "interference" from monopoly or government or physical accident or trade union coercion. Whether or not all races are equal in civilizing potential, is there any conceivable evidence that could convince firm liberals that they are *not* equal or Senator Ellender that they are? Again, obviously not. All conceivable evidence will be explained away in order to defend the chosen doctrine.

It is a characteristic of ideological thinking, whatever the given ideology, that it cannot be refuted by logical analysis or empirical evidence. Actually, the internal logical structure of a developed ideology is usually quite good anyway, rather like the logical structure of paranoiac obsessions, which ideologies resemble in other ways also; and when a logical gap appears—as happened to liberalism in the doctrinal shift from limited to welfare state—

sufficient ingenuity can always patch it up again, as we duly noted. The ideology is a way of interpreting the world, an attitude toward the world and a method for dealing with the world. So long as I adhere faithfully to the ideology there is no specific happening, no observation or experiment that can unmistakably contradict it. I can always adjust my categories and my attitude to allow for whatever it is that happens or that I observe; if necessary I can shut my eyes.

We all feel intuitively that a discussion or argument with "my kind of people" is very different from a discussion or argument in which some other kind takes part. The former is likely to seem more fruitful, as "getting somewhere." The latter is often frustrating. Not only are those people of the other kind wrong; what they say is usually also irrelevant, and it is hard to see what point they are trying to make, even if they knew how to make it. "My kind of people" means, as the phrase is used, those who share my ideology, or my lack of ideology, if I am among the eccentric minority that has none.

Mr. Hutchins mistakes the "universe" in which his universal dialogue takes place; it is not the world of time and men and galaxies, but only a "universe of discourse." The basic ideas, beliefs and values of his ideology constitute the frame, the setting, for the dialogue; and an argument or fact that juts outside that frame or departs from the setting becomes garbled and unintelligible. As the Washington school discussion syllabus explained: "In a democracy everyone has the right to his own convictions and attitudes toward others, but…all attitudes and convictions must be based on truth and reason." It is the ideology that defines what will be accepted as truth and reason.

A discussion with a convinced ideologue on matters covered by his ideology is sure to be a waste of time, unless you share the ideology. What is there to discuss? His ideology is proof against the shock of any seemingly conflicting facts which you might bring forward. He will either reinterpret those facts so that they become consistent with his ideology, or deny them. There are no facts that could convince an intransigent John Birchite that there are no communists in the upper echelons of the American government. A debate between Arthur M. Schlesinger, Jr. and William F. Buckley, Jr. can be a good show (and has been), but not a genuine discussion.

Many liberals, especially among non-intellectuals, are not rigid, orthodox ideologues. Though they are adherents of the liberal ideology in a general, often largely unthinking way, there are gaps and flexible joints in their chitin. Between such loose liberals and those non-liberals who are not themselves unbreachably armored, communication, dialogue and discussion are possible. Of course even hardened ideologues are sometimes transformed, but not often by evidence or reasoned argument; usually by a deep shift in emotional allegiance, or the accumulated weight of direct experiences that the ideology proves unable to assimilate, or by fear or greed. As a rule, a man, when his ideological lenses are shattered, is in haste to replace them with another set ground to a new prescription. The unfiltered world is not his dish of tea.

SEVEN

A Critical Note
in Passing

I

SO THAT THE COMPLETE SYNDROME may be freshly and simultaneously before us, I shall now make a summary list, though this will oversimplify, of the nineteen liberal ideas and beliefs that were discussed in Chapters III-V. But in order to know what a thing is, we must understand what it is not. To clarify the liberal beliefs still further and to help, perhaps, to objectify our estimate of them, I shall draw up a list of nineteen corresponding contrary beliefs, also stated summarily, and printed in a parallel column. In each case more than one contrary belief, in fact an infinite number of contraries, are logically conceivable; but since our positive interest is merely to throw more light on the meaning of liberalism, I have given only one of the possible contraries, as it happened to occur to me in first writing the list down.

Elements comprising the doctrinal dimension of the liberal syndrome:	*One possible set of contrasting non-liberal elements:*

L1. Human nature is changing and plastic, with an indefinite potential for progressive development, and no innate obstacles to the realization of the good society of peace, justice, freedom and well-being.

X1. Human nature exhibits constant as well as changing attributes. It is at least partially defective or corrupt intrinsically, and thus limited in its potential for progressive development; in particular, incapable of realizing the good society of peace, justice, freedom and well-being.

L2. Human beings are basically rational; reason and science are the only proper means for discovering truth and are the sole standard of truth, to which authority, custom, intuition, revelation, etc., must give way.

X2. Human beings are moved by sentiment, passion, intuition and other non-rational impulses at least as much as by reason. Any view of man, history and society that neglects the non-rational impulses and their embodiment in custom, prejudice, tradition and authority, or that conceives of a social order in which the non-rational impulses and their embodiments are wholly subject to abstract reason, is an illusion.

L3. The obstacles to progress and the achievement of the good

X3. Besides ignorance and faulty social institutions there are many society are ignorance and faulty social institutions.

other obstacles to progress and the achievement of the good society: some rooted in the biological, psychological, moral and spiritual nature of man; some, in the difficulties of the terrestrial environment; others, in the intransigence of nature; still others, derived from man's loneliness in the material universe.

L4. Because of the extrinsic and remediable nature of the obstacles, it follows that there are solutions to every social problem, and that progress and the good society can be achieved; historical optimism is justified.

X4. Since there are intrinsic and permanent as well as extrinsic and remediable obstacles, the good society of universal peace, justice, freedom and well-being cannot be achieved, and there are no solutions to most of the primary social problems—which are, in truth, not so much "problems" as permanent conditions of human existence. Plans based on the goal of realizing the ideal society or solving the primary problems are likely to be dangerous as well as utopian, and to lessen rather than increase the probability of bringing about the moderate improvement and partial solutions that are in reality possible.

L5. The fact that an institution, belief or mode of conduct has existed for a long time does not create any presumption in favor of continuing it.

x5. Although traditional institutions, beliefs and modes of conduct can get so out of line with real conditions as to become intolerable handicaps to human well-being, there is a certain presumption in their favor as part of the essential fabric of society; a strong presumption against changing them both much and quickly.

L6. In order to get rid of ignorance, it is necessary and sufficient that there should be ample, universal education based on reason and science.

x6. There is no indication from experience that universal education based on reason and science—even if it were possible, which it is not—can actually eliminate or even much reduce the kinds of ignorance that bear on individual and social conduct.

L7. The bad institutions can be got rid of by democratic political, economic and social reforms.

x7. There is no indication from experience that all bad institutions can be got rid of by democratic or any other kind of reform; if some bad institutions are eliminated, some of the institutions remaining, or some that replace them, will be bad or will become bad.

L8. It is society—through its bad institutions and its failure to elim-

x8. There are biological, psychological and moral as well as social inate ignorance—that is responsible for social evils. Our attitude toward those who embody these evils—of crime, delinquency, war, hunger, unemployment, communism, urban blight—should be not retributive but rather the permissive, rehabilitating, education approach of social service; and our main concern should be the elimination of the social conditions that are the source of the evils.

causes of the major evils of society. A program of social reform combined with a merely permissive, educational and reformist approach to those who embody the evils not only has no prospect of curing the evils—which is in any event impossible—but in practice often fosters rather than mitigates them, and fails to protect the healthier sectors of society from victimization.

L9. Education must be thought of as a universal dialogue in which all teachers and students above elementary levels may express their opinions with complete academic freedom.

x9. Unrestricted academic freedom expresses the loosening of an indispensable social cohesion and the decay of standards, and permits or promotes the erosion of the social order. Academic discourse should recognize, and if necessary be required to recognize, the limits implicit in the consensus concerning goals, values and procedures that is integral to the society in question.

L10. Politics must also be thought of as a universal dialogue in which all persons may express their opinions, whatever they may be, with complete freedom.

x10. Unrestricted free speech in relation to political matters— most obviously when extended to those who reject the basic premises of the given society and utilize freedom of speech as a device for attacking the society's foundations—expresses, like unrestricted academic freedom, the loosening of social cohesion and the decay of standards, and condones the erosion of the social order.

L11. Since we cannot be sure what the objective truth is, if there is any such thing, we must grant every man the right to hold and express his own opinion, whatever it may be; and, for practical purposes as we go along, be content to abide by the democratic decision of the majority.

X11. Whether or not there is any truth that is both objective and capable of being known to be so, no society can preserve constitutional government or even prevent dissolution unless in practice it holds certain truths to be, if not literally self-evident, then at any rate unalterable for it, and not subject to the changing will of the popular majority or of any other human sovereign.

L12. Government should rest as directly as possible on the will of the people, with each adult human being counting as one and one only, irrespective of sex, color, race, religion, ancestry, property or education.

X12. A number of principles have been appealed to as the legitimate basis of government, and most of these have been associated in the course of time with bad, indifferent and moderately good government. Government resting on unqualified universal franchise— especially where the electorate includes sizable proportions of uneducated or propertyless persons, or cohesive subgroups—tends to degenerate into semi-anarchy or into forms of despotism (Caesarism, Bonapartism) that manipulate the democratic formula for anti-democratic ends.

L13. Since there are no differences among human beings considered in their political capacity as the foundation of legitimate, that is democratic, government, the ideal state will include all human beings, and the ideal government is world government. Meanwhile, short of the ideal, we should support and strengthen the United Nations, the World Court and other partial steps toward an international political order and world government, as these become successively possible in practice.

X13. In their existential reality, human beings differ so widely that their natural and prudent political ordering is into units more limited and varied than a world state. A world state having no roots in human memory, feeling and custom, would inevitably be abstract and arbitrary, thus despotic, in the foreseeable future, if it could conceivably be brought into being. Though modern conditions make desirable more international cooperation than in the past, we should be cautious in relation to internationalizing institutions, especially when these usurp functions heretofore performed by more parochial bodies.

L14. In social, economic and cultural as well as political affairs, men are of right equal. Social

X14. It is neither possible nor desirable to eliminate all inequalities among human beings. Although reform should be designed to correct existing inequalities and to equalize the conditions of nurture, schooling, residence, employment, recreation and income that produce them.

it is charitable and prudent to take reasonable measures to temper the extremes of inequality, the obsessive attempt to eliminate inequalities by social reforms and sanctions provokes bitterness and disorder, and can at most only substitute new inequalities for the old.

L15. Social hierarchies and distinctions among human beings are bad and should be eliminated, especially those distinctions based on custom, tradition, prejudice, superstition and other non-rational sources, such as race, color, ancestry, property (particularly landed and inherited property) and religion.

X15. It is impossible and undesirable to eliminate hierarchies and distinctions among human beings. A large number of distinctions and groupings, rational and non-rational, contributes to the variety and richness of civilization, and should be welcomed, except where some gross and remediable cruelty or inequity is involved.

L16. Sub-groups of humanity defined by color, race, sex or other physical or physiological attributes do not differ in civilizing potential.

X16. Whether or not sub-groups of humanity defined by physical or physiological attributes differ congenitally and innately in civilizing potential, they do differ in their actual civilizing ability at the present time and are likely to continue so to differ for as long in the future as is of practical concern.

L17. The goal of political and social life is secular: to increase the material and functional well-being of humanity.

X17. Among the goals of political and social life, well-being is subordinate to survival; and all secular goals are in the last analysis subordinate to the ultimate moral or religious goal of the citizens composing the community.

L18. It is always preferable to settle disputes among groups, classes and nations, as among individuals, by free discussion, negotiation and compromise, not by conflict, coercion or war.

X18. Disputes among groups, classes and nations can and should be settled by free discussion, negotiation and compromise when—but only when—the disputes range within some sort of common framework of shared ideas and interests. When the disputes arise out of a clash of basic interests and an opposition of root ideas, as is from time to time inevitably the case, then they cannot be settled by negotiation and compromise but must be resolved by power, coercion and, sometimes, war.

L19. Government, representing the common good democratically determined, has the duty of guaranteeing that everyone should have enough food, shelter, clothing and education, and security

X19. Except in marginal and extreme cases, the duty of government is not to assure citizens food, shelter, clothing and education, and security against the hazards of unemployment, illness against unemployment, illness and the problems of old age. | and old age, but to maintain conditions within which the citizens, severally and in association, are free to make their own arrangements as they see fit.

I REPEAT THAT THE SECOND ('x') LIST is presented only for the sake of the first ("L"), only to throw additional light on the meaning of the first, and not at all to argue any virtues the second list might be thought to possess, or to recommend it to the reader. I should, however, note that, besides the specific differences in content between each of the nineteen beliefs in the L-list and its opposite number in the x-list, there is a difference in structure as well as content between the two sets of nineteen taken in their entirety.

The L-list is the verbalization of a single, more or less systematic ideology: the ideology of modern liberalism. The x-list, though it perhaps has a recognizably "conservative" cast, does not constitute an ideology, not any ideology at all. The nineteen x-beliefs are related much more loosely to each other, both logically and psychologically, than the nineteen L-beliefs. Thus the two sets are not true opposites of each other, though each individual pair consists of logical contraries. The two sets are two different kinds of thing, like a house and an apple. More generally, the alternatives to an ideology are not solely other ideologies. There is also the possibility of abandoning ideologies and ideological thinking altogether.

A convinced liberal believes all of the nineteen L-beliefs, or is at any rate logically committed to belief in all or nearly all of them. But the x-list is not so all-or-nothing. Both logically and psychologically, it is not only possible but frequently the case that a person should believe six or eight of the x-beliefs and doubt or reject the rest. For several, he might substitute the corresponding L-beliefs; and for others, alternate beliefs that I have not stated.

II

THIS BOOK IS IN NO WAY concerned to refute liberalism. The question of the truth or falsity of an ideology is in any case of minor importance. Human beings believe an ideology, as a rule, not because they are convinced rationally that it is true but because it satisfies psychological and social needs and serves, or seems to serve, individual or group interests. Still, I do not want to hide my own conviction—nor could I, if I would—that the nineteen constituent beliefs in the liberal list are, so far as they can be judged in terms of truth and falsity, false on the available evidence; and that, though they may not be internally inconsistent, they are pragmatically contradictory in the sense that they lead in practice, and necessarily lead, to results that violate their own premises and intentions.

Though I shall not attempt to offer a sufficient case for this summary judgment, I will motivate it briefly with respect to two or three of the crucial liberal beliefs, not so much in order to prove those beliefs false as to suggest that they are at any rate not self-evidently true.

Let us consider, then, the liberal theory of human nature. According to liberal doctrine, human beings are not innately corrupt or defective or subject to essential limitations in their psychological and social dimensions. (Obviously there are certain physical limitations to which human beings are subject; though these, and their possible consequences for individual conduct and social life, are usually not stressed in discussion of the human potential by liberal ideologues.) Human beings are capable of an unlimited, or at least an indefinitely great, advance toward the good life and the good society. There is nothing ineradicably evil in human nature or the human psyche. On the contrary, the primary motivation of human beings is, or can become, rational; so that once education gets rid of ignorance, prejudice, superstition and frustrating customs, human beings will conduct themselves reasonably and will thus be able to build a reasonable society of peace, freedom, justice and material well-being.

At the height of the Victorian period, when the articulate part of the world was enjoying the century of approximate peace bestowed by the British Empire, the spreading fruits of the steam engine and the factory system, and the softening early effects of humanitarian and parliamentary triumphs—in that age of what seemed to most educated men, except for a few perverse poets and artists, an historical dawn if not quite yet full sunshine, this liberal portrait of human nature, inherited from the eighteenth-century Enlightenment, was not altogether implausible even from a non-ideological perspective.

Even then, some scrupulous observers were troubled when they recalled that, as understood by all the centuries of Christianity—the body of faith and belief under which the civilization of Europe and the Americas had taken form—and by all other of the great world religions, man is a creature by essence limited and bounded, his potential goodness corrupted by a portion of evil that by his own efforts cannot be overcome, fated to walk in the valley of the shadow of an alien material universe, under unreprievable sentence of death. Those who were inclined to dismiss religious doctrine as superstition might nevertheless have noted that it was borne out in full and terrible detail by the entire history of man, in every continent, climate and region of the earth, in every society at every stage of development from primitive tribe to mighty empire, constructed by whatever race, black, brown, yellow, red or white. Only those who know very little about the history of mankind can suppose that cruelty, crime or weakness, mass slaughter or mass corruption, are exceptions from the normal human rule. A doctrine of human nature that paints a picture of what man might be that is in direct contradiction to what he has always and everywhere been may be a comfort to the spirit, but is not to be taken very seriously as a scientific hypothesis.

The fundamental law of every genuine science is the postulate that the pattern of what happens in the future will probably resemble that of what has been observed to happen in the past. Any belief requiring the assumption that the future will be radically different from the past is not only false on the evidence—it could not be otherwise, since the only evidence available to man is the observations he has made in the past—but non-scientific in kind, no matter how many invocations the believer makes to Science and Reason. If there was a Victorian moment that perhaps excused a brief optimism over the chance that the human future might be radically unlike the past, what can a reasonable man, once he frees himself from ideology, conclude from the record of our own era? The grimmest lessons of the past about the inherent limits and defects of human nature have been continuously confirmed by wars with tens of millions dead, by mass persecutions and tortures, deliberate starvation of innocents, wanton killings by tens of thousands, the ingenuities of science used to perfect methods of mass terror, new forms of enslavement, gigantic genocides, the wiping out of whole nations and peoples. True enough, the record of the present as of the past is not an unmixed black; the crimes and horrors are mingled with achievements, mercies and heroism. But in the face of what man has done and does, it is only an ideologue obsessed with his own abstractions who can continue to cling to the vision of an innately uncorrupt, rational and benignly plastic human nature possessed of an unlimited potential for realizing the good society.

It is not merely the record of history that speaks in unmistakable refutation of the liberal doctrine of man. Ironically enough—ironically, because it is liberalism that has maintained so exaggerated a faith in science—almost all modern scientific studies of man's nature unite in giving evidence against the liberal view of man as a creature motivated, once ignorance is dispelled, by the rational search for peace, freedom and plenty. Every modern school of biology and psychology and most schools of sociology and anthropology conclude that men are driven chiefly by profound non-rational, often anti-rational, sentiments and impulses, whose character and very existence are not ordinarily understood by conscious reason. Many of these drives are aggressive, disruptive, and injurious to others and to society. Some of them, as seen by modern science, are destructive to the self: seeking pain, suffering, even death. And these negative impulses (if they are to be designated so) are no less integral to the human psyche than those positive impulses pointing toward the liberal ideals.

The liberal assumes, and must assume, that men, given a knowledge of the problem and freedom to choose, will opt for peace, justice and plenty. But the facts do not bear him out, either for individuals or for societies. Individuals choose, very often, trouble, pain, injury, for themselves and for others. Societies choose—as Egypt, Indonesia, Ghana and many another nation are choosing in our day as soon as they have the chance—guns instead of butter, empire instead of justice, despotic glory instead of democratic cooperation. Of course the liberal can always say: that is because they, individuals and societies, were not sufficiently educated and were too much handicapped by the bad institutions held over from the past. To that argument there can be no answer, because in making it he is speaking as an ideologue, and all evidence becomes irrelevant.

It is also ironic that liberalism—so prevalent among modern intellectuals and so widely regarded as the truly creative outlook in modern society—has failed to attract any of the major creative writers of our century. Professor Lionel Trilling, who seldom deviates from the liberal line on specific political or social issues though he is mildly heterodox in theory, discussed this little remarked but surely significant fact in an article published in 1962 by the magazine *Commentary*. He pointed out that none of the major writers has been a liberal and that most of them have been anti-liberal; and that there is no great twentieth-century literary work infused with the liberal ideology as *De Rerum Naturae*, the *Aeneid, The Divine Comedy, Don Quixote, Faust* and *War and Peace* were infused with other ideologies. In the twentieth century, Professor Trilling declares, there has been "no literary figure of the very first rank...who, in his work, makes use of or gives credence to liberal or radical ideas." Many secondary writers and a substantial majority of critics have been and are liberals; but Henry James, Marcel Proust, Ezra Pound, William Butler Yeats, James Joyce, André Gide, Thomas Mann, T.S. Eliot—all of whom the liberals so much admire, so frequently imitate and so endlessly comment on—have all been, often explicitly and scornfully, anti-liberal.

The findings of the modern scientific study of genetics seem to strike a multiple blow at the liberal conception of man and his prospects. The fixity of unit characteristics, their biological transmission through the genes according to mathematical laws of probability, and the non-inheritability of acquired characteristics combine to reinforce the non-liberal belief that human nature has a permanent sub-stratum, that there are ineradicable differences among men not traceable to social circumstance, and that there are limits, often quite low, to what even the most perfect education could accomplish. Genetics certainly gives no support to any doctrine holding that education and social reform could transform man into a creature so radically different from what he has been as would be the case if he dropped his aggressive, destructive and other troublemaking traits. The conclusions to be drawn from genetics would, indeed, seem to be even more drastically counter to the liberal faith in secular progress. It seems to be generally agreed that under the conditions of modern life, the sectors of the human population with inferior genetic assets—inferior, that is, from an intellectual, moral and civilizing standpoint—are increasing, rather rapidly, relative to those with superior assets.

Because the ideology of modern liberalism has become so powerful an influence in contemporary American thought and conduct, it is worth noting that the liberal doctrine of human nature is sharply at variance with the view that prevailed among the Founding Fathers of the republic. At this critical point they parted company with the European Enlightenment, from which, in other respects, they drew so many of their opinions. Most of them believed, with John Adams, that "human passions are insatiable"; that "self-interest, private avidity, ambition and avarice will exist in every state of society and under every form of government"; and that "reason, justice and equity never had weight enough on the face of the earth to govern the councils of men."

IGNORANCE, LIBERAL DOCTRINE TELLS US, is in the last analysis the only obstacle to the good society—peaceful, free, just, prosperous and happy; and ignorance can be dispelled by a rational education accepting the axioms of academic freedom and free speech. Even the problem of reforming bad institutions is secondary to education, because once education overcomes ignorance, then men—men as defined by liberal ideology—will know what is wrong with the institutions, and will take steps to correct them. What do the facts show?

The facts show plainly that there are many obstacles on the road to the good society that are at least as formidable as ignorance: obstacles, such as I have cited, innate to the human organism and psyche; obstacles planted in the physical nature around us; the accumulated weight of history that unavoidably presses on all of us. The facts, moreover, do not show any positive correlation between education and the good life, for society or even for the individual.

Athens was the most educated society of the ancient world and in some respects of all time; and Athens fell as much from inner decay as from external foes. Germany has been the most literate, the most thoroughly educated nation of the twentieth century; and Germany bred Hitler, Nazism and the gas chambers. The Russian drive for totalitarian world power becomes only better equipped and more threatening as the formerly illiterate Russians become more educated. The universities of India and the Arab world, and also of Europe and America, have bred more communists than have the backward villages.

In the United States, all of our children go to school; but in many of our cities they are much worse behaved and more dangerous to society than their unschooled ancestors of a few generations ago. Modern Japan is a completely literate nation, but her literacy did not draw her back from the Marco Polo Bridge or Pearl Harbor. Lenin and his closest associates, Goebbels, Goering, Hess and Schacht if not Hitler himself, Klaus Fuchs and Alger Hiss, ten thousand traitors, a million suicides and tens of millions of neurotics, have all been highly educated men. After all, has not Satan always been known to be the most intelligent of created beings; and was it not by leading them to eat of the Tree of Knowledge that he drove Adam and Eve from Paradise?

There is still another difficulty in the liberal belief that the removal of ignorance, as the key obstacle, will bring the good society. Suppose we ask, how is ignorance to be overcome? By universal institutionalized schooling, presumably. This is the remedy that the liberals have always advocated, where they have not taken it for granted. By its own rules, liberalism cannot accept as the proper method for eliminating ignorance the sort of educating in traditions, conduct, folkways and uncritical beliefs that a child gets from home and family, or the religious educating done through the church: on the contrary, home, church and family are seen as likely sources of the errors, superstitions and prejudice that proper education must overcome.

Now the fact is that we *do* have universal institutionalized education, or come close to having it, in the advanced nations. But this has *not* removed ignorance, especially about political, social and economic matters; and to whatever extent it may have done so in some countries, the removal of ignorance has *not* brought any notable advance toward the good society. The nineteenth-century liberals overlooked, and the twentieth-century liberals decline to face, the fact that teaching everyone to read opens minds to propaganda and indoctrination at least as much as to truths; and on political and social matters it is propaganda and indoctrination rather than truth that universal education has most conspicuously nurtured. All modern dictators quickly establish universal education, just as they institute a really universal franchise, and rigorously carry it out—without discrimination on the basis of sex, religion, color or whatever— if it was not already in operation. And we have already noted that some of the least ignorant nations of our day have, or have had, the worst governmental regimes.

LIBERALISM, WE HAVE FOUND, is committed to a relativist theory of truth. Liberalism holds that there is no such thing as objective truth; or, if in some abstract sense there may be objective truth, that it is impossible for us to be sure that we know it. That theory is the ultimate justification for universal free speech and democracy: no man has the right to believe that his truth has any priority in the marketplace over any other man's. Indeed, his truth is in no way privileged even over the other man's error, for who can know, and know that he knows, which is which? Truth too, at least with respect to political, economic and social affairs, must accept the verdict of democracy's tribunal. Everyone should speak his piece, advocate his own truth, and then let the majority decide.

Aristotle was the first of the many philosophers who have pointed out that a wholly relativist theory of truth cuts the ground from under its own feet, is self-refuting. As a relativist, I say that there is no way to be sure of the truth, and that therefore every man is entitled to his own opinion. But how do I know that it is true that there is no way to be sure of the truth? And how can I prove to you that every man is entitled to his own opinion if you deny this? By my own principle, may not your denial be just as true as my assertion? We are thus plunged into an unending series of mutual contradictions, with no way of reaching a conclusion. Suppose that you deny and reject the whole doctrine of liberalism. Then, by that doctrine itself, you are not only entitled to your opinion, but there is just as much chance that your opinion is true as that liberalism is true.

The fact is that all human discussion, all communication among human beings—and thus every form of human society—must assume that *not all* opinions are true, that some of them are false, that there is an objective difference between truth and falsity; and that if you and I hold contrary views, then at least one of us is wrong.

There may be a trace of sophistry in this Aristotelian critique; and some modern logicians believe they avoid the theoretical dilemma it poses by introducing the idea of logical types or levels. Even so, liberalism confronts an inescapable practical dilemma. Either liberalism must extend the freedoms to those who are not themselves liberals and even to those whose deliberate purpose is to destroy the liberal society—in effect, that is, must grant a free hand to its assassins; or liberalism must deny its own principles, restrict the freedoms, and practice discrimination. It is as if the rules of football provided no penalties against those who violated the rules; so that the referee would either have to permit a player (whose real purpose was to break up the game) to slug, kick, gouge and whatever else he felt like doing, or else would have to disregard the rules and throw the unfair player out.

This practical dilemma has been driven home in our day by the growth of totalitarian movements operating within the structure of democratic and liberal society. It suggests a grave weakness in the liberal ideology, one that has troubled many liberals. Surely there would seem to be something fundamentally wrong with a doctrine that can survive in application only by violating its own principles. I plan to return to this dilemma, and some of its consequences, in another context.

THERE ARE A NUMBER OF other practical dilemmas that modern liberalism cannot avoid. Take, as one additional example, the meaning of the liberal declaration against social hierarchies, segregation, discrimination, against what sets one group of men apart from others. Certainly some sorts of discrimination are of a kind that seems cruel and unjust to almost everyone. But the trouble is that human beings—the human beings of the real world—are hierarchical and segregating and discriminating animals. There has never been a human society anywhere, at any time, from the most primitive tribe to the freest republic to the most civilized empire, in which there have not been segregations, discriminations and groupings: into young and old, male and female, warrior and peasant, slave and citizen, black and brown and white, believer and unbeliever, tall and short, rich and poor, egghead and blockhead. There is always apartheid—the South African word means merely "apartness"—in some degree, on some basis or other. Even in college there are clubs and fraternities, freshmen and seniors, athletes and brains, chess players and beer drinkers and aesthetes. Prison and concentration camp are no different from other forms of human society. The French writer David Rousset, who was for some years an inmate of Nazi concentration camps, wrote a brilliant study of what he called "The Concentrationary Universe." Its main point is to record the existence within the camps of the same patterns of social division and discrimination that exist in the outside world; and his findings have been confirmed by many ex-inmates of the Soviet camps.

Now the fact that social discriminations always exist does

not justify this particular discrimination, whatever it may be. Perhaps we ought to get rid of this one, or at least try to mitigate its degree. But it shows that the attempt to get rid of all discriminations, all apartheid, is illusory. The undiscriminating effort to end all discrimination must necessarily fail. Either the old groupings remain, perhaps with new protective disguises; or they are replaced by new and different types of discrimination that may be worse than the old: party member and outsider; bureaucrat and plain citizen; college graduate and non-graduate; secret policeman and concentration camp candidate.

THE CRITICAL COMMENTS MADE in this section deal with what might be called formal elements of the liberal ideology. I have reviewed evidence—accessible to everyone from his own experience and reading—indicating that the liberal theories of human nature and social progress and the liberal belief that ignorance is the primary obstacle to the good society are false. And I have shown that the logic of the liberal doctrine of free speech and the liberal program to remove all social discrimination is self-refuting in practice.

Other of the liberal beliefs can be analyzed along similar lines. For example, it can be shown, and has been shown by a number of writers,[1] that the idea of the general will and popular sovereignty in the form required by liberal ideology is inconsistent in theory and impossible in practice. However, I shall close this parenthesis here, since a further elaboration of the formal critique is not relevant to the purposes of this book.

---

1. I have discussed the work of several of these writers in *The Machiavellians*; and in Chapters 21-25 of *Congress and the American Tradition* I have made an extended analysis of certain indigestible ingredients of the liberal theory of democracy.

It is of course possible to analyze the merits and demerits, or simply the meaning, of liberalism from quite different perspectives. Without reference to the truth or falsity of liberal beliefs, we might consider the psychology and sociology of liberals, liberalism as a moral code, liberalism as a political device, or the pragmatic consequences of widespread acceptance of the liberal ideology; and some of these considerations will be dealt with, one way or another, in chapters to come.

EIGHT

Do Liberals Really Believe in Liberalism?

I

THE JUDGMENTS THAT LIBERALS render on public issues, domestic and foreign, are as predictable as the salivation of Pavlovian dogs. Whether it's a matter of independence for Pogoland or school integration for some Southern backwater; the latest loyalty oath or a nuclear test ban; the closed shop or the most recent inquiry of the Committee on Un-American Activities; foreign aid or poll taxes; the United Nations or Fair Employment; whether it's X, Y or Z, you can know in advance, with the same comforting assurance with which you expect the sun to rise tomorrow, what the response of the liberal community, give or take an adverb or two, will be. The editorials in the *Washington Post, New York Times, New Republic*, or indeed Paris' *Le Monde* or London's Sunday *Observer*; the liberal columns, speeches and sermons; the deliberations of the faculties of any Ivy League university;[1]

---

1. A friend of mine, who is a lone non-liberal in a large department of

the discussions of the Foreign Policy Association, League of
Women Voters or American Association of University Professors—the small flourishes of special rhetoric in their commen-
taries are like the minor decorations permitted on a rigorously
fixed style of painting, architecture or music.

These myriad but manifestly not random judgments were
the raw data from which I started in composing this book. I
addressed, in effect, the liberal community, saying: Tell me,
please, where I may discover what the underlying principles
are that give this marvelous confidence and cohesion to the
specific judgments all of you are able to make so spontaneous-
ly for the ordering of your lives and the lives of the rest of us;
tell me, so that I too can perhaps learn by deliberate study to
share your ability, since I seem not to have been endowed with
it by nature.

But my request, I found, was not easily fulfilled. I could
not locate any book, for example—though my liberal friends
have produced thousands upon thousands of books—where I
could read the major principles of liberalism exhibited in an
orderly manner, save for that one modest and rather superficial
little volume by Professor Schapiro, whose name is not elevated enough to count very much on those loftier planes where
our opinions are made and remade. There are plenty of books

---

the humanities division of a large university, told me wonderingly: "My
colleagues have read hardly anything of history, political theory or political
philosophy. They know nothing of economics, geography or strategy. They
are acquainted with only the thinnest surface of current events, gleaned by
skimming through the daily paper and perhaps *Time* or *Newsweek*. Yet,
when any important public event happens anywhere in the world, every one
of them reacts with the speed and automatic certainty of a fully programmed
computer to give the orthodox liberal evaluation which will be confirmed by
the recognized public spokesmen within a day or two."

wherein this principle or that, and sometimes three or four together, are discussed in learned or inspiring prose; and one can sense the organic doctrine hovering like a brood-hen over many an historical, political or moral treatise. That is enough, certainly, for liberals themselves, who have the whole system of principles woven into the fabric of their spirits; but it does not answer an alien's need.

When, despairing of the printed record, I sought a verbal answer from experienced and literate liberals, I was told: Well, modern liberalism believes, fundamentally, in Freedom, in the Dignity of Man, in Peace, in Welfare.... Yes, of course. Undoubtedly we all believe in Freedom, Peace, Welfare and the Dignity of Man. But alas, that didn't get me very far forward. What is the content of Freedom, Dignity, Peace and Welfare in our age? By what programs are they fulfilled, defended and enlarged? With whose help—and against whom? The really troubling questions remain.

So I then concluded: since I cannot get an answer from others, I will have to find the answer myself, by carrying through a project of logical exploration, to unearth the set of ideas, principles and beliefs that can explain and motivate the kind of specific opinions that liberals hold and the kind of judgments they render. But when my project began to yield some results that were communicated to others, liberals among them, through lectures, seminars and conversations that were preliminary stages in making this book, this liberal or that would throw up his hands and protest: Oh no, that's not me you're talking about! That's maybe Condorcet or Fourier or some other romantic fellow from ages past. Or it's those sticky chaps in Americans for Democratic Action, whom I don't have much truck with. Or that's what any sensible person thinks, not just us liberals.

I think I can guess why many liberals shy nervously away from the explicit statement of the liberal principles. Part, at least, of what they suddenly see is unfamiliar, and they are not sure they like it. Modern liberalism, for most liberals, is not a consciously understood set of rational beliefs, but a bundle of unexamined prejudices and conjoined sentiments. The basic ideas and beliefs seem more satisfactory when they are *not* made fully explicit, when they merely lurk rather obscurely in the background, coloring the rhetoric and adding a certain emotive glow. "Democracy," "equality," "popular government," "free speech," "peace," "universal welfare," "progress," are symbols that warm the heart; but the mind has a hard time getting through the smoke that surrounds them.

Naturally this is true not only of liberalism but of most ideologies and attitudes. Very few persons bother to inquire into the logical foundations of their day-by-day judgments and rules of conduct, nor is there any reason why many people should. And nearly everyone who does make such an inquiry is likely to be disturbed by what he finds out: that is, he is likely to be rationally dissatisfied with one or more of the principles that logical analysis proves to be the basis for the judgments and evaluations he is in the habit of making.

I certainly do not want to end up sticking pins into a straw man. I want my portrait of liberalism to be so undeniable a likeness that liberals themselves, liberals especially, will recognize and accept it, after a little prodding perhaps, no matter how they may feel about whatever interpretative comment goes along with it. But at the same time there is no reason why liberals should be permitted to evade responsibility for their beliefs, and for the logical implications and the practical consequences of those beliefs. Liberals, surely, are logically committed to belief in *something*—whether they wish to admit it or not; and it must be something noticeably different in many respects from what conservatives, say, or reactionaries or fascists are committed to. So far as the liberal ideology can be stated as a more or less systematic set of ideas and beliefs, I have now stated it, and the result is before us. If liberalism is not what I say it is, then what is it?

II

LET US WORRY A FEW PAGES longer the question: Do liberals "really believe" in liberalism? We may translate more exactly: Do those persons who are generally known as liberals and who regard themselves as liberals really believe the nineteen propositions on our diagnostic list, or nearly all of them?

If we are using the word "believe" in a psychological sense, in which "to believe so-and-so" means "to give conscious assent to so-and-so," we will find that many liberals do believe all nineteen propositions, and that all liberals believe most of them. Certainly a man who disbelieved a majority of the nineteen would not regard himself, or be regarded, as a liberal.

There are some liberals, however, who will say that they disagree with several of the nineteen propositions. Most of such psychological non-assent is not significant. The reason for it, as I have already mentioned, is merely that most people don't think in general terms anyway and don't take the time, even if they have the skill, to examine their own ideas with logical precision: most people, that is to say, quite literally "don't know what they believe." But there are also some sophisticated and even philosophical liberals who dissent quite consciously and rather volubly from a few of the diagnostic nineteen; and I shall return in a moment to the problem this raises for the attempt to arrive at a satisfactory definition of the liberal ideology.

If we are thinking of "belief" in what might be called a "pragmatic" rather than a psychological sense, we will find a considerably wider variation in the relation of liberals to liberalism. To believe in liberalism in this pragmatic sense would mean not merely to say you believed in it, but to act in your private and public conduct in accordance with its principles and injunctions. Undoubtedly there are many persons generally regarded as liberals, including some who also regard themselves as liberals, who do not thus believe in liberalism; who do not, for it comes down to this, practice what they preach. Sometimes, as in the case of many politicians who find the liberal label a useful tool of their profession, the discordance comes from a straightforward cynicism. "In an era of democracy," Robert Michels observed several decades ago, "all the factors of public life speak and struggle in the name of the people, of the community at large. The government and rebels against the government, kings and party leaders, tyrants by the grace of God and usurpers, rabid idealists and calculating self-seekers, all are 'the people,' and all declare that in their actions they merely fulfill the will of the nation....Even conservatism assumes...a democratic form. Before the assaults of the democratic masses it has long since abandoned its primitive aspect....A...candidate who should present himself to his electors by declaring to them that he did not regard them as capable of playing an active part in influencing the destinies of the country, and should tell them that for this reason they ought to be deprived of the suffrage, would be a man of incomparable sincerity, but politically insane."[2]

---

2. Robert Michels, *Political Parties* (New York: Hearst's International Library Co., 1915), pp. 2-15, *passim.*

Sometimes, as happens within the community of every faith, the deviation from the code springs not from the cynicism of a deliberate rascal but from the weakness of a sincere believer. The best of liberals, even like St. Paul's just man, can fall, if not seven times daily, at least every now and then: can find himself, perhaps, lying on the delicious white sand of a sunny beach where Negro or Jewish foot ne'er trod; or stuffing a few extra ballots into the box to make quite sure that the will of the people coincides with his personal program for the march toward the good society. But amiable peccadilloes of this sort, that make the whole world kin, will not be charged, by one who thinks ideologically at any rate, to the account of principles. Indeed, it is not infrequently the sinners who are the most passionate in affirming all the articles of the creed.

However, my interest here is in neither the psychological nor the pragmatic meaning of belief, but what might be termed the logical meaning. Whether or not liberals consciously assent to the beliefs into which I have resolved the liberal ideology, and whether or not their conduct is uniformly in accord with them, these are the beliefs that articulate liberalism into a rational (even if not reasonable) system, that can provide a logical (even if false) explanation for the specific opinions, programs, projects, aims and preferences of liberals.

A rather simple mental exercise should help convince us that these beliefs, or beliefs very similar to them, are the ones required to fulfill that logical task. *If* we assume these nineteen beliefs to be valid, *then* the judgments that liberals pronounce and the proposals they advocate make good sense. Concerning, for example, racial integration in the United States: if the races are indeed equal in civilizing ability, if education and democratic social reform will cure society's ills, if discrimination is socially wrong and government has the universal duty to correct social wrongs, if legitimate government is democratic and democracy rests on the one-man one-vote rule, if tradition and local custom weigh nothing against principle, then, as liberals believe and demand, all forms of racial discrimination should be forbidden, by law and at once. But if the basic liberal beliefs are false or questionable, if even a single one of those just listed is false, then the *logical* argument for the liberal view on racial integration dissolves. The liberal view may still be correct, but it no longer has any rational frame; it becomes a matter of prejudice, sentiment or faith. Now it may be that the best way to deal with matters of this sort is by sentiment, prejudice and faith; and it may be that in any case a rational frame is only a cover for this non-rational trio: but for liberalism, whose formal appeal must be to reason and science, such admissions are taboo. The liberal therefore cannot cut himself off from the only beliefs that can seem to provide him with a shelter of logic.

So, too, concerning liberal judgments about social welfare, academic freedom, decolonization, the United Nations, foreign policy toward right-wing dictators, penology, aid to underdeveloped nations: the liberal can give his conclusions a logical justification only with the help of the principles we have reviewed. If these principles are abandoned, many of the specific liberal opinions and proposals are likely to seem absurd as well as arbitrary. Principles aside, could anything be more absurd, for example, than to expect an Indonesia, a Vietnam, an African ex-colony or Caribbean duchy, to behave like a constitutional republic?

This is the most important sense in which liberals "really believe" in liberalism. Without the nineteen propositions, they have no logical legs to stand on. The liberals, whether they like it or not, are stuck with liberalism.

III

AN OPTIMISTIC THEORY OF HUMAN nature and history has a major role, perhaps the crucial role, in the liberal ideology. It may be asked: Is this theory really a necessary part of liberalism? Even if the liberal forebears of the eighteenth and nineteenth century used to believe it, as they undoubtedly did, cannot the late twentieth-century liberals dispense with it? And is it not a fact that some present-day liberal thinkers have denied it, while holding to the other liberal beliefs more immediately related to political and social affairs?

It is true that among the more sophisticated of our liberal thinkers there are some who have denied the optimistic theory of human nature and history—and a good many more, both sophisticated and naive, who forget, overlook or ignore it. This is not surprising. Once the optimistic theory has been separated out from the bundle, made explicit and placed in the dock for judgment, men acquainted with modern science, art and literature cannot defend it openly without risking conviction for intellectual obsolescence. I have already mentioned Max Lerner as a liberal whose hankering after Freud has inclined him toward heresy in his ideas about man. Sidney Hook, who has always had some trouble preventing facts from interfering with his ideology,[3]

---

3. Professor Hook, partly because he saw the truth about Bolshevism before he got his ideological glasses fitted, has had occasional trouble keeping step in the liberal army. He is perhaps to be considered a fellow traveler of liberalism rather than a liberal *tout court*; guilty of liberalism, we might say, by association.

has followed John Dewey in seeking the help of dialectical formulas that synthesize the classic dogma (Man is Evil) with the Enlightenment dogma (Man is Good) into an account that is sufficiently qualified in every direction to cover every contingency.

Professor Charles Frankel, in *The Case for Modern* [i.e., *Liberal*] *Man*, announces that it is his "purpose in this book to re-examine the credentials of [liberal] philosophy, and to do so by considering the most representative and influential indictments which have been drawn up against it."[4] And in the event he shows that he has a formal or cocktail-party acquaintance with many of the facts and arguments that can be introduced as evidence in the case against modern liberalism. But there was never any need for the defendant to fear the outcome of the trial. Professor Frankel's judgment had been firmly decided before court opened, as he quite frankly admits in his introductory pages:

> This book is a defense of the revolution of modernity [a term he equates with liberalism]. It is an attempt to show that these doom-filled prophecies [of the critics of liberalism] are unwarranted, and that the hopes with which the modern era began are still the hopes by which we may steer our course....I believe that these liberal ideas, notwithstanding all the criticisms that are being made of them, are essentially right—right in their logic, right in their estimate of what is possible, and right in their estimate of what is desirable.[5]

---

4. Charles Frankel, *The Case for Modern Man* (New York: Harper & Bros., 1956), p. 8.

5. *Ibid.*, pp. 2, 6.

The pledge of allegiance is gallant and unqualified; and any difficulties that remain after the jousts with the critics Professor Frankel dissolves by denuding the theory of all factual reference that anyone could put a finger on.

But it is Arthur M. Schlesinger, Jr. who has made the boldest gambit. In Chapter III of *The Vital Center*, Mr. Schlesinger substitutes the terms "progressive" and "progressivism" for "liberal" and "liberalism." He attributes to progressivism an extreme and somewhat caricaturized version of many elements of the liberal ideology, in particular the doctrines of progress and human perfectibility. He then renounces progressivism so defined, in the name of what he calls "radical democracy." Since Mr. Schlesinger is intellectually stylish, his own comments on human nature (*anno* 1948, when this manifesto of the coming New Frontier was mostly written) are sprinkled with references to Kierkegaard, Dostoevsky, Nietzsche, Proust and other writers whose opinions on human nature and conduct are far from flattering.[6]

But the denials are like Peter's. An optimistic theory of human nature and history is integral to, logically inseparable from, the whole body of liberal doctrine. When they come out of their theoretical detours and get down to their own ideas and programs, Professor Frankel's "modernity," Professor Hook's "democratic socialism," Mr. Schlesinger's "radical democracy" and Mr. Lerner's "radicalism" (or whatever he calls it) turn out

---

6. It is worth noting that Professor Frankel, who in his books still remains something of a scholar as well as a pamphleteer, takes a rather dim view of these chroniclers of the spiritual underground. He realizes how vulnerable it leaves liberalism, intellectually, "that liberal voices should be speaking, as they now are, in such strange accents, in the accents of Burke and Kierkegaard and Dostoievsky and Heidegger." (*The Case for Modern Man*, p. 43.)

to be polished-up versions of the standard liberal design, just as does Mr. Hutchins' scholastic-flavored democratism.

The payoff invariably comes in the exhortations of the concluding paragraphs. In, for typical example, *The Vital Center*'s rousing farewell chapter ("Freedom: A Fighting Faith"), the orthodox rhetoric, for all the qualifications, proves irresistible. "Freedom must become, in Holmes' phrase, a 'fighting faith.'...The thrust of the democratic faith is...toward compromise, persuasion and consent in politics....In place of theology and ritual, of hierarchy and demonology, it sets up a belief in intellectual freedom and unrestricted inquiry....Man is instinctively anti-totalitarian" (yes, instinctively).

We need not abandon our optimism, only recognize that "optimism about man is not enough....The historic methods of a free society are correct so far as they go; but they concentrate on the individual; they do not go far enough....An adequate philosophy of free society would have to supplement the [historic] tests by such questions as this: Do the people have a relative security against the ravages of hunger, sickness and want?...It has become the duty of free society to answer these questions— and to answer them affirmatively if it would survive. The rise of the social-welfare state is an expression of that sense of duty....The reform of institutions becomes an indispensable part of the enterprise of democracy. But the reform of institutions can never be a substitute for the reform of man."

We may note in each case how Mr. Schlesinger's words merely reformulate the substance of one or more of the nineteen elements of the liberal syndrome. In those last two quoted sentences there reappears unchanged the orthodox doctrine: the only obstacles to the good society are ignorance and bad institutions; both obstacles can be removed with the help of a fighting faith in radical democracy—that is, in liberalism. "Wherein lies the hope?" Mr. Schlesinger asks, and answers in Walt Whitman's words: "In 'the exercise of Democracy,'" now raised to a capital letter. The millennium, Mr. Schlesinger goes so far as to grant, may not be fully realized, since democracy or Democracy, following John Dewey, is "a process, not a conclusion." But to the question that he asks in his penultimate paragraph, "Can we win the fight?"—it is not quite clear what the fight is for: the "process," it would seem, strictly speaking, but it is also "against communism and fascism," "against oppression and stagnation," "against pride and corruption," and for restoring "the balance between individual and community"—to the question whether we can win, Mr. Schlesinger leaves us in no doubt that we can if we "commit ourselves with all our vigor" and believe "in attack—and out of attack will come passionate intensity."[7]

Men as bright as Messrs. Schlesinger, Hook, Frankel, Lerner and Hutchins know very well that the optimistic theory[8] of man and society is a grave weakness in liberalism's doctrinal equipment; and that is why they try to shake it off, why they avoid its company, and protest when they meet it face to face that it is no friend of theirs. But if man's nature is not plastic and ever subject to beneficent change, not perfectible in large if not quite infinite degree, ready to blossom when the winter cover of ignorance is lifted, then what happens to the liberal confidence in universal education and universal democracy—

---

7. Arthur S. Schlesinger, Jr., *The Vital Center* (Boston: Houghton Mifflin Co., 1949), pp. 245, 247-51, 256, *passim*.

8. It should be noted that a pessimistic theory of man and society is not the only alternative to an optimistic theory. Actually, both optimism and pessimism are equally irrelevant to an objective and empirical theory.

with full freedom of speech and opinion, of course—as the necessary and sufficient key to progress, to peace, justice and well-being?

What if some men, and some tendencies within all men, prefer lies to truth; suffering, including self-suffering, to pleasure and happiness; crime to honest work; fighting to cooperation? What if they use free speech for deceiving instead of educating, and the free ballot as a device for consolidating despotic power instead of fulfilling the will of the people? What then happens to Mr. Hutchins' "universal dialogue," to the gallant hopes that Walt Whitman and Mr. Schlesinger stake on "the exercise of Democracy"?

What if the government that truly embodies the democratic will of the people turns out to be a hideous tyranny, and not the free, scientific and open society of John Dewey's turgid prose? What if his progressively reared children, unhampered by superstition, custom and traditional disciplines but left free to develop their own free natures, turn out to be not liberals but monsters—turn out to be, let us say, the delinquent monsters that today roam the cement jungles of our great cities? No, we must repeat: if human nature is scored by innate defects, if the optimistic account of man is unjustified, then is all the liberal faith vain.

IV

'IN THE END,' PROFESSOR FRANKEL suddenly admits, throwing in the sponge, "to believe in 'the goodness of man' is not to commit oneself to any particular description of human behavior. It is not to say that men's good deeds outnumber their evil deeds, or that benevolence is a stronger disposition in men than malice. It is, quite simply, to adopt a policy—the policy of looking for cures for human ailments, and of refusing to take No for an answer."[9] That is to say: the meaning of the liberal belief about human nature, like that of the liberal beliefs about progress and history, about education, reform and equality, and indeed like the meaning of the beliefs comprising any and all ideologies, is not solely and not primarily a matter of truth and falsity. It is exceedingly naive to suppose that we have solved the problem of an ideological belief, or even understood it, by proving it true or false.

"Derivations," wrote Vilfredo Pareto (using that term in the sense I am giving to "ideologies"), "comprise logical [i.e., scientific and true] reasonings, unsound reasonings, and manifestations of sentiments used for the purpose of derivation: they are manifestations of the human being's hunger for thinking. If that hunger were satisfied by logico-experimental [i.e., scientific] reasonings only, there would be no derivations: instead of them we should get logico-experimental [scientific] theories. But the human hunger for thinking is satisfied in any number of ways; by pseudo-experimental reasonings, by words that stir the sentiments, by fatuous, inconclusive 'talk.' So derivations come into being."[10]

The various liberal beliefs that we have reviewed—each of them a rather complex affair—do contain or entail cognitive assertions that are either true or false; in nearly every case, as a matter of fact, false. But the matter does not end there. In spite of liberalism's assumption to the contrary, a doctrine's objective claim

---

9. Frankel, *op. cit.*, p. 115.

10. Vilfredo Pareto, *The Mind and Society* (New York: Dover Publications, Inc., 1963), Section 1401. Quoted with permission of The Pareto Fund.

to truth—especially about moral, political and social issues—is the least of the motives that lead men to believe in it; nor will an objective proof that the doctrine is false have much influence in leading anyone to abandon it. Moreover it does not automatically follow that if a doctrine is false, it is therefore "bad." Even though the doctrine is false, its consequences in practice, for individual conduct or for society, may still be superior to those from any available alternative.

The doctrines of the liberal ideology, then, besides making certain assertions that may be judged true or false, also express attitudes, values, ideals and goals. Some of these are palpable on the surface—any reader can intuit the sentiments expressed in Mr. Schlesinger's more excited passages, such as some of those I have quoted—and others are hidden more or less deep under the verbal wrappings. Now we cannot prove attitudes, values, ideals and goals to be false or true in the same sense that we can prove cognitive assertions to be true or false. We can merely try to understand them clearly, to estimate their probable consequences, to relate them to the pattern of human life as we have become acquainted with it, and then to judge them, if we feel called on to judge, as acceptable or unacceptable. A man's goal might be to stay drunk all his waking hours. We can't exactly prove this false by logic and scientific evidence. What we can do is to trace out its probable results, and show what these mean in terms of health, family, friends, job and so on. This is enough to convince some people that the goal of perpetual drunkenness is unacceptable. There are others, however, who like their liquor enough not to care about the meaning and consequence of a drunken life, or who are incapable of staying sober. The philosopher Morris Cohen told the story of a patient with incipient Bright's disease for whom the doctor prescribed a quart of buttermilk daily. After trying the remedy a few weeks, the patient reported back: "Doctor, I'd rather have Bright's disease."

In judging the sentiments, values and attitudes associated with a given ideology, there are two special difficulties. Are there, in the first place, any objective criteria that can be applied so that an analysis will have some chance of reaching an agreed conclusion? Anybody who knows the tricks can find out fairly easily whether the logical structure of a doctrine is consistent or not. The question of factual truth is more complicated; but there are fairly well understood rules of evidence that usually can lead to an objectively probable result, if we are willing to consider the evidence objectively—which, of course, we are usually not where morality and politics are concerned. In the case of sentiments, values and attitudes, we can refine and clarify our judgment by observation, study, research, analysis and meditation; but in the end, I suppose, we must either accept or reject. If some ultimate clash of temperament, interest or ideal is at stake, however concealed, then we are not going to get agreement. There will just have to be disagreement; and if the disagreement is of a kind that necessarily leads to practical conflict, then one side will have to prevail.[11]

---

11. To illustrate this point further, by an unimpeachable example, I had planned to reproduce one of Jules Feiffer's strip cartoons that summed it up perfectly in his very special medium. My publishers sent a routine request to Mr. Feiffer for permission to do so. Mr. Feiffer replied that he refused, on the ground that his opinions are not the same as mine and he does not want to run the risk that any work of his should help my purposes. It is an impressive demonstration of the power of ideology that it can compel so talented and witty (if, like his verbal analogue, Murray Kempton, rather sentimental) a young man to sound like such a stuffed shirt. At the same time I am grateful that he has thus provided an example, even more revealing than his walled-off cartoon, of liberalism's rational dialogue in action.

The second difficulty is related to the first. I too (whoever I happen to be) express sentiments, values and interests in all my words—except perhaps when I use mathematical symbols, and maybe then—whether or not my words are also making cognitive assertions that are true or false. So when I write about the sentiments of others—of liberals, say—I cannot avoid expressing my feelings about their feelings. Suppose X says: "The late Eleanor Roosevelt was unfailingly thoughtful and generous in her attitude toward others, particularly toward the neglected and unfortunate." And suppose Y says: "The late Eleanor Roosevelt was always sticking her nose into other people's affairs." It is quite possible, I think we all might agree, that those two sentences are identical in cognitive meaning; that, interpreted solely in the cognitive or propositional dimension, they are equivalent and, as a matter of fact, true. And yet there does seem to be a world of difference between them. Perhaps we need to state both in order to understand Mrs. Roosevelt.

Aristotle remarked with his usual good sense that it is foolish to expect greater accuracy in our knowledge of a given subject-matter than the nature of the subject-matter permits. In turning from the examination of liberalism as a set of doctrines to a sketch of liberalism as a cluster of sentiments, attitudes and interests and as a mode of conduct governed by certain typical values or goals, the microscope of logical analysis will be less useful, for the most part, than the everyday observation and experience open to common sense. Our account will have to be more flexible, somewhat impressionistic here and there, and at times a little arbitrary in omitting qualifications and exceptions that could be discovered by minute enough inquiry. But it can be accurate enough for my purpose, which is not to portray every last detail of every individual liberal's liberalism, but to determine the meaning of modern liberalism as an historical tendency, and the function that it fulfills in our epoch.

NINE

The Liberal's Order of Values

I

AS A RULE IT IS NOT THE several values (ideals, goals) to which a man adheres that reveal most about his character and conduct, but rather the order of priority in which the values are arranged. It tells us little about John Doe to know that for him life is an important value. So it is for nearly all men; not quite all, but nearly all. But we will have learned much about John if we find out whether life is for him a value more important than any other; or, if not, what other value is more important than life. Better Red than Dead?... Liberty or Death?... Death before Dishonor?... My life, that another may live?...

Suppose that we use the term "Liberty" to designate national independence and self-government—the meaning that was presumably in Patrick Henry's mind; "Freedom," to designate the freedom, or liberties, of the individual; "Justice," to mean distributive justice of a more or less social welfare sort—that is, a reasonable amount of material well-being for everyone along with an absence of gross exploitation or discrimination;[1] and "Peace," to signify the absence of large-scale warfare among major powers.

Liberty, Freedom and Justice are the three primary social values or goals that have been approved or at least professed by nearly everybody—not quite everybody, but nearly everybody—in Western civilization, whatever the political philosophy or program, since the Renaissance. The fourth—Peace—has moved into the front rank during the present century, especially since the advent of nuclear weapons.

Most people want, or think they want, all four of these values; but, the way the world goes, it is not possible to realize the four equally on all occasions. One value must be subordinated or sacrificed to another, or others. Whether we wish to or not, each of us is compelled for practical purposes to arrange the four values in a certain hierarchy—if liberals will permit the word—or order of priority.

For the older liberalism of the nineteenth century, the standard order, starting with the value that was regarded as the most important, was:

Freedom

Liberty

Justice

Peace

---

1. I am thus using the term "Justice" in a broad sense that covers both "economic justice" and "social justice"; and as part of the latter I mean to include the ideal of eliminating discrimination, or at least gross and coercive discrimination, on such grounds as race and color. The present movement in the United States against racial discrimination is often referred to as a campaign for "civil rights" or for "freedom." It is more useful to understand it as a struggle for "social justice," interpreted along more or less egalitarian lines, and to consider civil rights and freedom as applying primarily to individuals rather than groups, races or classes.

For twentieth-century liberalism up to a decade or so after the First World War, the order became:

Justice
Freedom
Liberty
Peace

From that time until after the Second World War, the last two tended to shift positions, so that the liberal ranking became:

Justice
Freedom
Peace
Liberty

Since the coming into being of full-scale nuclear systems, the standard liberal order has become:

Peace
Justice
Freedom
Liberty

This evolution expresses summarily the rise in the relative importance, for liberalism, of the ideas of social reform and the Welfare State, and the gradual shift of stress from national sovereignty to internationalism.

The significance of these ratings becomes more marked when we contrast them with non-liberal orders. For example, the form of contemporary self-styled conservatism that is really a kind of right-wing anarchism accepts an order that is the same as that of nineteenth-century liberalism, except for a displacement of Peace:

Freedom

Peace

Liberty

Justice

However, this ideology (for this form of conservatism is also an ideology) grades the last three so much below the first that they must almost be thought of as belonging to a different scale; and it tends to interpret Freedom primarily in terms of laissez faire economics.

The form of contemporary conservatism that might be called traditional—which is not an ideology—would not judge, or feel, that there is any fixed order of priority for the major social values. Under the specific circumstances of this specific time, it would probably rate the four here under consideration as:

Liberty

Freedom

Peace

Justice[2]

II

FOR CONTEMPORARY LIBERALISM, then, the standard, typical or average order of priorities runs: *Peace, Justice, Freedom,*

---

2. I have developed this little game of value-permutations from a suggestion in a manuscript written by Ralph McCabe. I should perhaps note that the subject-matter of this section continues to be located within the framework of "ideology." By this I mean that I am here presenting the value systems, as I

Liberty. Before discussing certain special features of this liberal order, I want to clarify what is involved more generally when several non-identical values are arranged in a priority sequence.

My values function as guides to my judgment and conduct. I judge the worth of an act or line of action in their light, and I strive to realize them in practice. I strive, in fact, to realize *all* the values I hold, as fully as possible. Along with more personal values (pleasure, friendship, love, money, salvation, whatever they may be) I seek, as social or public values, Peace *and* Justice *and* Freedom *and* Liberty, all four. No critical problem arises so long as there is no conflict among the various values; but in the real world there is frequently both competition and conflict; and in many cases the conflict is insoluble in the sense that no matter what action I take I will have to negate and sacrifice at least one of the values. There cannot be Peace in this situation, we find, unless the claims of Liberty (i.e., national sovereignty and self-government) are diminished or neglected. There cannot be Justice—for this minority group, perhaps, under the given circumstances—without restricting the Freedom of some other group, or even of the majority.

A liberal (or a conservative or a communist) may explain to me that these conflicts are only temporary and superficial. His values (he is confident) are consistent and supplementary. In the long

---

previously did the doctrinal system, from the inside, without necessary reference to how they are actually related to the external world of space, time and history, or even to the actual motives of those who believe they hold the values, as those motives might be judged, after due investigation, by an external observer. From the fact that I sincerely want freedom (or whatever), it does not follow that I will act in ways that will in reality promote freedom; and in spite of the subjective sincerity of my wish, it might still be the case that an external observer would conclude that my real goal is power or privilege for myself or my group.

run or the last analysis or somehow or other (he believes), raising Everyman's standard of living (Justice) will guarantee Peace and Freedom too; or (if his ideological starting point is different) Freedom (of the market) will prove the high road to Justice, Liberty and Peace. So it may be in the world of ideologies or the Earthly Paradise; but in the real world the conflicts continue to exist, and to afflict us with the pangs of decision. I am not referring to choices between "good" and "bad," "right" and "wrong," "justice" and "injustice," between, that is, white and black. In these there is no formal difficulty; the moral man knows that white is his proper choice, even when in his moment of weakness he opts for black. The painful decisions that concern us here are those between two or more courses of action along each of which some positive values will be realized and some will be sacrificed.

In such circumstances we have got to establish—in practice even if unrecognized in theory—an order of relative importance among the different values; we have got to act as if some "goods" are better than others. Freedom to do business or to decline to do business with whomever one chooses is a genuine value; but this freedom (the liberal feels) is rightly sacrificed in order to end the correlated discrimination (injustice) to Negroes. Liberty must be ready, if the dilemma confronts us, to give way to Peace.

The actual problems can be intricate. It isn't always a direct choice between Freedom, say, and Justice, with one assigned an automatic priority over the other. Often it is a question, in both directions, of how much: how much Freedom are we willing to endanger or forego in order to achieve this particular enhancement of Justice, or to increase the odds on Peace at this particular juncture? There are not many individuals, though there are some, who always and invariably, under all circumstances, rate value A over value B. An absolute pacifist does: indeed, he rates

Peace not only over any other public value but over all others; and an anarchist so rates Freedom. (Perhaps that suggests the correct definition of "extremist.") But though most people arrange their values less rigidly, nearly everyone exhibits on average, whatever he may say, a recognizable and predictable order of preference. The laissez faire economist or businessman is all for Justice and Peace and Liberty, of course, but we know that when the practical choice must be made between any of these and Freedom of the market, Freedom is an odds-on favorite. When a man proclaims, "Better Red than dead!" he is really saying that however much he may also want Justice, Freedom and Liberty, he will always prefer Peace if a choice must be made.

I RETURN THEN TO THE contemporary liberal order: *Peace, Justice, Freedom, Liberty*; and I direct attention, first, to the middle relationship, Justice over Freedom. I am sure that the rating, Justice-Freedom, holds for contemporary liberalism taken collectively, taken in its broadest sense as a social or historical tendency—and so taken, it is very broad indeed. But it does not hold for every individual liberal. There is a minority of liberals for whom Freedom—individual freedom, especially freedom of speech and opinion—takes precedence, or seems to, over Justice. Roger Baldwin, for so many decades the director of the American Civil Liberties Union, is no doubt one of the clearest examples. Not that Mr. Baldwin does not believe in social justice, universal welfare, social security, etc., and peace too: he would not be a liberal if he didn't, and no one would question his claim to the title. But if the issue came down to a choice between freedom and justice, as it does now and then, Mr. Baldwin would usually, I think, choose freedom; has, in fact, usually chosen freedom. I don't mean choose just for himself: that he would rather starve than submit to tyranny, and that sort of thing. My reference is to social and public values. I think that Mr. Baldwin would judge starvation better than submission to tyranny—if there were no way to escape from the dilemma—for human beings generally, for society, as well as for himself; or, to put the problem on a less extreme level, that he would choose a lowered general standard of living plus more freedom as against a higher standard plus less freedom.

There are other liberals of Mr. Baldwin's type. I imagine that Professors Henry S. Commager and Zechariah Chafee are two, and quite possibly one or two of the members of the Supreme Court. But I have an idea that there are fewer of this type of liberal extant than there seem to be. This is one of the many cases in which the words men use are inaccurate tests of their real attitudes.

Nearly all liberals—and most non-liberals also, for that matter—invoke the name of Freedom the way a drill sergeant invokes his favorite obscenity. It takes closer study to find out just what they mean by that term and how they rate it under pressure. Very often we find that what is really being talked about has little to do with individual freedom, but is basically a question of advancing the interests of an economic, racial or religious group that the Freedom-invoker feels has a status below what it ought to be. Sometimes it is easy to prove that individual freedom is not really involved. For example, a liberal may call on Freedom in demanding that trade unions should have the right to recruit members without interference, to strike, to enjoy immunity from anti-monopoly legislation, etc.; and also to establish a closed shop, with automatic deduction of union dues from the paychecks of all workers. Without attempting to judge the merits of these two sets of proposals, it is obvious enough that by any normal understanding the second—that is, the compulsory closed shop and dues checkoff—is not an enhancement but a deprivation of *individual* freedom. This is accepted because of the belief that the enhanced social power of the unions taken as groups or collectivities will help raise the living standards and political power of the members.

In this practical showdown, Justice is preferred to Freedom; a certain amount of individual Freedom is sacrificed to the presumptive advance of social Justice. And you will search a long time to find a liberal who will disagree with this specific choice, no matter how fervent are his usual hymns to Freedom. Of course, if he is slick at words he will put together an elegant explanation of how the seeming curtailment of individual freedom in the particular instance, by improving the security and mobility and this and that of each worker and lessening his helplessness before the phalanx of monopoly capital, has the ultimate effect of increasing the worker's genuine individual freedom. But that sort of talk shifts us from the real world into the fantasy world of pure ideology, where anything goes and there's no point arguing. (Let me stress, however, that I am not discussing here whether the liberal view on trade unionism is right or wrong, good or bad. I am only offering evidence for the conclusion that in the case of most liberals today, individual Freedom has a lower priority than social Justice.)

What we have come to call "social security" is another important and striking example. The United States, like most other Western nations and all communist nations, provides certain welfare services to all citizens through a system run by the central government and financed by compulsory payments from all wage earners. (The exclusion, which always turns out to be temporary, of a few categories is irrelevant in principle, since both inclusion and exclusion are by group, not by individuals.) Now whatever can be said for and against this sort of social security system, and there is a lot that can be said on both sides, it most certainly and unambiguously reduces at least some elements of individual freedom.

Suppose I, an individual citizen, don't want governmental social security? Suppose I prefer to provide for illness and old age in my own way, or maybe just don't give a damn? My preference in the matter of course makes no difference. I must nevertheless pay my social security percentage—an always increasing percentage, it goes without saying—regularly; and my employer, too, if I have one, must pay for me.

But don't most people, the great majority, prefer to have their social security handled through the centralized governmental system? Very probably—although they would quite possibly be just as satisfied with a decentralized, regulated system after the manner of our electric power system, such as is found in one or two European countries; but, certainly, the great majority like *automatic* social security. I—this supposititious I—have no objection; let every man choose whatever system he wants; let it even be ruled that he *must* choose some system, so that he will not perchance become a public charge, thereby misusing his individual freedom to the injury of the freedom of others; only leave open an alternate choice for the deviants, doubtless a very small minority, who want to do it their own way. But no: the liberals' Welfare State demands one hundred percent compliance, with or without voluntary consent.

Even the liberal achievement in making desegregated schooling the law, though not yet everywhere the practice, of the land cannot be called an unmixed victory for individual freedom. Let us grant the Supreme Court's finding in *Brown v. Board of Education* that compulsory segregation in the public schools violates not merely the rights of Negroes as a group but the freedom of Negroes as individuals—though it must continue to puzzle a naive observer that the Court, in order to reach that conclusion in 1954, had not merely to amend but to contradict its own prior law and doctrine. Whatever the legal and constitutional niceties, it is plain to common sense that as a Negro I have more freedom if I can go to the school of my choice than if I must go to this school only—or, rather, to this particular type of school with respect to racial matters: the public school system allows no individual choice of school in any case.

Nevertheless, this expanded freedom for the Negro is obtained only at the cost of a decreased freedom for white children and their parents. Within the framework of the public school system—and it is not excluded that the principle will become compulsory for private schools also—white students are not free to go to schools for whites only, though this might be their choice, or their parents' choice, if they were free to choose. Even the Negro families have lost one bit of freedom in payment for that which they have gained: for they too, where *Brown v. Board of Education* has effectively extended its sway, are no longer free to send their children to schools segregated by race, though some might wish to, conceivably even a majority here and there. In theory one might imagine families, white or black, wanting schools segregated by some other outlandish principle than color of the skin—color of the eyes, say, height, athletic prowess, ability at chess. According to the liberal principle in action, parents do not possess the freedom to decide what sort of school they want their children to be educated in; and yet that too is undoubtedly a freedom. Here, also, the other side of liberalism's Freedom-stamped coin turns out to be Coercion.

It may be said more generally that the use of legal, police and other governmental sanctions to end social discriminations against racial, religious or other distinctive sub-groups inevitably means some restriction on the individual freedom of some persons, perhaps of a majority or even of everyone: at the very least no one is any longer free to discriminate in the proscribed ways. This is by no means a mere quibble. In the United States, the spread and stricter enforcement of anti-discrimination laws and regulations, both State and Federal, are progressively limiting my freedom to hire whom I choose, to decide whom to sell to or buy from, to associate with whom I please, to choose my neighbors, and so on, as well as to determine what sort of school I want my children to attend. It would be mere ideological hypocrisy to pretend that these are not genuine freedoms; freedoms, moreover, of very considerable significance for the individual. Modern liberals (and a good many non-liberals also) believe, or assume, that the goal of ending social discriminations amply justifies the sacrifice of these freedoms,[3] and perhaps it does, of course. In this field there is wide and daily confirmation of the fact that for modern liberalism's normal order of values, Justice has priority over Freedom.

THERE IS ANOTHER COMPLICATION in assessing the place of Freedom in the modern liberal's litany. In the degree that we give Freedom priority over other values, it gets closer to becoming, logically speaking, a universal. When it gets absolute priority, with all other values assigned not merely to a lower but a different order, then we have reached the pure ideology of anarchism. Short of that logical end point, the assignment of Freedom to the top of the value list would mean that we want—more than anything

---

3. But there would be some dissent among liberals if the individual freedom to be sacrificed were freedom of speech.

else if not quite more than everything else—freedom for each, any and every individual; that our stand for freedom has nothing to do with the specific individual or type of individual in question. Men should be free, should enjoy so far as possible every concrete freedom, whether they are Tom, Dick or Harry; black, brown or white; Christian or Buddhist or pagan. If it turns out that our defense of freedom in practice favors these individuals but not those, this group but not that one, then we must conclude that it is not actually Freedom that we are preferring but some other attribute pertaining to the individuals or groups that enlist our concern.

Let me illustrate this abstract-sounding point. Suppose you observed that over a period of time I was frequently exercised over threats to the freedom of Christians, but seldom if ever over threats to the freedom of Jews. You would then be entitled to suspect that it was not just freedom, plain and simple, that I primarily valued. Or if I were easily aroused about invasions of the rights of employers but not of the rights of employees.

Now I think it can readily be shown that most liberals—not all but most—exhibit a number of unbalances of this sort in their practical pursuit of freedom. Their sentiment toward violations of freedom is not an indiscriminate absolute, but rather, in Sir Arnold Lunn's phrase, a "selective indignation." It is easier for a liberal to feel indignant at, even to notice, a presumptive violation of the freedom of a communist than of a Nazi, or of a suspected communist than of a suspected Nazi. Though a few liberal protests were put quietly on record, not many liberal tears were shed over the notably un-liberal procedures of the government of Israel in the Eichmann affair. The mention of the trial of Sacco and Vanzetti can still rouse millions of liberals to fever-pitch, but hardly anyone even remembers who Draza Mihailovich was, much less what his trial was about.

Liberals the world over have lately been very impassioned indeed in defense of the freedom of Negroes to attend universities in the Southern states of the United States; but few liberals have expended much feeling over, have even bothered to note, the daily and gross violations of the freedom of Christians in most communist countries—in several of which, as it happens, known members of Christian churches are not, generally speaking, permitted to enter universities. Angola's liberation from Portugal is demanded by a thousand times more liberals than condemned India's armed conquest of Goa. Liberals everywhere, among them the President-to-be of the United States, bestirred themselves for years in support of the rights and freedoms of Algeria's Moslem revolutionaries—including the terrorist bands of the FLN: but the liberal dismay over the lost freedoms and rights of a million Christians of European origin, whose only home was and for generations had been Algeria, was too faint to be heard in the passing journalistic breeze. The patterned asymmetry of this selective indignation is related to a still more general and important trait of modern liberalism, to which I shall return in Chapter XI. But I have pointed to enough here, I think, to suggest that behind the shiny values that are the nominal goals of liberal conduct there may lie impulses, drives and interests that are not given open recognition in the official ideology.

The relation between Freedom and Justice is the source of another of those dilemmas that are to be found within the structure of modern liberalism. Giving priority to one or the other can be thought of as defining two different kinds of liberal that are readily recognizable in the flesh: the older-fashioned kind, a dwindling tribe, that puts Freedom first and is usually seen riding hell for leather on a civil liberties issue—the old-fashioned free speech, free assembly, academic and religious freedom sort of civil liberties, not the new-fangled social, economic and UN Declaration brand; and the modernized liberals who feel most strongly about feeding the hungry, housing the homeless, and equalizing the unequal.

This difference in human character type corresponds to a theoretical conflict within the ideology of modern liberalism: the conflict between the principles of free speech and the other individual freedoms on the one hand, and the principle of egalitarian social justice on the other. Essentially, it is a conflict between individualism and regimentation: the individualism that the liberal ideology derives from its past and the regimentation it has absorbed in the present. This conflict is real, and can be hidden but not solved by discussion, negotiation and compromise. It is a fact that liberalism's inherited principles presuppose individualism, and a highly atomistic individualism at that. It is equally a fact that the Welfare State and plebiscitary democracy mean a good deal and an increasing deal of regimentation. One or the other must give way; and, on the evidence of the past generation, there is little doubt which is the tottering horn of that particular dilemma.

III

IN THE CLASSICAL LIBERALISM of the nineteenth century, Freedom was the unchallenged first among values, and this older ranking is retained, though somewhat blurred, in the tendency that is called "liberalism" on the European continent.[4] The

---

4. In Britain, however, the Liberal Party, official custodian of British "liberalism," has shifted a good deal of the way toward the "modern liberalism" that is the subject of this book.

decline in the relative importance assigned to Freedom and the correlated rise in the rank of social Justice, reform and mass welfare quite evidently mark a major historical transformation. In Chapter V we examined the logical maneuvers by which this transformation was accomplished. Here we are concerned with the psychological and moral dimensions: with liberal sentiment, with the relative intensity of diverse liberal interests, with the ideals and goals that guide liberal conduct.

The "Freedom" that came first in the older liberalism included what I have been calling "Liberty" as well as individual freedoms. That is to say, the older liberalism did not sharply distinguish between Freedom and Liberty; the two terms were used interchangeably. The self-government and independence—"self-determination"—of nations and peoples was thought of as closely analogous to the freedom of individuals and it was assumed—erroneously, as experience was to demonstrate—that they mutually promoted and supplemented each other. In the first section of this chapter I listed Freedom and Liberty, in that order, as the first two values in the older liberalism's order of priority. It might have been more accurate to list a compound Freedom-Liberty as first, followed by Justice and Peace.

In accord with this value rating, the older liberals tended to be patriotic and nationalist. They believed in the self-government, independence and sovereignty of their own country, and also in the right of other nations and peoples to be independent and self-governing. They were ready to fight, and did fight, not merely to defend their own country but to advance its interests and influence; and many of them, as a whole series of romantic biographies attests, were eager to enlist in the battles for independence that were being fought by other nationalists in the Balkans, Italy and South America. There was little trace of pacifism in nineteenth-century liberalism; rather more imperialism than pacifism, indeed. As rationalists they believed that discussion, negotiation and democratic voting are the preferred methods for settling disputes, and that, other things being equal, peace among nations is better than war. But Peace had a modest priority; there were a number of other things, Liberty prominent among them, more important than Peace.

These attitudes of the older liberalism are partly reproduced in our day in the Afro-Asian anti-colonial "liberation" movements, many of whose leaders became acquainted, through Western schooling, with the liberal doctrines, and introduced elements from liberalism, or at any rate from the liberal vocabulary, into their local political struggles.[5] Moreover, the modern liberals of the advanced nations preserve the older attitudes and the older order of values with respect to the liberation movements in the underdeveloped regions. They proclaim the supreme right of each of the underdeveloped nations and peoples—even when the nations have never before had historic existence and the "people" have never formed a cohesive group—to self-government and independence at whatever political, economic and social cost, and they give practical support to the struggle to assert that right; and they are ready to accept fighting when that becomes the method of conducting the struggle.

However, the emotional and moral as well as doctrinal relation of modern liberals to the advanced Western nations, and in particular to their own country if this is itself an advanced Western nation, has been transformed. In the first place, the

---

5. The discussion of the "dialectic of liberalism" in Chapter XII will consider more extensively the relation of the anti-colonial struggles to modern liberalism.

concepts of individual freedom (what I have been designating simply as "Freedom") and national freedom ("Liberty") have been dissociated from each other. Both have been downgraded, but the second considerably more, and more unequivocally, than the first. Concomitantly, Peace, which occupied a relatively lowly place in the nineteenth century, has rapidly risen until, for many liberals if not yet for modern liberalism collectively, it is now at the head of the list.

"Liberty," in the sense that I have assigned to it, means self-determination for the political or social group in question, the political group with which I primarily identify myself. For our grandfathers and their fathers and grandfathers before them, this group was in the first instance the nation, and in a more nebulous but still real sense, "their"—that is, Western—civilization, of which the particular nation was a part or "member," and thus distinct in kind from nations that belonged to other civilizations. For the nation to have Liberty (to be "free") meant that it should be self-governing, independent and thus "sovereign." For the civilization, it meant, or would have meant if the problem had been thought about along these lines, that Western civilization should preserve a distinctive character of its own; that it should not be, in whole or part, politically or spiritually subordinate to any other civilization (or non-civilization); that it should in fact be (or be regarded as) the highest form of civilization, properly ascendant over all others.

To downgrade Liberty means to dilute the idea of the sovereignty of the nation and of the uniqueness and superiority of the civilization, and to reduce the importance that we attach to these in the scheme of public values. In terms of attitude, it means, concretely, that patriotism plus Christian faith are to one or another extent replaced by internationalism: not just an "international outlook" that views world affairs in global terms, with due realization that under modern circumstances there is a multiplicity of interests besides those of our own nation and culture that must be taken into account, but an active international*ism* in feeling as well as thought, for which "fellow citizens" tend to merge into "humanity," sovereignty is judged an outmoded conception, my religion or no-religion appears as a parochial variant of the "universal ideas common to mankind," and "the survival of mankind" becomes more crucial than the survival of my country and my civilization.

It is easy to see that, as Liberty moves down the value scale, Peace moves, in an almost automatic correlation, up. The big wars of recent centuries have been fought over the conflicting sovereign claims of the nations, mixed with clashes arising from religious and cultural differences. When nations and distinct civilizations are felt to be of lesser importance, big-scale wars cease to make sense; war has become, as we have frequently been told during the past decade, "unthinkable."[6] There is nothing left worth fighting big wars for. In the internationalized, or internationalizing, society, the resort to force becomes "police action."

In Chapter V we saw how the logic of the ideology of modern liberalism—its theory of human nature, its rationalism, its doctrines of free speech, democracy and equality—leads to a weakening of attachment to groups less inclusive than Mankind, to a conviction that democratic discussion, negotiation and compromise are the only proper methods for resolving conflicts, and to

---

6. These dicta are usually reinforced by references to the destructive power of modern weaponry. Actually, the conclusion emerges from the inner logic of the liberal ideology, and is not dependent on the state of armaments; the existence of the new weapons has served only to bring the conclusion to the surface, not to produce it or even, for that matter, to justify it.

a trend toward international government. This does not mean that all modern liberals are unpatriotic, pacifists, and World Government enthusiasts; though quite a number of them, and a growing number, are one or the other or all three. In particular, many liberals are pacifists. If we use the term broadly, to include moderate as well as absolute pacifists, it will cover a majority of liberals. However, it is not so much the terminal positions as the tendencies which the logic irresistibly determines. Liberalism has during the past several decades become *less* patriotic (in the old-fashioned sense), *more* pacifist, and *more* internationalist. Everybody knows this. It is shown publicly a thousand times a day.

These tendencies are a commonplace of modern argument and rhetoric. From the publication of Norman Angell's *The Great Illusion* sixty years ago, a geometrically expanding mountain of books, articles, speeches, charters, editorials and columns have explained that war between nations is out of date, nations themselves obsolete, universal disarmament mandatory, and growing international organization necessary to salvation. A political figure who suggests that Peace may not be unqualifiedly the supreme object of national policy runs the risk of being scalped at sunrise by the leading hatchetmen of liberal journalism. In this postwar period it has required dozens of Canadian forests to sustain the output of books proving that sovereignty must go.

In language provided for him by a staff that included several of liberalism's most accomplished ideologues, President Kennedy affirmed this "strategy of peace" (as his concluding phrase correctly named it, since the plan of action takes Peace as the supreme value or goal) in his address of June 10, 1963, at American University in Washington: "I have, therefore, chosen this time and place to discuss...the most important topic on earth: peace....I speak of peace, therefore, as the necessary rational end of rational

men....We have no more urgent task." With strict logic the President added the necessary corollary respecting weaponry: "Our
primary long-range interest in negotiating [about arms control]
is general and complete disarmament." His chief aide for policy
planning, the liberal ideologue Walt Whitman Rostow, had included the third and completing link of the logical chain in *The
United States in the World Arena*: "It is a legitimate American
national objective to see removed from all nations—including
the United States—the right to use substantial military force to
pursue their own interests. Since this residual right is the root of
national sovereignty and the basis for the existence of an international arena of power, it is, therefore, an American interest to see
an end of nationhood as it has been historically defined."[7]

It is hard to be sure that the remarks of a political leader are
not passing demagogy. This speech of the late President's may
not state his own serious thinking, but it is no less significant
as an expression of the liberal ideology that is the source of the
speech's ideas and outlook, as of Mr. Rostow's books. Remarks
like these that have just been quoted—which can be matched a
million times over—reveal that when modern liberals talk about
Peace and Liberty they are dealing with ideological absolutes,
not with the empirical facts of contemporary world affairs. In
substance, they present a purely deductive theorem, like a theorem in a closed system of geometry, proving that the three Absolutes—Peace, Disarmament and the end of Nationhood—mutually imply each other. (Though this last step is usually omitted
by prudent ideologues, "the end of Nationhood" is, in turn,
equivalent to universal World Government.) Granted suitable

---

7. Walt Whitman Rostow, *The United States in the World Arena* (New
York: Harper & Bros., 1960), p. 549.

definitions, this is valid enough as an abstract theorem, but it tells us nothing about the actual problems of the real world.

Every informed person agrees that under contemporary circumstances national sovereignty must be modified and restricted. Indeed, every informed person, if he stops to think about it, knows that national sovereignty is in fact and always has been modified and restricted, that "absolute sovereignty" is a fiction that has never existed. Every nation, in charting its own course, has had to take into account, to one degree or another, the geography, resources, power and interests of its neighbors, and to temper or adapt its own sovereign claims accordingly. In our time, rapid communication and transport have made all nations neighbors of each other; and this fact as well as the existence of weapons of mass destructive potential must inevitably be allowed for in the practical exercise of sovereignty. Moreover, no sensible person, whatever his ideology if he has one, is going to suggest that under modern technological conditions a nation has the absolute sovereign right to make its own arbitrary decisions about the allocation of radio-TV channels, the rules of air and sea transport, the international control of epidemics, and so on. But the modifications and restrictions that these modern circumstances require do not inevitably mean the liquidation of sovereignty and "the end of nationhood," any more than the acceptance of rules of the road taking into account the existence of heavy traffic means an end of driving your own car where you want to go. In fact, "nationhood" could achieve a richer meaning as the nation becomes more complexly and intimately related to the community of nations, somewhat as a man does not lose but rather enlarges his individuality through marriage and business and citizenship.

The idea that nationhood, sovereignty, what in this chapter has been called "Liberty," must and should be adapted to changing circumstances is not, therefore, a belief peculiar to modern liberalism. What is distinctive is its view that nationhood and sovereignty should be not merely adapted and altered, but minimized or even altogether ended, and that Liberty has become a lesser or even a negative value. I stress here not the logic of liberal doctrine, which we have seen leads to such conclusions, but the associated liberal feelings and attitudes that translate the doctrine into morality and conduct.

The average liberal is just not so concerned about, not so emotionally involved in, nationhood, national patriotism, sovereignty and Liberty as is a fellow citizen to his ideological Right. It does not shock him when bearded young men say they will never fight for their country, nor is he indignant even when they express preference for a country other than their own. If a mob in an underdeveloped land smashes the consulate or embassy of his nation, he is not much aroused; indeed, he may well conclude, after interpreting the facts, that justice was on the side of the rioters. He feels little thrill when the flag goes by, and quite probably finds pledges to the flag or oaths of allegiance actively distasteful. He approves many of the weighty books setting out to show the relativity and morality equivalence of diverse religions and cultures, and to decry the backwardness of those Westerners who still believe that in some rather important sense Western civilization is superior to Buddhism, Islam, communism, atheism and animism, and therefore worth preserving. If he is not himself a pacifist, as many of his fellow liberals are, he does not *condemn* pacifists or pacifist organizations; in fact, he usually praises what he calls their idealism, defends them against critics, and gives them smiles and cups of coffee when they picket his government's installations. He is likely to have an opinion more lenient than that of non-liberals concerning the deviations from earlier norms of patriotic citizenship by men like Robert Oppenheimer or Alger Hiss, particularly if their actions can appear to be motivated by humanitarian or universalist goals of a logical order higher than nationhood. It does not grieve him that his country should lose a colony or strategic base, or be humiliated by a vote in the United Nations; if his is an advanced nation of the West, he may rather rejoice thereat (as he may have contributed actively to the result) because it will seem a step toward the global Justice and Peace that he seeks. He will not feel uneasy, certainly not indignant, when, sitting in conference or conversation with citizens of countries other than his own—writers or scientists or aspiring politicians, perhaps—they rake his country and his civilization fore and aft with bitter words; he is as likely to join with them in the criticism as to protest it. It does not seem to him an anomaly that his own nation's communication industry should on a massive scale print the books, produce the plays and movies, present the television scripts of those who hate his nation and his civilization, and seek, often avowedly, the destruction of both.

The cluster of attitudes and feelings which constitutes liberalism in the affective dimension is of decisive practical importance. It indicates what liberals will work and struggle, sacrifice and die for, and in what order. Many liberals (though not all) would reject as a slander and smear, the statement that they are not "patriots"—although they never themselves use the word except in a scornful phrase applied to war veterans, Daughters of the American Revolution and Empire Loyalists. But it is certainly a fact that the average liberal, for good or ill, is not a patriot in the sense of fifty years ago. That a man was a patriot meant that in political life his primary emotional involvement was with his country. Stephen Decatur was entirely accurate in his summing up of true patriotism: the patriot desires that his country shall always be in the right, but his country comes first even if it is not right. That is, in terms of the analysis we have used, for the patriot Liberty is unequivocally first in the order of public values. But for the modern liberal, Liberty is not first. If he judges his country wrong on a given issue, including the very important issues, he is willing that it shall lose out, he prefers that it lose out, he may even help make sure it loses. If the United Nations vote or the World Court decision goes against his country, then, he believes, the United Nations or the World Court should be upheld and his country give way. If he thinks that his country's weapons or strategy "menace peace," then Peace, he feels, not his country's military plans, should take precedence. It is the duty of his country to aid an underdeveloped nation even if that nation offers no reciprocal benefit, even if it is unfriendly or downright hostile; in other words, Social Justice, too, like Peace, comes before Liberty. There is nothing arbitrary in this pattern of liberal feeling or the conduct to which it normally leads. Liberals would be subjectively immoral, would be disloyal to their liberalism, if they did not feel and judge and act so.

It may be that under sufficient pressure from reality these patterns of feeling, like the doctrinal syndrome to which they are linked, might crack up like spring-thawed ice, and that the older loyalties and ideas would force through the ideological crust. In the case of individual liberals this does undoubtedly continue to happen when the penetrating chip goes down. But for liberalism as a social tendency, the crust seems to be growing more rather than less solid in most of the advanced Western nations; and perhaps most of all in the United States. While the test ban and Sino-Soviet negotiations were simultaneously going on in Moscow during July 1963, a French liberal—Jean-Jacques Servan-Schreiber, editor of the weekly *L'Express*—summed up what is perhaps the decisive value issue, with traditional Cartesian rigor: "Henceforth, serious political leaders throughout the world divide into two distinct categories: those for whom peace is more important than all else; and those others who do not agree with that evaluation."

IV

WE MAY NOW ASSEMBLE the main public values of modern liberalism, as made explicit in this chapter and implied in Chapters III-V, into the sketch of a kind of moral portrait of the typical modern liberal. In the case of each value, we may assume a corresponding sentiment, emotion or impulse. And in order to provide a suitable background for the portrait of the liberal, I will place next to each liberal value the contrasting value from the cluster that defines a typical conservative of what I have called the traditional variety. These terms as I am here using them should not be taken in an absolute sense, however. As we have already noted, the liberals and conservatives within our civilization, except on their outer flanks, share most of the same values and sentiments; but in different degree, with different emphases and priorities. They exhibit different tendencies, not different natures. Still, these graded differences can be sufficiently decisive.

1. A liberal, as we have had several occasions to remark and as everyone knows, tends to welcome change; tends not merely to accept change that happens to come his way, but actively to foster innovation. If some liberals lack quite that "passion for reform" that Professor Schapiro attributes to them, they all do favor many and far-reaching reforms. They all feel responsible

for "doing something" about the grave social problems that are never absent from the world we live in. They are prepared, in fact, if the reforms are slow in coming, to accept revolution, if the revolution in question or in prospect can be thought of as in some way "popular" or "democratic," and "against reactionary forces." Nearly all liberals have looked kindly on, have often actively supported, at least in the early stages, all revolutions from the Left that have occurred during this century; and there have been a lot of revolutions. This was as true in the case of the Russian revolution of 1917 as of Castro's revolution in 1960; of the Algerian Arabs' revolt against France as of the Indonesians' revolt against the Netherlands. If a goodly percentage of these revolutions has gone sour, this does not in the least affect the true liberal's optimistic attitude toward the next one.

The conservative, in contrast, tends to stress continuity rather than change, and what might be called "renewal" rather than reform—especially drastic and rapid reform—or revolution. "To be conservative," writes Professor Oakeshott, "is to prefer the familiar to the unknown, to prefer the tried to the untried, fact to mystery, the actual to the possible, the limited to the unbounded, the near to the distant, the sufficient to the superabundant, the convenient to the perfect, present laughter to Utopian bliss." Like all men, the conservative must suffer the inescapable changes that time inevitably brings, but, as Professor Oakeshott adds, "a man of this temperament will not himself be an ardent innovator."[8]

2. The modern liberal tends to be egalitarian in sentiment, and to stress the ideal of equality among men with respect to their political, economic and social as well as legal rights, very

---

8. Michael Oakeshott, *Rationalism and Politics* (New York: Basic Books, 1962), pp. 169, 171.

broadly interpreted, and in increasing measure with respect to their conditions of life. He favors an active public policy, at all levels of government, to accomplish this equalizing. In recent years, he has been most intensely concerned, on a local, national and international scale, with equality among the different races of mankind.

The conservative, while sharing the ideal of an equality of legal rights and agreeing on a goal of at least lessening the inequality of rights and privileges in other fields, prefers a more deliberate pace, and greater reliance on gradual shifts in community attitudes through education, experience and the indirect effects of modern economic structure rather than through the coercive intervention of government. And the conservative does not believe in equality in the abstract, "in general," even though he may believe in this particular kind of equality under these particular conditions. He not only accepts but approves the hierarchical structure of society, with a large variety and range of stations and conditions.

Some of the difference here is only in degree, no doubt, but of a degree sufficient to lead to wide divergence in many public fields from education to housing to tax policy, and in private conduct. Conservatives, some conservatives, may agree with liberals about, for example, the concept of "equality in education" that is expressed in the demand for racial integration of schools. But those conservatives will not feel as profoundly and passionately about it as the liberals, nor will they give the goal of school integration so total a precedence. The conservatives will restrict the means they employ to achieve such goals to discussion, gradual public education, and normal legislative or judicial action. You will not find many conservatives among the whites who join with Negroes in the picket lines, lie-downs and

Freedom Marches of the recent mass movements proclaiming the goal of racial equality.

3. In economic matters interpreted in their broadest sense, the modern liberal tends toward such values as security, cooperation and collective welfare: the values, in short, that determine the conception of the Welfare State.

The conservative tends to stress opportunity and initiative more than cooperation; freedom of the marketplace more than security; and individual development more than collective welfare.

Naturally the conservative and liberal both assert that his way is the better route to *both* individual good and social good. The difference, as usual, is in the ordering. For the conservative, if individuals severally seek their own worldly (and heavenly) salvation, there will be the best chance that the good of society will also be most effectively promoted. For the liberal, if society, guided through government, assures the collective welfare, there will be the best chance that individuals will severally attain their happiness.

4. The modern liberal is internationalist in outlook; the conservative's attitude retains more of the traditional sort of national patriotism. There is no doubt that this is one of the most unmistakable differences between the two species, and one that has, moreover, repeated and extensive practical consequences. In our day, the attitude toward the United Nations as the most obvious expression of the internationalist trend is one of most accurate shibboleths; all liberals, from its beginning, have been favorably inclined toward the United Nations and hopeful about its potential, even when it has stumbled badly; most conservatives—it is never possible to generalize too sweepingly about "all conservatives"—have been skeptical if not suspicious and downright hostile, even when it has scored an undoubted plus.

5. The liberal's internationalism is associated with a deeper attitude. He often thinks and feels in terms of humanity as a whole, of mankind; he worries about "the survival of mankind," and recognizes "a duty of mankind." The conservative, more localized in both thinking and sentiment, tends to feel that humanity is a bloodless abstraction, and that the prime social realities are not categories defined by abstract reason but the concretely bound and hierarchically arranged groups handed on by human history: family, community, Church, country and, at the farthest remove, civilization—not civilization in general but this historically specific civilization, the civilization of which *I* am a member. The conservative is likely to find a duty to mankind not so much non-binding as incomprehensible.[9]

6. The modern liberal tends to judge peace to be the highest social value—higher than any other social value and (in the judgment of many liberals) higher than all others—and the supreme object of public policy. No conservative will judge peace higher than all other social values, and few will judge it higher than any other. And the conservative will place more stress, in theory and practice, than will the liberal on the strength, including preeminently the armed strength, of his country and its allies.

---

9. This incomprehension is mutual. I discussed several of the ideas of this chapter, and applied some of them, at a seminar most of the members of which were sophisticated liberal intellectuals. They found it incomprehensible when I seemed to them to be suggesting (as I was indeed suggesting) that the use of force by the United States to prevent consolidation of a communist beachhead in Cuba was not equivalent morally to the use of force by the communists to set up and maintain the beachhead. (Similarly, the members of SANE find incomprehensible the judgment that nuclear tests conducted under the control of Western nations are morally not equivalent to tests conducted under communist control; or H-bombs in Western possession not equivalent, morally, to H-bombs in communist possession.) Curiously enough, however,

THE CONSERVATIVE DRAWN BY these six coarse strokes must be regarded as a theoretical construct, introduced only to heighten the liberal values by contrast. And it should be added that the sketch of the modern liberal here outlined in the color of his primary values should be considered an ideological more than a psychological portrait. Innovation, reform, equality, cooperation, collective welfare, security, internationalism, the survival and betterment of mankind, peace: these are the values or ideals that characterize modern liberalism as a functioning tendency within our society. These are the values that accredited liberals profess. To the extent that affairs tread the liberal line, these values guide the steps that are actually taken, the programs that are pushed, the laws that are proposed or enacted, the policies domestic and foreign that are pursued.

Not every individual who publicly professes or even follows the liberal line, however, has the same subjective relation to these values. He may vote in Congress, or advocate in his column or editorial page, egalitarian reforms for education or housing or what not; but he may be a dreadful snob in his personal life. The public champion of integrated schooling who would never dream of letting his own children attend an integrated school, and who would suffer a permanent trauma if his daughter sat at a soda fountain with a Negro, is a familiar enough figure in liberal society. Practical politicians can espouse liberalism for the best of all practical reasons without having any feeling about its beliefs and values one way or another. "A politician," Pareto observes in a

---

the members of the seminar thought it not only comprehensible but virtually self-evident that the use of force by persons revolting against colonial rule was not equivalent morally, but differed rather as white from black, to the use of force by a colonial power seeking to maintain its rule. This seeming anomaly in liberal logic will be explained in Chapters XI and XII.

comment paralleling another I have earlier quoted from Robert Michels, may be "inspired to champion the theory of 'solidarity' by an ambition to obtain money, power, distinctions. Analysis of that theory would reveal but scant trace of his motives, which are, after all, the motives of virtually all politicians, whether they preach white or black. First prominence would be held by principles *a* that are effective in influencing others. If the politician were to say, 'Believe in "solidarity" because if you do it means money for me,' he would get many laughs and few votes."[10]

On the other hand, there undoubtedly are many liberals whose subjective feelings correspond very closely to these professed and operational values—who really do feel the passion for reform, the sense of true equality with all their fellow men, the wish for universal cooperation, the desire to give everyone food and clothing and dignity, the duty to mankind, the burning hope for an end to war; who feel so, and who try to act in accord with those feelings. I attended a small, lengthy and unrecorded conference in 1962 that discussed the problem of the theoretical foundation for the American foreign aid program. My assigned seat was next to a fine young man who was a friend and aide of President Kennedy's, assigned at that time chiefly to such matters as the foreign aid program, the Peace Corps and civil rights. I recall very vividly how at one point he declared with utter sincerity, his voice vibrating with emotion and his eyes shining: "So long as a single being anywhere in the universe [just so] suffers from hunger or any economic privation or any injustice, this nation has the duty to help him or her"—or "it," I suppose he should have added for grammatical completeness.

---

10. Vilfredo Pareto, *The Mind and Society* (New York: Dover Publications, Inc., 1963), Section 854. Quoted with permission of The Pareto Fund.

But the diverse subjective feelings are primarily a private affair, of personal and some psychological interest. The public consequences flow from the public ideology, its correlated impulses, interests and social forces, and its implementing programs as these are translated into public program and external action, whether the individual liberals who proclaim the program and perform the actions are saints, villains, fools or hypocrites.

TEN

The Guilt of the Liberal

I

IT HAS BEEN MORE THAN ONCE remarked that modern liberalism, as manifest within the relatively privileged strata of Western society, bears, only lightly concealed, a heavy burden of guilt. To uncover a layer of guilt inside the liberal breast is not, to be sure, a startling discovery. Guilt seems to be an emotion, feeling, idea, conviction—whatever it is to be called—that is very widely distributed among men. If one were not committed to a denial of any permanent human nature, one might almost conclude that it is part of man's essence.

In Franz Kafka's novel *The Trial*, Joseph K.—"K.," symbol of the mathematical constant, Everyman presumably as well as author and particular reader—is informed by authoritative sources that he is under indictment. K. never succeeds in finding out the specifications of the charge. But it becomes quite clear that they are of a capital order, and that he is indeed guilty, since he has already been condemned to death, with no possibility of reprieve. Everyman, conservative and liberal, communist and fascist, atheist and churchgoer, is of course exactly in K.'s situation; and, no matter what his doctrine, he feels at least sometimes the reality of that situation: that is, feels guilty; and occasionally he feels guilty not about this or that deed or thought, but guilty in general, guilty about nothing in particular, that is, about everything. Guilt, and the feeling of guilt, are facts of the human situation.

Christianity, the traditional religion of Western civilization, faces the reality of guilt, provides an adequate explanation for it, and offers a resolution of the anxiety to which it inevitably gives rise. Each man is guilty merely by being a man, because the entire human race, in the person of its progenitor, committed a supreme crime. The exact content of this crime, or sin, is obscure; but its infinite measure is known from the fact that it was done in defiance of the Will of the infinite Being who is Creator at once of the world and of man himself. Every man is therefore born with this guilt; and, since it is infinite, neither any man nor all men together can, solely by their own efforts, wipe it out. God Himself, however, freely chose the only possible solution, if there was to be a solution: that He, the infinite Being, should Himself become incarnate as man, and sacrifice Himself, so that through this infinite sacrifice man, and men, might be redeemed from their infinite guilt. The sacrifice having been carried out, men may be released from the guilt by being baptized in His name, believing in Him and doing His will.

This Christian doctrine does genuinely solve the problem of guilt; or at any rate, gives a framework, so long as it is believed, within which the problem in all its complexities becomes tractable to both understanding and emotion. Liberalism, however, is secular, secular at least in tendency and emphasis even when individual liberals are or regard themselves as Christians. Many liberals or liberal ancestors—of the eighteenth-century

Enlightenment, for example—have openly broken with Christianity. Many more continue to consider themselves Christians but have abandoned most of the orthodox dogma and doctrine, which they often reinterpret as myth, metaphor or symbol. Moreover, for most persons today, non-liberal as well as liberal, religious belief has become departmentalized, restricted in its influence on life and conduct, and relatively independent of political, economic and social views. But the Christian solution of the problem of guilt is valid only if the relevant Christian doctrine is true; and it can be psychologically effective only when the doctrine is believed, whether or not true, and believed not in a mere formal and atomistic way, as one truth among the many others, but integrally and totally, as pervading all of life and experience.

Let us consider the situation of a member of our affluent society, and let us assume him to be from the more rather than less affluent half, who is no longer deeply committed in spirit to the interlocked Christian doctrines of Original Sin, the Incarnation and Redemption, which constitute the Christian solution. His guilt nevertheless exists; he is conscious of it, and feels the anxiety that it generates. What is he going to do about it, and think about it?

Liberalism permits him to translate his guilt into the egalitarian, anti-discrimination, democratist, peace-seeking liberal principles, and to transform his guilty feeling into that "passion for reform" of which Professor Schapiro speaks. If he is an activist, he can actually sign on as a slum clearer, Freedom Rider, Ban the Bomber or Peace Corpsman, or join a Dr. Schweitzer or Dr. Dooley in the jungle. But activists of that literal sort are always a minority. The more significant achievement of liberalism, by which it confirms its claim to being considered a major ideology, is its ability to handle the problem of guilt for large numbers of persons without costing them undue personal inconvenience. This it does by elevating the problem to representational, symbolic and institutional levels. It is not necessary for me to go in person to the slum, jungle, prison, Southern restaurant, state house or voting precinct and there take a direct hand in accomplishing the reform that will unblock the road to peace, justice and well-being. Thanks to the reassuring provisions of the liberal ideology, I can go about my ordinary business and meanwhile take sufficient account of my moral duties by affirming my loyalty to the correct egalitarian principles, voting for the correct candidates, praising the activists and contributing to their defense funds when they get into trouble, and joining promptly in the outcry against reactionaries who pop up now and then in a desperate effort to preserve power and privilege.

The key fact toward which I am pointing here is really very simple, a product not of complicated analysis but of common-sense observation. My own observations have confirmed it time after time over a good many decades, and I cannot believe that my experience is so very different from that of other men; besides which, it is discussed, directly and indirectly, in the writings of many liberals and non-liberals. Indeed, I remember very well the first time I became aware of this key fact I am trying to get at here; it was about thirty-five years ago.

I became acquainted then with the first fully ideologized female liberal I had known. She was a member of a fairly sizable and important class in modern American society: the class of indoctrinated liberal, sometimes more Left than liberal, women turned out over a period of many years by Vassar and her sister institutions of the female Ivy League, many of them destined to become the rather formidable wives of men who have had much to do with making liberalism our prevailing national ideology. At one time I was, in a modest way, something of a student of this species.

This first specimen I knew well was the daughter of a wealthy investment banker. Her family had the usual large house just off Fifth Avenue in the East Seventies, summer place on the Long Island Shore, and auxiliary outbuildings here and there. She used to invite budding young intellectuals, a few of her classmates, and sometimes a communist or young trade union organizer, to dinner; and as the butler and footmen passed the food and wine there would be animated discourse about that hardy perennial of economic disaster, the West Virginia coal fields, along with the rise of anti-Semitism in Germany, sharecropping in the South, the latest demonstrations by the unemployed, and British oppression in India, all dealt with from a systematically progressive point of view.

It was obvious on the face of it, and in the rhetoric they used and the sentiments they expressed, that this girl and many of her friends felt guilty, felt a personal sense of guilt, toward the poor, the wretched and the oppressed; and that this sense of guilt was an important, perhaps the decisive, ingredient in the liberal ideas they had adopted concerning the condition of the poor and wretched, its cause and its cure—ideas that were, it may be added, far from accurate on most counts. The particular girl whom I am here remembering was entirely sincere in both her feeling of guilt and its translation into principle. It led her, shortly after the period of those dinners, to leave her family household and set up on her own in a sparely furnished apartment, where the only inharmonious object held over from the old days was her magnificent mink coat which she had taken along in all innocence, I believe, never having thought of it as a luxury. She married a determinedly non–Ivy League type and they actually did spend several years working for unemployed leagues and the United Mine Workers in West Virginia.

Along one perspective, liberalism's reformist, egalitarian, anti-discrimination, peace-seeking principles *are*, or at any rate can be interpreted as, the verbally elaborated projections of the liberal sense of guilt. I, who have enough to eat and a sufficiently comfortable life, feel guilty—even though I have no direct personal relation with you—because you are hungry or deprived of civil rights or suffering political oppression. More exactly, the sequence is the following: I feel guilty, and I do not know why; you are hungry, etc.; I attach my guilt to your unhappy state, trying to explain my guilt to myself, to give it some sort of objective, motivating structure. All this may be too obvious to need saying. And it *is* obvious, but it is necessary to insist that it is not self-evident and not an inevitable outcome for the guilt experience.

The generalized feeling of guilt toward mass wretchedness and oppression[1] is so widespread today and so pervasive a characteristic of public rhetoric that many persons do not realize it to be a rather new arrival in history. Comparatively few people

---

1. This generalized feeling of guilt toward an anonymous mass is altogether different from a specific feeling of personal guilt toward a specific individual or group of individuals with whom I have some sort of specific relation, and whose lives have been or can be affected fairly directly by my conduct. A Christian, though his religion solves for him the general problem of guilt, continues to feel guilty if he does specific wrong to other individuals (or to himself) or if he omits doing the specific goods that are within his power and province. Even if I don't feel guilty because Papuan headhunters murder each other, I ought to feel guilty—and will feel guilty, liberal or not—if *I* murder somebody.

felt this sort of guilt before the present century, and virtually no one before the second half of the eighteenth century, though there has never been any lack of wretched and oppressed in this world.[2] Nor is a feeling of guilt the only motivation there has been and can be for the attempt to improve the condition of the poor. The hardy breed of Calvinist-slanted early bourgeois, or bourgeois-minded, felt plenty of guilt, but none over the poor and wretched who, their doctrine told them convincingly, had only their own shiftlessness and extravagance to blame for their troubles. In many cultures the more fortunate were contemptuous or simply indifferent toward the wretched. Many have reconciled themselves to the sorrows of mankind by accepting them as God's will; and others, like Lucretius, have viewed them with a calm objectivity as part of the way things are. And I or another might choose to try to better the lot of the wretched because I thought it God's command that I should do so or out of a feeling of noblesse oblige, from charity or civic duty or because I preferred a happier world for its own sake: none of which motives need presuppose any sense of guilt on my part.

The liberal's feeling of guilt at the condition of the wretched and oppressed is irrational; and irrational precisely from the point of view of the liberal ideology itself. According to liberal doctrine, the poverty and oppression are the result of ignorance and faulty institutions handed down from the past; they are none of my doing. Why then should I feel that any guilt attaches to me, individually and personally, because there are the poor and the enslaved? It has lately become morally fashionable to

---

2. It is estimated that at least two of the current three billion world population are so impoverished as to suffer from involuntary malnutrition; and certainly fewer than half a billion live at even a minimum level of comfort.

say: "The white people of the United States have exploited and oppressed the American Negroes for three hundred years and now it is the moral obligation of the whites to make up for all the suffering they have caused." And analogously: "The white Europeans kept hundreds of millions of black, brown and yellow Afro-Asians in colonial subjection for up to five hundred years and now it is the moral obligation of the Europeans to make up for that crime not only by freeing all the colonies but by giving them massive help to attain quickly a high standard of living." (It will be noticed that by these injunctions the ideal of equality of treatment for the heretofore privileged and underprivileged groups has evolved into the demand for an inequality in favor of the underprivileged; and this transformation has been openly acknowledged by the leaders of both American Negro organizations and the new African countries.)

Now it may be that American and European whites have such moral obligations, but it is certain that they cannot be derived from liberal principles. Liberal theory is atomistic and quantitative, and in particular rejects "organic" conceptions of society, which liberalism believes to be correlated with reactionary and fascist types of social regime. The idea that I, today, am organically part of a "white race" that was doing something—anything at all—to American or African Negroes or Indonesian brown men or Hindus or Bantu is total nonsense from the point of view of liberalism's philosophical conceptions. In fact, the very concept of a "race" of human beings is so difficult to reconcile with liberal doctrine that many liberal anthropologists and philosophers—including the late Franz Boas and his pupils, who constitute the most influential American school of anthropology—rule it out. If a race doesn't even exist, it is hard to see how it can be guilty. And there is a milder paradox, for liberal theory, even in the idea of an "integration" to be achieved through a struggle by Negroes for "their rights": the struggle is conceived in terms that differentiate the Negroes from the rest of the population; but the goal, in terms that assimilate the Negroes within the population.

However, theoretical paradoxes, inconsistencies or confusions are of little importance. The feeling of guilt with its accompanying anxiety is rooted much too profoundly to be affected by the quibbles of reason. Guilt is integral to liberalism, and the feeling of guilt is an integral element in the liberal motivation, with all the weighty consequences that follow therefrom for both individual conduct and social practice.

II

THE GUILT OF THE LIBERAL causes him to feel obligated to try to *do something* about any and every social problem, to cure every social evil. This feeling, too, is non-rational: the liberal must try to cure the evil even if he has no knowledge of the suitable medicine or, for that matter, of the nature of the disease; he must *do something* about the social problem even when there is no objective reason to believe that what he does can solve the problem—when, in fact, it may well aggravate the problem instead of solving it. "We cannot stand idly by while the world rushes to destruction...or women and children are starving...or able men walk the streets without jobs...or the air becomes polluted...or Negroes can't vote in Zenith...or immigrants live in rat-infested slums...or youngsters don't get a decent education..." or whatever. The harassed liberal is relentlessly driven by his Eumenidean guilt. It does not permit him to "let well enough alone" or "stick to his own cabbage patch"

SUICIDE OF THE WEST

or decide that the trouble is "none of his business"; or to reflect that, though the evil is undoubtedly there and he is sincerely sorry for its victims, he doesn't understand damn-all about it and even if he did he hasn't got the brains and resources to fix it up. He may not know much, generally speaking he does not know much, about economics, but that lack in no way inhibits him from demanding that industry and government do this, that or the other to cure unemployment; he may not have a single serious idea about strategy and international affairs, but he will nevertheless join his fellow liberals in calling for grandiose measures concerning arms, alliances, bases, and colonies; he may have no acquaintance with the actual problems of mass education, but he will nevertheless insist on the most far-reaching reforms of the school system.

The peoples of the new underdeveloped nations are hungry, poor and diseased. Therefore, by the logic of the liberal guilt, we have a duty to give them aid; and we do so, though the objective evidence may show that in at least a number of cases the aid given injures rather than helps the recipient—corrupts the officialdom perhaps, subverts the social order, or provokes wild inflation. Our government is obligated to send money to rehabilitate a chronically depressed domestic region; though the objective evidence may show that the area is depressed for good reason, and that the way to help its inhabitants is to get them to move somewhere else. Negro children have feelings of inferiority and alienation when they attend separate schools, so therefore they will go to school with whites. But what if, placed in direct confrontation with whites, the Negro children feel still more alienated? Indonesians have been poor under Dutch colonial rule; so therefore, etc. But after independence they are not merely poor but starving.... Latin America is in bad political, economic and social shape. So we will have a

$20 billion Alliance for Progress program. But, for this and that objective reason, the program will not improve the condition of Latin America, will most likely make it worse? No matter; there is a problem; where there's a problem we've got to apply a solution.

I do not raise the question whether in these cited cases the liberal solution is or is not valid, but merely that it doesn't really make any difference. The real and motivating problem, for the liberals, is not to cure the poverty or injustice or what not in the objective world but to appease the guilt in their own breasts; and what that requires is *some* program, some solution, some activity, whether or not it is the correct program, solution and activity. The good intention—slum clearance, racial equality, better health, decolonization, high standard of living, peace— plus plenty of action is assumed to guarantee the goodness of the program; and the badness, one might add, of those reactionaries who are rash enough to question it.

III

FOR WESTERN CIVILIZATION IN the present condition of the world, the most important practical consequence of the guilt encysted in the liberal ideology and psyche is this: that the liberal, and the group, nation or civilization infected by liberal doctrine and values, are morally disarmed before those whom the liberal regards as less well off than himself. I remember learning one manifestation of this attitude for the first time in practice in the same year that I met the female liberal to whose memory I paid tribute earlier in this chapter.

I was teaching then at New York University, which was a pioneer in racial integration; indeed, as a big university in so cosmopolitan a city as New York, with its large Negro community, the issue never really arose. I soon found out that there was an unwritten rule providing that Negro students should be marked about two grades higher than whites for a given level of work. If a newcomer on the faculty deviated in his innocence from this rule when he turned in his first mid-term grade sheets, discreet words to the wise were communicated to him by his older colleagues, so that no lasting damage would be done by an unsuitable end-of-term grade that would have gone into the student's permanent record. One literal-minded young instructor, who refused to take those prudent hints, found himself the physical focus of the Dean's office, the student's parents and uncle, a delegation from the NAACP, and a suave representative of City Hall.

Naturally the liberals on the faculty—that is, most of the faculty—had no difficulty justifying this rule to themselves, though they never did get around to recognizing it in public. The Negro students, they could explain, had come from inferior, usually segregated schools; they did not have an educated family background; conditions at home were difficult; they had to work on the side; it was important not only for them but for their people, the city and the nation that they should not be discouraged; and so on. Still, the fact remained; and this urbane New York University custom can be matched by a thousand comparable practices today, yesterday and tomorrow. I recall an evening not long ago that I spent with one of the country's most distinguished historians, who is a liberal *à outrance*. As the night wore on, he got somewhat more tight than was his habit; and at one point he remarked, more to his fifth gin and tonic than to the rest of us: "In the last ten years I've had several hundred Indians and Pakistani and lately Africans in my graduate courses, and I've given out many an 'A,' and never flunked any of them; and there hasn't yet been a single one who was a really first-class student."

These academic forgeries are petty enough affairs, but often the moral disarmament is more startling, and more consequential. Consider, for example, terror: I mean the terror that tortures and kills people, a rather pervasive trait of our time. The terror carried out by the French paratroops in Algeria—let us take a specific case—and subsequently by Europeans of the so-called "Secret Army" aroused the full-scale, sustained indignation and protest of liberals in Europe and America. But somehow the indignation was less ardent and the protest much muted in the case of the terror that was carried out by the Arabs' so-called "Army of National Liberation"; though, in point of fact, the Arab terror came first, was far more ferocious, lasted much longer—still goes on, indeed—and has had a hundred times as many victims, most of them, as it happens, fellow Arabs.

The Algerian case is in no way exceptional. The Mau Mau terror in Kenya in the early 1950's, exercised almost entirely against other Negroes, was one of the most bestial in history. However, Western liberals never became much worked up about it, and were stirred to much greater passion and political activity against the stern and occasionally brutal—but incomparably less savage—police measures taken against it by the British authorities. There has never been a liberal protest against the outrages committed by the South African Negroes. There has never been a liberal condemnation of the savage terrorism that the Angolan revolutionaries unleashed in 1961 in their attempt to overthrow Portuguese rule in Angola, during which they killed thousands of persons, mostly Negroes, by burning, torture, sawing and miscellaneous brutalities. The liberals' condemnation has been reserved exclusively for the Portuguese who fought back, perhaps for an unjust cause but for the most part without terrorist excesses.

As with terror, so with colonialism. Liberal opinion has

demanded and demands that the advanced Western nations—Britain, France, the Netherlands, Belgium, Portugal—liquidate forthwith all forms of direct and indirect colonial rule, without reference to economic or strategic interests or the readiness of the peoples for independence or the question whether independence will in truth benefit or harm them, or to any other factor save the abstract badness of colonialism. Liberals implement this injunction by giving political, propaganda, financial and other practical support to the anti-colonial movements and their leaders, and by trying, usually successfully, to swing their own governments and the United Nations into action on the anti-colonial side. But when an underdeveloped nation goes actively colonial—when Nehru moves into Goa, or Sukarno into New Guinea or northern Borneo—there is at most a little clucking from the liberal back bench. No public protests; no letters to the newspaper; no resolutions in the United Nations; no invitations to resistance leaders; no Committees to Aid the threatened Papuans or Sarawakians (or whatever they are properly to be called).

Analogously, in the United Nations: any amount of stupidity, rudeness, demagogy, barbarism or sheer ignorance from a spokesman of the ex-colonial and other underdeveloped nations goes unreproved; and no reference is made to the tyrannical and savage deeds that may be taking place in his home country.

Within the United States, as in other advanced Western nations, the same moral asymmetry is present. The liberal community not only flagellates itself with the abusive writings of a disoriented Negro homosexual, but awards him money, fame and public honors. The spokesmen of the Black Muslims can openly preach racial hatred, violence and insurrection to their heart's content, with never a challenge from police, courts or the self-appointed guardians of civil liberties. The guilt of the liberal is insatiable. He *deserves*, by his own judgment, to be kicked, slapped and spat on for his infinite crimes. The shooting of a Negro in Mississippi, purportedly the act of a crazed and isolated white man, reverberates from liberal sounding boards into weeks of world headlines; the shooting of white men in Maryland by rioting Negro gangs slides back into an obscure and unread paragraph. The truncheons of hard-pressed police struggling to preserve the minimum elements of public order against unloosed chaos become Satanic pitchforks; the rocks and broken bottles of the mob, angelic swords. The force that blocks an entrance to a factory which a union leadership has declared on strike is a courageous defense of the rights of man; the force that might seek to use that entrance for its intended and lawful purpose is a cowardly blow by the hirelings of the privileged.

Judging a group of human beings—a race, nation, class or party—that he considers to possess less than their due of well-being and liberty, the liberal is hard put to it to condemn that group *morally* for acts that he would not hesitate to condemn in his fellows—not to speak of reactionaries; his feeling of guilt and his egalitarian principles, which incorporate and express that feeling, do not seem to give him the *right* to condemnation. Even if, because of an imperious practical situation, he finds himself resisting the pretentions of the underprivileged group, he does so with a divided conscience. If he has to shoot one of its members—and sometimes in the end he must, and rather more of them than if he had stood firm a little earlier—he feels a moral twinge that often spoils his aim, as he pulls the trigger.

When the Western liberal's feeling of guilt and his associated feeling of moral vulnerability before the sorrows and demands of the wretched become obsessive, he often develops a generalized hatred of Western civilization and of his own country as part of the West. We can frequently sense this hatred in the paragraphs of such American magazines as *The Nation* and *Dissent*, Britain's *New Statesman*, France's *L'Express* or Germany's *Der Spiegel*. A Western retreat or humiliation at the United Nations or Suez, in Cuba or space or Southeast Asia, becomes the occasion not for analysis, regret, sorrow or stocktaking, but for vindictive and smugly pleased I-told-you-so's.

In one of the critical discussions to which much of the material of this book was submitted as it moved along the production line, a liberal commented, after I had used the Algerian case as an example of the moral asymmetry: "It is true that there is among liberals this asymmetry of which you speak, this selective indignation; and it is true that in relation to the Algerian affair, the liberal protest was directed against the French paras, not the fellaheen. However, this is in keeping with the highest dictates of morality, which has always decreed that we must be much stricter with ourselves than with others. The French are ours, fellow members of Western, Christian civilization, educated and materially privileged. That they should descend to acts of terror, even if on a minor scale, deserves our moral condemnation much more than the terror of the Arabs, belonging to a different civilization with ideals we deem lower than ours, for the most part illiterate and impoverished, and for a century and a half subject to the oppression of a foreign power."

The force of his observation was somewhat weakened by the fact that this particular liberal happened to be not a Christian but an avowed atheist, of Jewish origin, who denies that Western civilization is in any respect superior to any other civilization, and who, in the Algerian affair, from the beginning identified himself not with the French but the anti-French side. If his argument were valid, the realities of his own point of view should have led him to excuse the French and direct his condemnation toward the Arabs. But the argument itself, though it draws on a profound moral truth, is not really relevant to the problem to which it is here applied; and even if it were, it could not be properly used by a liberal.

It is true that as a moral being, I ought to judge myself more strictly than others, ought to forgive others more readily than myself, and ought to be especially generous in forgiving the lowly and unfortunate; and to forgive irrespective of race, color, creed or previous condition of servitude. But this means others as individuals and myself as an individual. The metaphor by which we extend moral categories to groups—a race, class or nation—is doubtful and confusing. A group does not possess either intellect or will, the presuppositions of moral conduct; and is therefore, strictly speaking, outside the range of moral judgment whether in praise or blame. And liberals most particularly, in terms of their own doctrine, have no basis for those moral distinctions among groups—in favor of, specifically, the poor, wretched and oppressed—that they do nevertheless habitually make. Reasoning from quantitative and atomistic premises, as I have noted, liberalism has always rejected Platonist, Hegelian and other realist or organic conceptions of society that assign some sort of subsistent reality to the group. It makes a certain amount of sense for a Hegelian to speak of the historic guilt of this race or that empire, or the moral claim of that people; but it makes no logical sense for a liberal to do so. It is the guilt, not the reason, of the liberal that is being expressed in these attitudes.

Moreover, whatever may be the respective crimes, virtues and deserts of various races, classes and nations, civilized society requires a certain rule and order to hold back from the edge of anarchic savagery where it is always precariously poised.

Human beings must have at least a minimum security in life and property, must be able to move through the streets and between the cities, must accept certain common rules in their mutual intercourse, or civilization does not exist. If this necessary order is subverted, the civilization is destroyed, whether the subversion take place from the best or worst of motives, whether or not it is in some supposedly moral sense justified, whether it is carried out by saints or devils. At some point the guardians of a civilization must be prepared to draw the line.

I V

CHRISTIAN DOCTRINE, IF IT IS TRUE, solves the problem of guilt in general and provides a structure within which the individual who believes in Christian doctrine may solve the problem of his individual guilt. But though guilt has so integral a role to play in the liberal attitude and conduct, liberal ideology does not succeed in solving the problem of guilt. As we have seen, it does not supply an intelligible explanation of the fact of guilt. Nor does it offer the individual any final answer to—that is, redemption from—his individual guilt.

The work of secular education and reform undertaken to appease the liberal's guilt at the same time expresses and even irritates it. This must be, for there is no end, no terminal point, of the work of secular education and reform. This vacuum is reflected in the ideology and rhetoric of liberalism; it accounts for the emphasis on continuous change, on method rather than results, on striving and doing rather than sitting and enjoying. "We are forced back on the reality of the struggle," Arthur Schlesinger concludes in his usual somewhat breathless tone. "The choice we face is not between progress with conflict and progress without conflict. The choice is between conflict and stagnation.... Out of the effort, out of the struggle alone, can come the high courage and faith which will preserve freedom."[3] Within the universe of liberalism there is no point at which the spirit can come to rest; nowhere and no moment for the soul to be able to say: in His Will is our peace.

---

3. Arthur M. Schlesinger, Jr., *The Vital Center* (Boston: Houghton Mifflin Co., 1949), pp. 255-56.

≡≡≡

ELEVEN

Pas d'Ennemi à Gauche

I

THE MORAL ASYMMETRY SPRUNG from the guilt felt by liberals toward the wretched of the earth overlaps, though it is not identical with, a primary rule of liberal strategy. This rule, which anyone may verify by a cursory study of liberal behavior over a moderate period of time, may be stated as follows: *The main enemy is to the Right.* Viewing liberalism from the outside, a more exact wording might be: *The preferred enemy is to the Right.* This rule is a matter of feeling, principle, conduct and history. It is a basic parameter of liberalism understood as a personal attitude and as a political tendency.

Referring to the development of progressive and radical political views in their own country from the eighteenth century on, the French put a similar point still more unconditionally: *il n'y a pas d'ennemi à gauche*—there is no enemy to the Left. That formulation is perhaps too extreme for the main body of modern liberalism—though it undoubtedly holds for liberalism's own left flank, as represented, for example, by most of the authors of *The Liberal Papers.* But all wings of liberalism unite in finding that the main enemy, the preferred enemy, the enemy that one enjoys coming to grips with, is to the Right.

This rule is a matter, to begin with, of feeling. A liberal may agree that there is or can be a "threat" from the Left; but to a liberal, a threat from the Left does not *feel* the same way as a threat from the Right. As the liberal sees it, some persons on the Left are doubtless mistaken in some of their views, even rather badly off course; but the liberal feels instinctively that their "intentions" are good, that they are aiming at the right goals, and that you therefore have a chance to sit down and reason things out with them, to negotiate differences. Even communists, bad as they are, are not hopeless. You can discuss test bans and disarmament with them, work out agreements covering this or that particular crisis, seek out areas of common interest, carry on trade, expand communication through cultural and scientific exchange, take measures to reduce tensions, and so on. In domestic affairs, you will often find the communists lining up on the decent side of such issues as civil rights, congressional inquisitions, academic freedom, colonialism and peace.

But those extremists over on the Right are a different breed, as the liberal feels them. There's no getting anywhere with them by reasonable methods and compromise. Not only are their methods disruptive, provocative and inflammatory; their goals are all wrong, and even the intentions of many of them are obviously vicious. For that matter, people on the Right are so full of reactionary prejudices and anti-intellectual bias that it's really pointless to try to work things out, so far as they are concerned, by discussion and negotiation. With them it's just a question of who is stronger.

The Western liberal community united into a solid and impassioned front against the totalitarian threat of fascism and

Nazism; called long before 1939 for the fullest sanctions, up to and including war, to bring them down; and joined full-bloodedly in the demand that the anti-fascist war should be fought through to unconditional surrender. Against the no less totalitarian threat of communism, there has never been a solid and uncompromising liberal attitude, much less a united liberal determination to use measures of a firmness thought routinely appropriate in dealing with fascism.

Many liberals—many thousands of liberals—have found it to be in no way incompatible with their principles that, among the sponsors of public committees, causes, organizations and petitions, their names should appear alongside the names of communists or known communist fellow travelers. Those same liberals would have cut their throats, politically speaking, if they had been publicly associated in such manner with fascists or fascist sympathizers; would indeed have refused, do still refuse, to permit any public link between themselves and any right-wingers much short of fascism.

To meet the menace of Nazism or any sort of fascism, to bring to heel apartheidism or a colonialist imperialism governed by a rightist regime, it seems to liberalism self-evidently proper to call for boycotts, embargoes, refusal to purchase goods made in the fascist or right-wing countries, ostracism of the musicians, artists, writers or professors who go along with their regimes, cessation of mutual tourism and of cultural contacts except through outlawed refugees, support of revolutionary opposition, denunciation of compromise as shameful appeasement; and for war itself in the end if all else fails to bring the enemy down. But the response to communist and other far-out leftist regimes is gentler; more, shall we say, rational, more in keeping with the rationalist principles of the liberal creed. In relation to these, liberalism senses at once the promise held out by an *increase* in cultural exchange, a mingling of peoples with peoples, a multiplication of international gatherings, of gradually expanding trade, enlarging tourism, negotiations official and unofficial on many topics at many levels, searching for those areas of common interest and concern, and a general readiness to try all available means that might keep the dialogue going according to Mr. Hutchins' prescriptions.

No dialogue with Franco, however: even if Franco's system, though a long way from democracy, is not and never has been totalitarian, and can be called "fascist" only by a snowball use of words; even if Spain has not been and could not be a serious threat to American or world security. But Franco is a man of the Right, and must pay for his rightist sins even unto the second and third decade after his wars have finished. For many American, British and French liberals of the older generation, the Spanish Civil War of 1936-39 was the determining episode of their ideological lives. They have retained a permanent emotional and moral commitment to the side they continue to call "the Republicans," much as many veterans of the First World War kept a lifelong commitment to the strange comradeship of the trenches, or as businessmen relive in their emotional and drunken moods their college days, or as a romantic's soul returns always to his first young love.

For these liberals, time does not cloud the clarity of the choice they made in the complex Spanish combat, nor does the accumulated record suggest to them that the realities of 1936-39 may not have been quite so unequivocal as they then seemed. The outrages done by Franco's minions of the Right, the interventions by Nazis and fascists, the sorrows of the anti-Franco exiles, are kept fresh in memory. But the facts

about the outrages done by the Republicans and their associates; about the control of the international brigades by the
Soviet secret police and the liquidation of anti-communists;
about the assimilation of so many of the anti-Franco veterans
into the international communist apparatus, often into its es-
pionage and terrorist sections; about the exploitation of the
Spanish question to the manifest detriment of Western unity
and strength—somehow such facts, though it is no longer possible for anyone to deny them, do not penetrate the ideologized
fibers of a liberal psyche. With his mind, the liberal knows that
there was much frightfulness on both sides of the Spanish Civil
War, and totalitarian intervention in both directions, so that
the moral claims with respect to the war's conduct fairly well
cancel out. And if it were a case where a clear balance of moral
evil were chargeable to the Left's account—as, say, in the matter of the Moscow purge trials that were simultaneous with the
Spanish Civil War—he would hasten to remind us that water
so long over the dam had best be forgotten. But Franco is to
the Right; and the main enemy, the preferred enemy, the eternal
enemy is and must be to the Right.

The program of Americans for Democratic Action has illustrated with laboratory purity the application of the enemy
to the Right rule to Franco's Spain. Over the years—including
Stalinist years when there was no chatter about peaceful coexistence or internal Soviet liberalizing, as well as post-Stalinist
years when strategic bases in Spain became important elements
in the Western defense system—the official ADA program,
re-adopted regularly by each annual convention, declared: "We
unequivocally condemn the fascist regime in Spain. We favor
political and economic support to the government-in-exile and
to the democratic forces within Spain." (That is, ADA stated its

support of an anti-Franco revolution.) Let us add that more than fifteen years after the end of World War II, the ADA program was still reminding its members and the public that "Germany's record of cruelty and inhumanity should not be forgotten." But nowhere in its program or in any other policy declaration has Americans for Democratic Action ever called for support of the struggle for liberation in the countries captive to communism in Eastern Europe. With the Soviet Union we are advised to show "an understanding of legitimate aspiration," and to keep trying both "negotiation" and "conciliation" while waiting for "relaxation and greater personal freedom within the Soviet regime." Playing similarly by the rule, Americans for Democratic Action, like most liberals, has long recommended giving diplomatic recognition and United Nations membership to Mao Tse-tung, and withdrawing recognition from Chiang Kai-shek.

Tito is of the Left, and toward the Left charity comes readily into the liberal heart. It quickly covers with its gentle veil the tens of thousands of corpses of his countrymen over which Tito marched to his seizure of power—including so many thousands of the finest men of those Christian families who for so many centuries defended the European marches; the fraudulent trial and killing of the Yugoslav patriot who had led the fight against the Nazis; the fraudulent trial and imprisonment of Yugoslavia's religious leader; the thousands of administrative arrests; the infamous deeds of the secret police; the property stolen and families broken up; his own closest colleague jailed for speaking a small part of the truth: there is no point stirring up old coals on the Left. Tito is to be immediately welcomed as a colleague in the United Nations of peace-loving states, while Franco is sternly kept outside the gate; Tito is to be nourished with money, food and goods, while liberal groans attend the granting of any concession to Franco even as part of hard-headed bargaining that gains crucial strategic concessions in return.[1] Pablo Casals, liberal ideologue in his own right as well as major figure in the liberal litany, will play no more in Spain after Franco. But in the spring of 1963 he played in Budapest. Yes: Budapest.

Boiling in oil is too generous a fate for a brute like Cuba's Fulgencio Batista. And he was a savage brute, most certainly—though savage mostly to certain of his own countrymen, not much to others. In dealings with the United States, for example, he granted the first missile tracking site on foreign soil, supported its international policy without deviation, gave the Pentagon every military facility it sought, and welcomed trade and business. Still, let us grant that Batista deserved boiling. But that bearded young romantic, Fidel Castro, when he first appeared on the horizon? A little wild, perhaps, with a few bad companions. But expressing the aspiration of his people for freedom, justice and well-being...Someone to work with, to help, to advise, to make plenty of allowance for....These were the things the liberals were telling us in the months before and for a while after Castro took power.

---

1. On October 2, 1963 (twenty-four years after the end of the Spanish Civil War, God save the mark!) the lead editorial of the *New York Times* was entitled, "Let Us Sell Wheat." It argued in favor of the proposal to sell a large quantity of wheat to the Soviet Union, and commented in a lofty vein: "The free world is not going to triumph over communism in Europe, in China or in Cuba by trying to make people go hungry. This is a case where good morals, good politics and good business go together." Immediately following, as if with the deliberate purpose of making the liberal rule unmistakable, came an editorial entitled, "Keeping the Spanish Bases." This discussed the five-year renewal, just then concluded, of the agreement under which the United States maintains naval and air bases in Spain—against the threat, as it happens, of the Soviet Union. The agreement is not endorsed, but merely

In April 1960, fifteen months after Castro seized power, Professor Robert J. Alexander,[2] writing in *ADA World*, the official organ of Americans for Democratic Action, continued to give duly abject expression to the liberal sense of guilt in telling us that the denunciations of the United States by Castro were well deserved because they were "largely due to the recent history of our relations with the Latin-American countries." Six months later *ADA World* indignantly protested the notion that Castro might be linked with Moscow and the communists. "Castro's hold," declared this keeper of the liberal seals, "comes from what he has done for his people, not what he has done for the Russians." As late as February 1962, when Cuba was being rapidly transformed into a Soviet base, *ADA World* not only protested fiercely against the idea of United States support for any sort of armed action against Castro as "in violation of the Charters of the UN and the OAS," but insisted that it was "no time to take unilateral economic sanctions against Cuba." (Simultaneously, it is hardly necessary to add, Americans for Democratic Action were already calling for economic and political sanctions against South Africa and Portugal, and offering no objection to the military actions—and terrorism—that had begun in Angola.) For Castro was a man of the Left.

Without exception, as I have already noted, the preponder-

---

described as "a technical matter," on which, "once the decision was made, the price had to be paid." The *Times* permits its rhetoric to express its attitude: "Many Americans feel uncomfortable about this continuing relationship with the Franco dictatorship....Part of the cost was to assume a posture of friendship despite the widespread political criticism in the United States—not to say abhorrence—of the Franco regime....The same old bitter pill—that 1953 military treaty—has been given a new sugar coating."

2. Professor Alexander's writings have for some years had a major influence on opinion both public and governmental concerning Latin-American affairs.

ance of liberal opinion has been in favor of at least the early phases of every revolution in this century that has seemed to come from the Left and to be directed against the Right: of the Russian and Chinese revolutions both pre-communist and communist, the Indonesian revolution, the Algerian like the Cuban, Nasser's revolution or Kassem's, Betancourt's in Venezuela or Salal's in Yemen, the revolutions now (1963) in their preliminary stages in Angola, Southern Rhodesia and South Africa.

In the last chapter we remarked how the liberal's selective indignation is controlled by his feeling of guilt toward the poor and oppressed, who gain an immunity from the moral condemnation that is reserved for the powerful and privileged and for himself. Often, though not invariably, this moral attitude coincides in practical application with the strategic tropism that seeks the enemy to the Right. In many though not all cases the poor and oppressed are deployed among the contingents of the Left when they become active politically; and thus the liberal's automatic sympathy with them as wretched reinforces his strategic impulse to stand with them, or at least not against them, as Left; and both the feeling and the strategic rule tend to make him see their enemy as his own. Indeed, by a little ideological ingenuity, the feeling, moral judgment and strategic rule can be brought into full harmony. If it happens that a goodly number of the poor and oppressed do in fact line up with a man or leadership seemingly "of the Right"—as they have done with a Perón, a Franco, a de Gaulle, or even (to be quite honest about it) a Hitler—then we will merely explain that they have been deceived by demagogic Right forces that are exploiting the ignorance of the masses.

What kind of deed is it that is most sure to arouse, and to arouse most vehemently, a liberal's indignation? to arouse, in the first place, his mere interest, since no one can become indignant about something if he fails to notice it? Left-wing trade unionists and Marxian politicians massacred by Franco strike a liberal's attention more forcibly than nuns, priests and tradition-minded peasants massacred by Franco's opponents. A liberal, like every sane man, burns with appropriate indignation at the thought of the Nazi death camps; indeed, the liberal revives his horrified memory of them continually, long years after Nazism perished, with books, articles, movies and television spectaculars. But the thought of the deaths at Katyn Forest—the carefully scientific slaughter by the Soviet secret police of the bulk of the Polish officer corps, in which were numbered the elite capable of leading an independent Polish nation after the war—is dulled and sparks no flame. *Deaths in the Forest*, the remarkable book on Katyn by J.K. Zawodny, passed, when it was published in 1963, like a shadow in the night, like the other books on Katyn before it, beginning with the moving and wonderfully written *Terre Inhumaine*, by Joseph Czapski, the Polish artist and hero who was the first man outside the Russian apparatus to come to realize that thousands of his countrymen had suddenly ceased to exist.

We have already considered how this same selectivity permitted an elevated indignation at the terror of the European paras and Secret Army (constituting the political Right in the Algerian equilibrium, though most of the Secret Army's supporters were poor enough, and sufficiently wretched in the dismal prospect of exile), and at the same time an indifference toward, even a justification of, the much more extensive and ferocious terror of the Arab revolutionaries (in that context accepted as constituting the Left); and a similar indignation at Portuguese (the Right's) measures to put down the revolt in Angola along with indifference toward, even support of, Holden Roberto's (the Left's) measures—among them some new and ingenious methods of automated torture—to further that revolt. Nor is it hard to imagine the campaign of liberal indignation that would have resounded to the highest heavens if, in 1961, it had been Franco's agents instead of Israel's who had kidnapped, in Argentina, not Adolf Eichmann but an ex-officer of the GPU control squad of the Abraham Lincoln Brigade, and brought him to Madrid for trial in a glass cage.

The strategic rule and the segregated emotion hold for domestic as for international affairs, for small things as for large. Liberals are sensitive about violations of academic freedom, free speech and other civil rights; but their sensitivity is much more surely and more keenly aroused when the alleged victim is of the Left. In truth, most liberals do not notice and can scarcely believe that citizens of the Right are ever among the victims. And yet it is not so infrequently that someone adhering, in one way or another, to an ideological tendency to the Right of liberalism at least believes that his rights have been invaded: that he has lost his job on a college faculty because of his opinions rather than his professional performance; that he has been prevented from speaking in a forum where he was rightfully entitled to present his views; that a bureaucratic decree has blocked him from running his farm or business in the way he judges to be his right to do; that because of his political stand he has been unrightfully discriminated against in seeking to sell his labor or his talents. He may be sure that whatever its objective deserts, his case will never become a *cause célèbre* in the Fight for Civil Liberties. With luck it may be immortalized as a footnote in a liberal sociological essay proving that right-wing political views are the expression of the schizoid paranoia of the insecure lower middle class. More likely, it will vanish without a trace.

To a liberal it seems eminently normal that *all* members of the political science or history or economics or philosophy department of a university should be, as in many important cases they are, liberals plus a few somewhat left of liberal. But it seems shocking if a sizable percentage is of the Right, even a rather moderate Right. Nearly all liberals believe communists should be allowed to speak on college campuses, and most liberals believe communists should be permitted to teach in colleges; and there have been many liberal campaigns of protest against the attempts of some college administrators to prevent communists from speaking or to fire them from faculties. There is no comparable liberal solicitude for fascists or even for those belonging to what liberals like to refer to as "the Radical Right." Even the strictest civil-liberties liberals, who do defend in principle the right of fascists to speak in a public place, are seldom around when the issue comes up. In both Britain and the United States, liberals began in 1962 to develop the doctrine that words which are "inherently offensive," as far-Right but not communist words seem to be, do not come under the free speech mantle.

From the annual millions of examples of the liberal rule in action, let me select one other that has a classic quality for clarity of outline as well as the stature of the protagonist. In the spring of 1962, Supreme Court Justice William O. Douglas, liberal of liberals, delivered the fourth "James Madison Lecture on the Bill of Rights" to the New York University Law Center. He took as theme the evils in the world around us that resulted from the failure to understand and protect the freedoms proclaimed in the Bill of Rights. He cited just three specific instances: the suppression and persecution ordered by Premier Menderes of Turkey against press critics of his government in the late 1950's; the ex post facto laws passed by the military junta that seized power in South Korea in 1960; the "precautionary" arrests made by the Pakistani government in 1962. Now no one will dispute that these three acts did in truth violate Bill of Rights freedoms—though it might be added that other issues, perhaps not less important, were also involved. But how remarkable—or, rather, since he is so total a liberal, how inevitable—that it was three violations such as these and no others that came to Justice Douglas' mind as he surveyed the record of recent history: in each case, a violation by a man and government of the Right. In the lively sectors of his memory there were evidently not to be found those rather substantial violations of freedoms that occurred during those same years, they say, in Hungary; or Kwame Nkrumah's suppression, jailing and exiling of all his political opponents; or Gamal Abdel Nasser's equally one-party, one-opinion regime; or Sukarno's press and opinion controls; or Mao Tse-tung's handling of critics; or Julius Nyerere's declaration that there is room for only one party and one policy in Tanganyika; or....But it is irrelevant to draw out the list; for these are men of the Left.

I have heard many a liberal, many a time, wax indignant at the treatment accorded this or that leftward-leaning teacher who appeared as witness before the House Committee on Un-American Activities; but I have never heard any liberal become indignant over the brazen, shrewdly planned contumacious behavior through which Communist Party members called as witnesses, their Party lawyers and the audience assembled under control of Party agents seek to destroy the integrity of the legislative process; and I have very seldom heard a liberal so much as mention the elaborate manipulation of the minds of tens of thousands of students carried out over the years, under detailed Party directives and continuous Party supervision, by the thousands of Party members and fellow travelers who have taught in the American educational system.

II

IN REVIEWING THESE DIVERSE episodes and issues, I do not mean to raise the question whether the liberals' attitude toward Franco, Tito, Hungary, J. Edgar Hoover, the Soviet Union, Pandit Nehru or any other person, nation or event has been "right" or "wrong." Possibly it has been invariably right; possibly, always wrong; more probably, granted a significant norm for judgment, sometimes one and sometimes the other. But that is beside the present point. Nor do I mean to blame or condemn liberals for revealing a double standard in their conduct as well as attitude toward non-liberals of the Right and of the Left. Liberals are not the only human beings guided by that sort of double standard. My purpose has been only to illustrate by a sufficient number of varied examples that liberalism does in truth operate according to this double standard; that its location in what Professor Schlesinger likes to call the "vital center" is not equidistant from the Left and Right extremities; that it is a verifiable fact that liberalism finds, or tends to find, its main enemy, its preferred enemy, to the Right. This does not imply that liberals *never* see an enemy to their Left and never actively oppose persons or tendencies that are Left-of-liberalism. They do of course; and on some critical occasions, usually as a last resort when all mediating alternatives have been exhausted, some liberals will treat the further Left as for the given hour the main enemy. But this never gives a liberal an unmixed satisfaction; and he is especially uneasy when he finds that in his bout with the Left he has a self-invited ally from the Right at his side. His conscience can be really pure and his heart fully uplifted only when he is riding full tilt against a right-wing ogre.

Is there any doubt that it is indeed a strategic rule of liberalism to prefer to find and do battle with an enemy on the Right rather than to find him on the Left? Am I pounding here on an open door? Quite possibly so; I do not think there is really any doubt about the rule, and if there is, the confirming evidence is overwhelming. Still, I have found that some liberals, though like all liberals they feel and act according to the rule, do not want to acknowledge it. They feel a little shamefaced about this Enemy to the Right rule when it is brought fully out into the open; it seems to suggest a trace of both logical inconsistency and moral hypocrisy, like some other rules that incorporate a double standard. In one sense perhaps the suggestion is accurate. The formal principles of liberalism concerning rights, duties, equality, negotiating disputes instead of fighting about them, and so on are quite general. They do not show on their faces why terrorism or dictatorship is worse from the Right than from the Left, or violating a leftist's civil liberties worse than violating a rightist's; though, as always, a sufficiently ingenious dialectician can straighten out the logic, and a practiced casuist can no doubt untangle the moral knots. But in any case, whatever puzzle attaches to the rule from the standpoint of liberalism's internal doctrine or its moral self-righteousness, it is in a pragmatic sense a legitimate and inevitable expression of liberalism as a social tendency. It is not a merely arbitrary prejudice or quirk of temperament.

Liberalism is linked to the tendencies on its Left, and distinguished from the tendencies to its Right, by most, though of course not all, of its basic principles and primary values: by its conception of human nature, its secularism, its egalitarianism, its attitude toward change and social reform and indeed much of the content of the recommended reforms, its stress on an egalitarian social justice, its attack on social discrimination, and so on. Liberals frequently reflect this overlap, by implication at least, when they say of communists or left-wing socialists (right-wing socialists and liberals having become more or less wholly assimilated in our time): they have the correct ideals and goals, but their methods are wrong. To some liberals—I have known more than one such—communists seem not much more than liberals with guts; and even the liberal spokesmen of the American government refer to the "areas of common interest" shared with the communists, not to speak of the fifty-seven varieties of socialist. It is harder to think of a man with whom you have much in common as your sworn enemy, than of another who is "just not your sort of person." Or, enlarging the perspective: liberalism is itself of "the Left" (*la Gauche, il sinistrismo*), part of the great Left wave that we can trace back to the French Revolution and on into the Renaissance; and liberalism, even though it belongs to the rightward flank of the Left, feels more at home with its cousins of the Left than with the strangers of the Right.

Historically, moreover, it is against the social forces of the Right that the liberals and their ideological ancestors have usually found themselves fighting. What has come to be called "the Right" has been and is still bound up with organized religion, a hereditary aristocracy, the armed forces, landed property, business, "the interests" and "Robber Barons" (both terms coined by liberal ideologues), caste or racial discrimination: bound up, that is, with the superstitions, customs, prejudices, privileges and traditional institutions against which the impetus of liberalism, both theoretical and practical, has always been directed. In preferring and choosing the enemy to the Right, modern liberalism is true to its heritage.

The liberal tendency to see the main enemy on the Right is not, then, something accidental or temporary, but of the essence of liberalism. Modern liberalism reached what historians of the future will define as its zenith during the struggle against Hitler's Nazism and Mussolini's fascism—a struggle in which, of course, liberalism was allied with both socialism and communism. The menace of the Right then reached what seemed to be a new and peculiar intensity; and this menace constituted for liberalism a supreme challenge to which it triumphantly responded. It was through liberal leadership in so many phases of the anti-Nazi struggle that liberalism became intricately entrenched within the structure of Western society and dominant for the formation of Western opinion.

So necessary for liberalism is the enemy on the Right that when he does not exist, liberalism must invent him. This is why, I think, the Nazi menace is kept on the public stage by journalists, historians, movie directors, TV producers, novelists, preachers and demagogic politicians, with a prominence that has no objective historical justification. And I think this necessity had, too, a good deal to do with the symbolic and grotesque career of Senator Joseph McCarthy. McCarthy was in large part a liberal creation, as his liberal and suitably anti-McCarthy biographer, Richard Rovere, has concluded. A second-rate small-town politician, with no organization or machine, no competent staff or administrative talent, very little money at his disposal, not backed by any serious economic or social force, attracting mostly third-raters as his ardent admirers, McCarthy could not possibly have got very far without the help of the liberals.

The liberals required an enemy on the Right. All real ones of importance were beaten down or in quiescence, so in their desperation they invented McCarthy and McCarthyism. McCarthy was particularly needed by the faculties of the great American universities. Their members felt not only a gnawing vacancy on the Right; they were facing the most painful of all situations for liberal intellectuals—that of discovering themselves to be, though subjectively committed to non-conformism, conformist members of a virtually one hundred percent conforming community. By means of the created symbol of McCarthy the dangerous thrill of non-conformism was recovered—imaginatively, of course: in real life, a McCarthyite actually found in the university would have been shunted back to the farm leagues, or sent to a psychiatrist.

The McCarthy balloon collapsed, with disappointing speed, as soon as a few people decided to give it a prick or two. But the problem remains. Year after year the nostalgic liberal mythmakers renew the attempt to transform a moronic Jew-baiter, an addlepated ex-soldier or a retired candy merchant into a monster worthy to be target of the liberal sword. In November 1963, the liberals of all nations found themselves utterly unable to assimilate the fact that President Kennedy had been shot by a confirmed and long-time Marxist. The liberal ideology had to be summoned posthaste on a psychic rescue mission. Fact was quickly verbalized into myth, and soon everyone understood that, whatever the accidental appearances of the moment, the real culprit was—how could it have been otherwise?—the old, familiar and reassuring dragon, *the Right*.

In sum, then: if we are to understand liberalism existentially—not as an abstracted set of principles but as a historical tendency of human beings believing certain ideas, having certain sentiments, and acting along certain general lines—then we must recognize that the enemy to the Right is integral to its definition. Without the enemy to the Right, liberalism does not exist.

TWELVE

Dialectic of Liberalism

I

NON-COMMUNISTS HAVE OFTEN upbraided communists for
what are alleged to be gross inconsistencies in communist behavior. The charge goes as follows: You communists call for a
maximum of free speech, free press, free assembly and other civil
rights in the United States and other non-communist countries;
but inside the countries where communists are in power you
have suppressed, or virtually suppressed, all these rights. You
uphold the right to strike in non-communist countries, and very
often exercise that right in practice when you are in control of
trade unions; but in the communist countries it is criminal, in
some cases a capital crime, to strike or merely advocate striking.
In the non-communist countries you call for an end to war, for
disarmament and peace, and you support pacifist slogans and
organizations; but inside the communist sphere no pacifist talk
or pacifists are permitted and the entire economic plan is subordinated to armament; and communists give active support
to many wars and rebellions all over the globe. You demand
self-determination and independence for nearly any group,

however short a claim it has to being a genuine nation, in Africa, the Middle East or southern Asia; but you refuse to permit any free expression of national opinion within the nations—many of them of ancient lineage—inside your own bloc, and you send in tanks to put down the attempts to act independently. Similar examples could be multiplied to prove how you are both for and against free speech, for and against democracy, for and against peace, freedom of religion and self-determination. They all combine to show that either your official communist doctrine is a bundle of crass contradictions, or you communists are hypocritical liars, saying one thing with one side of your mouths and the opposite with the other.

The communist, however, is not prepared to accept either horn of that dilemma. If he is willing to admit you for a moment inside the threshold of the mysteries, he will explain as follows:

Your naive critique is only a reflection of your mental enslavement within the static framework of Aristotelian logic, which is unable to comprehend the reality of change, time and history— one more proof, by the way, that your way of thinking, like your world in general, is doomed to early extinction. If you were able to understand the historical dialectic—which, since you are not a communist, you cannot really do: only the living practice of communism makes possible a genuine understanding of the theory of communism—you would realize that there are no inconsistencies. In every case the seeming contradictories, in the reality of time and history, reinforce each other and fuse their dynamism into a synthesis at a higher historical level.

The communist camp is the *thesis* which represents the historical interests of the revolution, therefore of peace, freedom, justice, well-being, and the future of mankind in the coming epoch of a truly human history. Anything that strengthens the communist camp is right and just and good. In the present transitional era of world struggle, of wars and revolutions, the use of civil rights inside the communist camp to publicize opposition to the line of the Party and the revolution would only express the intrusion of counterrevolutionary influences, of capitalist hangovers and imperialist interventions; the proper purpose of public speech and assembly is to support, strengthen and improve the work of the revolution, not to sabotage it. Similarly, labor organization has the function of enabling the workers to contribute the maximum to the building of the revolution, not to tearing it down; besides which, strikes would be in any case an anachronism in a communist country, because it is the workers themselves through their revolutionary state, not capitalists and monopolists, who own the machines and factories. Since we still live in a world where the forces of reaction and imperialism are rampant and are daily plotting to drown the revolution in blood, our camp must be armed to the highest possible level precisely in order to serve the cause of peace, which is the cause of the revolution; and every blow struck in an anti-colonial revolt, or in a war for independence and liberation fought against an imperialist power or a reactionary social class, is a blow for peace. But to permit parts of the already communist—that is, truly liberated—region to break away under the alleged claim to the right of self-determination would be to surrender to the counterrevolutionary intrigues of the imperialist war-makers.

Exactly the same reasoning applies to the non-communist camp except, of course, in reverse. The non-communist camp represents the historical interests of the class oppressors and the counterrevolution, therefore of war, tyranny, poverty and the bloody, reactionary past and present of society only half lifted from barbarism. Anything that weakens the non-communist camp is right and just and good. Since free speech and assembly and other civil rights are useful for the operations of the revolutionary vanguard within the enemy camp, and for psychological and other fission maneuvers designed to erode the enemy will and his social structure, they are to be preserved and supported, though preferably withdrawn from use by militant anti-communists. Since strikes can be exploited to weaken the non-communist economy and to advance revolutionary ideas and personnel, the right to strike is similarly correct for the non-communist camp. And, self-evidently, any weakening of the armament of the non-communist camp or of the non-communist will to use its arms, through partial or outright pacifist propaganda and activity, is right and good and desirable, within the enemy's sphere.

The communists dress this analysis up in all sorts of Hegelian furbelows, but fundamentally they are making a straightforward point, however it may be neglected by non-communists. The meaning of universal ideas and principles, they are saying, cannot be discovered merely by definition and abstract analysis, but only by relating them to the specific conditions of time, place and circumstance in which they function; and further—this being the peculiar insight by which communism raises this notion above the common-sense level: the existential context always includes a clash, struggle or conflict of interests, forces, classes or institutions, whether or not the conflict is consciously recognized. Thus every universal idea—peace, law, freedom, democracy, justice, order, liberation—has both a plus and a minus value, dependent on which side of the given conflict is in question.

Undoubtedly the communists carry this dialectical analysis of theirs to logical extremes where it becomes lost in a maze of Hegelian-style metaphysics. Leaving that for the scholiasts, we may still recognize that a moderately dialectical approach is surely called for if we are to understand what happens in the actual world that has been, is and is likely to be for as far ahead as we need to be concerned with. But obvious as this may be when we focus attention on it, it is exceedingly difficult not to overlook it, or forget it, when we view the world through the lens of a universalistic and rationalist ideology such as liberalism. A liberal tends to feel and reason: peace is peace, free speech is free speech, law is law, democracy is democracy, justice is justice, then, now and forever, here, there and everywhere.

II

SUPPOSE THAT I AM approached by an armed robber. I preach to him the virtue of disarmament; he is persuaded, and throws his gun away; and I keep my wallet. This result will be pleasing to me, and most of us will judge the outcome morally praiseworthy. Still, it can hardly be said that disarmament meant the same thing for both parties, or that the net result was an equal gain to both—though of course we both ended up disarmed. The suspicion remains that I managed to put something over on my primitive and slow-witted accoster.

Change the circumstances slightly. Say that I, the good citizen, have the gun; and the would-be robber, only his two fists and a club, perhaps. But I don't like guns, thinking them dangerous for everyone concerned and also a barbaric way to settle disputes that ought to be dealt with rationally—by, let us say, a dialogue. So I enter into negotiations with my two-fisted friend, and we eventually agree to disarm—mutually, of course: I throw away my gun, and he throws his club, or seems about to when I get rid of the gun to prove my good faith. Again, the result yields an abstract equality: both sides disarm. But this has no relevance to the concrete meaning of what has happened: namely, a reversal in power relationship.

It should be obvious that from a practical standpoint disarmament measures—and even, through their psychological effect, mere disarmament campaigns that do not lead to specific measures—are to the relative advantage of the side that has the inferior arms, or no arms. My belief in non-violence may spring from the purest of ideals; but if I have no weapons and you have many, it will also prove a very useful belief if I can get you to share it sufficiently to lead you to throw away your big bombs, unload your revolvers, sheath your truncheons and kennel your police dogs.

The first large-scale disarmament campaign developed in the latter half of the nineteenth century. Its chief specific proposal was to prohibit a monstrous new weapon of annihilation: the steel-clad dreadnought. Not surprisingly, this demand was pressed most fervently by the nations of continental Europe, and resisted most firmly by Britain, which was the only country at that time equipped with the technology and industry to construct dreadnoughts. In the twentieth century it became the turn of British and American opinion to campaign for the prohibition of a monstrous new weapon, the U-boat—which happened to be the only device by which Germany might have challenged Anglo-American control of the seas.

All varieties of pacifism, though from the point of view of this or that individual they may rest on moral and theological beliefs, have similar connections in practice. The more my opponent is affected by pacifist ideas and feelings, the better it is for me, practically speaking. And this fact is so unquestionable that the propaganda and psychological warfare services of all modern governments have deliberately promoted pacifism among the enemy armies and civilian populations during the wars of this century. Several of the governments have included in their war preparations a preliminary sowing of pacifist ideas in prospective enemy quarters.

It is a mark of the ascendancy of the liberal ideology (with its attendant guilt) in the advanced Western nations, most particularly in the United States and Great Britain, that for the first time in history disarmament proposals and pacifist-tending ideas are being pressed not by the nations with inferior arms in order to weaken the stronger, but by the stronger in order to weaken themselves: to sacrifice their relative advantage, and thereby to lessen their ability to defend their interests and ideals. True enough, the governments of the Western nations have in some measure been trapped into disarmament-pacifism by the calculated manipulations of the communists and the intuitively shrewd demagogy of the Afro-Asian leaders. But quite apart from all deliberate efforts from the outside, the disarmament-pacifist trend in Western opinion is also self-imposed: a derivative of the rationalist habit of understanding "peace" as an abstract universal instead of a concrete and dynamic condition, and of the Western sense of guilt at the immensity of its own power.

Analyzed "dialectically"—that is, in relation to their existential and historical context—"disarmament" and "the search for peace" do not have a single, unambiguous meaning that can be established by a fixed definition. The operative meaning of such terms must be discovered in each case by relating them to the actions, interests and goals of the person or group that is using them. When Khrushchev speaks of "the struggle for peace," he is not being cynical, as many anti-communists believe. He is altogether sincere, since, for him, "the struggle for peace" *means* the fight for the worldwide victory of communism; and it is therefore consistent and natural that various sorts of coercion, violence and warfare should be included in the struggle for peace. This is not at all what Norman Cousins and the Rev. A.J. Muste have in mind in *their* "struggle for peace." They are thinking, vaguely to be sure, of a state of the world in which all men, basing their conduct on their "common humanity" and "common interests," will settle their differences by reasonable and democratic processes instead of by violence and war. And there is this additional "dialectical" difference between the meanings of their "peace" and Khrushchev's: the content that they give to the idea of "peace" is a figment of ideological imagination that has no relevance to the real world of space and time as it has been, is or could be; whereas Khrushchev's "peace" is a hardheaded program of action directly related to the world we live in. The inevitable result is that Messrs. Cousins and Muste's struggle for their empty dream of "peace" contributes in practice to the advance of Khrushchev's very realistic plan for peace.

The communists divide the world into "the zone of peace" and "the zone of war." "The zone of peace" means the region that is already subject to communist rule; and the label signifies that within their region the communists will not permit any political tendency, violent or non-violent, whether purely internal or assisted from without, to challenge their rule. "The zone of war" is the region where communist rule is not yet, but in due course will be, established; and within the zone of war the communists promote, assist and where possible lead political tendencies, violent or non-violent, democratic or revolutionary, that operate against non-communist rule. Clear enough, these definitions. You smash the Hungarian Freedom Fighters, and support Fidel Castro; you know where you are going.

But the liberal definition of "peace" is clear only as an abstraction; it is muddled as soon as any attempt is made to apply it, and it obscures instead of revealing a target. Thus liberals, and the Western nations influenced by liberal modes of thought, find themselves accepting, in the name of "peace," this communist division of the world into the two zones and the communist rules of conduct toward each. The burden of dissension, violence and revolt, often caused and always exploited by the communists, is borne in South Vietnam, Cuba, Katanga, Guiana, Laos, Angola, Venezuela, London and New York, for these all belong to the zone of war where violent trouble is endemic. But to avoid a "threat to peace," the communists are to be left undisturbed to maintain their peace in their own way in Hungary, North Vietnam, Tibet, Russia or wherever else in their ever-expanding zone.

LIBERALISM DEFINES FREE SPEECH and the related freedoms of assembly and association, as it does "peace" and "disarmament," in abstraction, without tying them to specific persons and circumstance. For liberalism, these freedoms are the procedural rules sustaining a democratic society that rests on the will of the majority and solves its internal conflicts of interest and opinion through continuous discussion, negotiation and compromise. But this meaning of free speech and the related freedoms is significant and operable only for those who share the wish or at least willingness to have and preserve some sort of free and constitutional society. For those others—and they are not few among us—whose aim is to subvert, overthrow and replace free and constitutional society, these freedoms of speech, assembly and the rest are merely convenient levers to use in accomplishing their purpose.

The liberal ideologue is thus caught in the inescapable dilemma of his own making that we have previously examined. If he extends the freedoms to the subverters, they will use them, as they have done in one nation after another, to throw the free society into turmoil and in the end to destroy it. But if he denies the freedoms to anyone, he will feel, does feel, that he has betrayed his own principles, "imitated the methods of the enemy," and thus joined the company of subverters. So, when a showdown with the subverters comes, as it comes from time to time to all nations, the liberals are demoralized in advance, if they do finally forget ideology and decide to resist, by the guilt generated from this feeling of self-betrayal. Let us note that this is a purely ideological trap. Common sense, unlike ideology, understands that you can play a game only with those who accept the rules; and that the rules' protection does not cover anyone who does not admit their restrictions and penalties.

LET US CONSIDER THE dialectic of "self-determination." Liberals accept, indeed actively favor and promote, self-government and independence for all peoples and nations—except, apparently, Katangans and Papuans—who want those blessings of liberty that are derived, or seem to be, from the principles of the liberal ideology. In this perspective, several score new or renewed nations have sprung into existence during the past fifteen years, and now have representatives occupying much of the street-side parking space in New York and Washington. To most liberals this seems a triumph of liberalism, and it is frequently so hailed.

As part of the process of gaining independence, various native leaders from the potential nations in question, many of whom have attended London University, Oxford, the Sorbonne and occasionally Columbia or Harvard, will have repeated the appropriate liberal slogans and aphorisms, sounding—especially on their tours through the United States lecture and TV circuits—like living syntheses of Locke, Jefferson and John Stuart Mill. They hire European or American professors to draw up constitutions and legal systems combining the best features of British and French parliamentarism, Anglo-Saxon common law, the Napoleonic Code and the United States Constitution. They designate themselves, at least in dispatches sent abroad, as President, Prime Minister, Premier or Cabinet member. Liberalism, the culmination and flower of Western culture, has advanced its dynamic frontier over another segment of the earth's surface, replacing the reactionary tyranny and exploitation of colonialism, imperialism, feudal sheikdoms and what not.

This makes a very satisfying picture, but it is not the way things look from the other side of the wall; in fact, they look considerably different even the smallest distance behind the surface. The revolutionary party, group or faction in the potential new nation does, certainly, want self-government and independence. However, the revolutionaries understand self-government and independence not as shining abstractions in the liberal prayer book, but as the effective instruments of power, privilege, jobs and glory for themselves and their associates. Let us add that the independence-minded group is usually a very small minority, which is compelled to use not merely propaganda and agitation on a wide scale but in many cases a systematic terror to get sufficient backing from the wider strata of the local population.

Independence for a revolutionary Arab Algeria is a great victory for human freedom, doubtless; but for the revolutionaries and their luckier followers it also means taking over the homes, shops, goods, factories and lands of a million Algerians of European origin at panic prices or by simple expropriations; acquiring the farms and vineyards that the labor, skills and capital of five generations of Europeans have painfully raised out of the desert; getting an easy chance at the profits of the great new oil and gas wells that French scientists, engineers, geologists and money have brought into production; and not least, the satisfaction of putting the infidel dogs finally into their place as the crescent of Islam replaces the cross struck from the temples.

Independence in East Africa is a dramatic achievement; and it is also the occasion when native black men, who have neither spun nor reaped, can take for nothing or next to nothing many of those splendid farms and ranches that the knowledge, effort, foresight, administrative ability and capital of Europe-sprung white men have slowly brought into being out of lands neglected and wasted for untold centuries. (Not, of course, that the land of most of those farms and ranches will continue for very long to nourish the bodies and economies of those regions, as it has been laboriously taught to do: it is already being broken up into scraggly plots of yams; the Masai will not have much time left for plowing and liming and fertilizing and spraying as their cows crop the forage to its roots to supply their diet of milk and fresh blood; an aspiring tribesman will not be concerned to number closely to the acre, in a petty white man's way, the head of cattle that prove his manliness and glory.)

Every observant visitor to the newly Balkanized Africa can report, though he is more likely to do so privately than in public, that the primary content of independence for many of the nationalist leaders is a car and chauffeur, a new house with servants, a bevy of mistresses, and plenty of beer and champagne consumed nightly in public competition with rivals to see who can finish with the largest number of empty bottles on his café table. Kwame Nkrumah may be "Mr. Prime Minister" in speeches to the United Nations, but at home his fellow citizens who wish to stay out of jail do well to remember that he is

"Osagyefo," the Redeemer. Julius Nyerere of Tanganyika, apple of many a liberal eye, had a law enacted requiring all vehicles going in either direction to pull to the side of the road and stop when he and his retinue of white-garbed security guards come in sight; but he insists that it is only by custom, not mandatory, that fellow citizens should bow down before him. He and Nkrumah agree with nearly all of their fellow African leaders, though the point ordinarily waits for post-independence to be mentioned, that multi-party democracy "in the Western sense" is not suitable for Africa just now; from the top of the new political pyramid, a one-party setup run by the regime in power is more "the African way"; and so it works out to be before long in one after another of the new African nations as it has in so many of the slightly less new Asian nations before them. It is fortunate for these newly risen potentates that they are for the most part men of the Left; if they were of the Right, all the furies of liberal rhetoric, we may be sure, would be thundering about their ears. Even as things are, a veteran liberal here and there can sometimes be heard swallowing hard at the report of the latest political outrage by one of these chiefs of state whom he and his fellow liberals and their common doctrine have helped boost into power.

I remember when Indonesia's Sukarno visited the United States a few years ago. In a couple of university lectures and a TV hookup he told us how his life and thought were modeled on Washington, Jefferson and Lincoln, with a dash of Franklin D. Roosevelt. And so he was seen and advertised by liberals as—supported jointly by Washington and Moscow—he led the battle for *merdeka* against the Dutch oppressor. Liberals eagerly waited for a new America, conceived in liberty and dedicated to the proposition that all men of all colors are created free and equal, to arise in the South Seas. With the heavy hand of the imperialist oppressor removed, democracy would blossom. No longer exploited for the benefit of alien monopolists, the people, working now for themselves and their own country, and helped by friendly older nations, would steadily expand their domestic freedom and lift their standard of living.

But Sukarno's idea of independence and *merdeka*, translated from abstraction into existence, means something quite different. For him it means a Javanese imperialism, ruled by himself and his palace associates in collaboration with the world's largest Communist Party outside the Iron Curtain. (Of course *merdeka* had, and continues to have, a still different, third meaning for the Indonesian communists, and for Moscow and Peking.) Westerners may do a lot of talking about opposition parties, but they are just a series of headaches for the Indonesian way of life, and we'll put a stop to their nonsense; either they fall into line or we liquidate them. As for the federalism business that was written into the constitution, it may have been a fine thing in American colonial days, but not in this part of the ocean: the function of the oil and rubber and spices of Sumatra, Celebes and the Moluccas is to contribute to the support of Java; any local ideas to the contrary are to be put down by machine guns and napalm. Liberal economists love to gather statistics about a rising standard of living; and doubtless it is a good plan, other things being equal, if others will pay for it—the two billion dollars' worth of goods stolen from the Dutch not having lasted long—but there are more important fish to fry. Too bad that the ordinary folk of Indonesia—for the first time in those islands so gently served by an abundant nature—don't have enough to eat. Our foreign exchange must be used to throw great monuments—international stadiums, cloverleaf highways, lofty hotels and public buildings—into the sky; and more particularly to assemble and maintain the planes and guns and ships to defend and expand the rising empire of the Southern Seas.

Nor is Sukarno the only budding imperialist, as the acts as well as the words of Nasser will readily remind us. Nasser, like several other empire-builders of this century, wrote down his imperial project in a small book[1] that any literate man may read: of the new Egypt, imperial base of the overlapping rings of Araby, Islam and Africa. The revolutionary nationalist leaders understand, as liberalism does not, though some liberals are beginning to do so, that what is ending in our age is not empire but merely the empires of the West.

'EQUALITY,' TOO, BECOMES a less simple notion when submitted to the gloss of the dialectic. If I have a thousand dollars and you have none, equality means that you gain five hundred dollars and I lose five hundred. If I have ten acres and you are landless, five are taken from me, by the principle of equality, and you get five. But the real relation is still more disturbing. If I have enough to eat and you are starving, equality may mean that we both go hungry.

Usually those of us who, adhering to the loosely defined egalitarian *tendency* of liberalism and thinking from the perspective of membership in a relatively affluent group—Western civilization, let us say—do not imagine equality in this rigorously mathematical way. We feel that the members of the other, less privileged group—differing in predominant color, race or religion, perhaps in distinctive culture or civilization—ought to

---

1. Published in the United States as *Egypt's Liberation* (Washington: Public Affairs Press, 1955).

be given equal rights and opportunities so that they will be able to follow our example, and to raise their level of life gradually to ours. To this end, and to speed up the process, we are prepared to give them help from our abundance. (We omit consideration of the question why they have so notably failed, in many cases over so many millennia, to do what we look forward to their doing in the next few decades.)

However, this more modestly egalitarian view of ours still differs enormously from the way things look from the other side of the balance. The members of the less privileged group, or at any rate its leaders, see plainly that we have more of the good things of this world and they have less. Any sort of equalizing means, when brought down to earth, that its members, or at any rate its leaders, take over something—power, of course, and privilege as well as material wealth—of what we've got, just as quickly as the transfer can be arranged. From the perspective of the less privileged group, anything less direct is hypocritical mumbo-jumbo. This business about gradual self-development with a five percent yearly rise in Gross National Product is good enough for the economic historians and foreign office authors of position papers, but it doesn't put many Cadillacs in official garages or pay a newly uniformed officer corps at a rate to keep it contented. Besides, it takes too much hard work. Looking over the percentage of the world's automobiles, telephones, bathtubs, shoes, iceboxes and summer homes owned in the United States, there are a great many new revolutionary nationalist leaders who can tell you how to get Americans neatly equalized with the rest of mankind a lot faster than by minuscule donations of a few billions of foreign aid dollars annually.

Nor does equality as applied to race and color escape unscathed from contact with the dialectics of reality. As liberals and at the same time members of the privileged nation, race and civilization, we are able to feel both just and generous in proclaiming the equality of all rights and liberties without respect to color, race, etc., and the end of all forms of political, economic, social or cultural discrimination. Naturally we don't for a moment really contemplate literal equalization of their condition and ours either in our time or our children's children's. We have sense enough, however drugged we may be with ideology, to know more or less what that would mean, if we have been round about the world a bit or just talked to someone who has visited awhile in Calcutta, Peking, Cairo, Timbuktu or Chicago's South Side; and we know it's not for us—not unless we're saints as well as liberals.

We don't mean what we say in any such crude and simple manner. We don't, but they do, those persons of those different colors, races, creeds and cultures hearing the fine-sounding principles that liberalism has formulated and taught them. And why shouldn't they take those principles to mean what they say in terms of their own lives and conditions? They have been lowly and wretched. Now, by the very invitation of the long-time lords of creation, they are to be raised up, clothed, fed, adorned and placed in the formerly reserved seats of power. And then very often—perhaps this too is natural enough, granted all the background—they go a step or two beyond even that pleasantly dialectical interpretation of equality.

We tell them that all races and colors, white, black, brown, red and yellow, are brothers, are equal before the eyes of liberal doctrine and the United Nations. But some of them think they know better, that experience has taught them more accurately than abstract principles, and that its lesson has been that races, colors, creeds and civilizations are not at all alike; and maybe, now that the white Westerners—we are mostly white, it is an inescapable fact—are climbing down, it's time for asserting not the empty illusion of brotherly equality but a new reality of changed priorities in the global scale. When Nyasaland celebrated its debut in self-government on February 1, 1963, Dr. Hastings Banda, the Prime Minister, another of the African leaders educated in the West and much admired by liberal opinion, proclaimed (as the crowd rang cowbells, danced and shouted *Kamuzu Ndi Nkango*—"Banda is a Lion"): "We are now a black country—in a black continent!" His conclusion does not differ in substance from that stated by James Baldwin at about the same time: "The only thing white people have that black people need, or should want, is power."[2]

The morality-play version of *The Trial* that is a feature of many gatherings of the Black Muslims carries the liberal's ideal of equality all the way through the dialectical ringer. Facing the jury representing the non-Western, non-Christian, non-white majority of the earth's population, the prosecutor declaims:

"I charge the white man with being the greatest liar on earth. I charge the white man with being the greatest drunkard on earth. I charge the white man with being the greatest swine-eater on earth....I charge the white man, ladies and gentlemen of the jury, with being the greatest murderer on earth. I charge the white man with being the greatest adulterer on earth. I charge the white man with being the greatest robber on earth. I charge the white man with being the greatest deceiver on earth. I charge the white man with being the greatest troublemaker on earth. So therefore, ladies and gentlemen of the jury, I ask you, bring back a verdict of guilty as charged."

---

2. James Baldwin, *The Fire Next Time* (New York: Dial Press, 1963), p. 110.

It requires only seconds for the foreman to announce the unanimous verdict: "We find the defendant guilty, as charged"; and only seconds more for the sentence of death.

The nineteenth-century French writer Louis Veuillot summed up the general law of this political dialectic: *Quand je suis le plus faible, je vous demande la liberté parce que tel est votre principe; mais quand je suis le plus fort, je vous l'ôte, parce que tel est le mien.*[3]

---

3. The spare elegance of the French syntax makes this impossible to translate. The meaning is approximately: "When I am the weaker, I ask you for my freedom, because that is your principle; but when I am the stronger, I take away your freedom, because that is my principle."

THIRTEEN

Again:
Who Are the Liberals?

I

IN CHAPTER II, I ANSWERED the question "Who are the liberals?" in a manner that Socrates would have termed "inductive": by pointing to existing persons and institutions that are called "liberal." By implication, several additional answers were given in the course of the intervening chapters: a liberal is a person or organization adhering to all or most of the nineteen beliefs listed in Chapters III-V; a liberal is a person characterized by the cluster of values and attitudes discussed in Chapters IX-XI. I want to add, in rough summary, what I suppose would be considered a sociological answer if it were phrased in the accredited terminology and accompanied by statistical summaries of elaborate questionnaires. I will now interpret the question "Who are the liberals?" to mean: what are the social groups, classes, strata, types or occupations that most incline toward liberalism? A group's inclination toward liberalism is shown, presumably, when we find a relatively high percentage of liberals among its members, along with a tendency of the "interest organizations" supported by its members to put forward a liberal program.

To be sure, there are orthodox liberals in every class and stratum of modern society, from kings to latrine attendants. No group has a total immunity to the virus of a major ideology. You can find persons who are convinced liberals even though it can be demonstrated that the consequences of liberal beliefs and programs are directly counter to the interests of the group to which they belong and their own individual interests; for the sake of the ideology in which they believe they are willing to ignore or to sacrifice those interests.

If liberals were scattered according to a random pattern throughout all social strata, liberalism would lack a significant "social dimension," and could be analyzed sufficiently in psychological and philosophical terms. But this is not the case. The fact is that there is a much heavier concentration of liberals in some social formations than in others; there are some in which liberals are as rare as triplets. It follows that there are social as well as psychological factors determining belief in liberalism; that through its capacity to fulfill certain social needs (or psychological needs characterizing certain social groups) and to advance certain social interests, liberalism has a closer natural affinity with some groups and some types of person than with others.

Let us begin in reverse, by noting some of the persons who are *not* liberals; more exactly, some of the social groups among the members of which there is a relatively low percentage of liberals. (I am limiting my inquiry here to the arrangements that may be readily observed within the advanced nations of Western civilization, in particular the United States.)

To begin with, very few professional (career) military men are liberals. Some military men have a certain number of liberal ideas; and in a nation like the United States or Britain, where liberalism has become the prevailing tendency in the makeup of public opinion, most military men, like everybody else, exhibit a certain amount of liberal coloration in their rhetoric. But few military men are orthodox liberals, and almost none are liberal ideologues. Liberalism and the military life just do not fit well together; a military man doesn't seem able to feel like a liberal and act like a liberal, even when he professes a liberal set of beliefs.

This incompatibility between liberalism and the military life, and many of the reasons for it, are obvious and well known. Concepts of equality, non-discrimination and universal democracy are hard to reconcile with the inequalities, authoritarianism, detailed discrimination and rigid hierarchy that are always and inevitably characteristic of military organization; even if they can be reconciled by some sort of complicated logical exercise, there remains a feeling gap. In his scale of priorities the soldier is professionally committed to place the safety and survival of his country first, and to be ready to sacrifice his life as well as his freedoms and comforts thereto; he must keep the values of social justice and individual rights secondary in rank, if he is to do his soldierly duty; and his devotion to peace, however fervently protested, will always be confused by the fact that his trade is war.

Liberals have always given implicit recognition to this natural state of affairs by their normal hostility to the military. There is nothing a liberal columnist more enjoys attacking than "the military mind." For a liberal audience it is considered an adequate refutation of a proposal or policy if it can be shown that "retired generals and admirals" support it. Every liberal realizes that when "the army" intervenes, or is thought to be intervening, in one of the bi-monthly Latin-American revolutions, it is acting as a limb of Satan. Learned treatises by Columbia professors or lurid novels by Hollywood-pointed journalists are assured of massive royalties if they reveal how fascist types in the Pentagon—if not stopped at the eleventh hour by Sir Galahad Liberal—are plotting to take over the country, and plunge the world into a nuclear shambles in the process.

Several circumstances are presently tending to breach the wall between liberalism and the military mind. Technological change brings into the military force more and more persons exercising "civilian skills" (administrative, technical, scientific) that lack the inbred immunity of the older, narrower military vocation to liberal ideas and values. As liberalism becomes ascendant in public opinion, the soldiers-to-be absorb liberal ideas from the educational process, and after entering military service continue to be bathed in liberal ideas and rhetoric pouring from newspapers, magazines, books, television and sermons. And as liberal civilians move into the positions of governmental power in a nation with a tradition of "civilian supremacy," they begin deliberate moves to alter the military mind according to liberal prescriptions, by suitable indoctrination and censorship, demotions or dismissals of stubborn anti-liberals, manipulation of key appointments and so on. But the military dough proves hard to knead. Generals and admirals can be found who will, up to a point, read liberal-written speeches and echo when questioned the opinions formulated by the reigning liberal ideologues. But somehow the liberalism doesn't seem to sink in; when the less supervised life of inactive service—or a guerrilla war—begins, the liberalism sloughs off in a month or two, and the rattle of the unregenerate military serpent is again heard in the land. You have to search through an unconscionable deal of letterheads of liberal organizations before you can come up with a pennyworth of military names.

A second group or class in which liberals are few and far between is that of the businessmen who both own all or a controlling share of their enterprises—especially in manufacturing, mining, transport, construction and other "primary" fields—and actively run them. In this class, the small businessmen (who often incline to what the French have come to know as "Poujadism") differ in typical ideology from the remnant of large operators, but both are overwhelmingly anti-liberal. It is from their ranks that many, perhaps most, of the advertisers in avowedly anti-liberal publications and contributors to anti-liberal organizations are drawn.

Among most sorts of what Americans call "businessmen" the conquests of liberalism are limited, as the anti-liberal programs of many major business associations indicate; but the active owners are considerably more anti-liberal than the rest. A fair number of the executives of various grades in the corporations that have shifted from stockholder to management control, in merchandising and in banking, investment, insurance and other services become liberals or at least take up a good many liberal ideas and beliefs; and the families with inherited wealth turn out some of the most conspicuous liberals—a product that seems to be an unstable blend of the standard guilt, a somewhat condescending idealism and rather sly calculation.

Among professionals the ratios are more complicated. Generally speaking, the percentage of liberals is low among independent, self-employed doctors, dentists, engineers, and others of what might be called the less verbal professions. Many of the doctors who work as salaried employees or administrators of governmental and other public agencies, or of research institutes, foundations, large clinics and even large corporations, are liberals, often thoroughly ideologized, when they have not moved beyond liberalism to socialism or communism. But in the United

States and the small number of other nations where medicine has not been fully nationalized, the percentage among the self-employed doctors is much lower. There is a similar difference in the other professions, though the ratio of liberals is probably higher among dentists, possibly because of their ambiguous social status, and among lawyers, whose profession is more verbal and more likely to make them feel at home among such abstractions as proliferate in liberal ideology.

Independent farm owners and operators are seldom liberals. When they seem to be—as the programs of some of the farm organizations might seem to suggest—their liberalism is in most cases a transparent disguise for solid economic demands. Indeed, liberalism flourishes much more readily in an urban than in a rural environment, in the big cities more than on the farms or in the small towns. This, too, has often been remarked, and is an axiom for practical politicians figuring how votes will go; it is perhaps the explanation why modern liberalism is more pervasive in England and the United States than on the European continent, where a much larger percentage of the population is still on the land and in the villages. When the rural population becomes "radical" in large numbers, it does not turn typically to liberalism in the modern sense but to less polished, wilder and more violent doctrines and programs: to cheap money panaceas, rural anarchism, communism, vigilantism, racial and religious "hate" movements, and for that matter fascism.

II

IN THE UNITED STATES a high and significant ratio of liberals is to be found on the faculties of the large colleges and universities outside the South. Even in the Southern universities and in the smaller colleges, except for some of the strictly sectarian institutions, the percentage of liberals on the faculties is in almost all cases considerably higher than in the communities from which the student body is drawn. This is true also of the secondary schools; and to a smaller degree of the primary schools as well, though in many areas the primary teachers are likely to be more closely tied to the rest of the community. But in many of the most influential universities—which in the long run dominate the entire educational system, since their graduates teach those who teach the teachers—the percentage of liberals has for several decades been very high indeed. In some of these universities such departments as Philosophy, Political Science, History, Government, Economics, Literature or American Civilization (various alternate names are used to designate the departmentalized fields into which the curriculum is divided) are manned one hundred percent by liberals. In many others one or two tame non-liberals are included within each department as if to display the liberal devotion to free speech by a kind of token integration.

In other advanced Western nations, also, the ideology of many teachers comes within the boundaries of modern liberalism as this book has defined it, or largely overlaps modern liberalism. There is often a more explicit admixture of socialism; but we have noted that contemporary reformist socialism and liberalism have moved into close coincidence. In countries like France and Italy, however, where there exist mass communist parties, a considerable number of teachers have moved on into communism or fellow-traveling. Such a leftward shift in the spectrum from liberalism toward communism takes place in these countries, in fact, not only among teachers but in most categories of the population.

Liberalism is prevalent among all sorts of opinion-makers as well as the teachers: editors, publishers, ministers and preachers, columnists, commentators, writers, miscellaneous intellectuals, all branches of the entertainment industry. (In these cases, too, the spectrum in France and Italy shows a displacement of part of the liberal band toward the further Left.) Generalizing, we may say that those who by career and occupation are *verbalists* exhibit an above-average predilection for liberalism.

Not surprisingly, social service workers, whose occupational interests are fully incorporated within the liberal ideology, are mostly liberals. By a somewhat lower but still high percentage, so are the multitudinous civil service workers and bureaucrats who man the gigantic mechanism of the Welfare State.

In fact, a second wide generalization seems valid: those who, as employees, administrators, staff members or in other capacities, make their living from tax-exempt institutions, including governmental and semi-governmental institutions, exhibit an above-average predilection for liberalism. Governmental bureaucrats are on average more liberal than the corresponding employees of private business; the permanent staffs of non-profit educational, philanthropic and scientific foundations are on average more liberal than the trustees, and more liberal than the staffs of profit-making organizations of a comparable type; and we have already noted that doctors working for governmental agencies or working full-time for hospitals, universities or group health organizations are on average more liberal than doctors self-employed in individual practice. This institutional category overlaps the category of verbalists: teachers, ministers, employees of university and governmental publishing houses, and many public relations experts are verbalists who make their living from tax-exempt institutions.

In the last section I mentioned that, though the liberal concentration among businessmen is generally low, it is relatively higher in the management strata of "publicly owned" enterprises (that is, those run by management itself or by some fiscal control group) than of those run by an individual, family or small group having a major ownership interest. It may be observed that managerial liberalism tends to be more moderate than the liberalism of the verbalists: tends to be the sort of centrist liberalism represented by many of the publications of the Committee for Economic Development in the United States or the Bow Group in Britain, or by what Professor Arthur Larson christened, during his brief moment of public blooming under the Eisenhower sun, "modern Republicanism."

A pure ideologue believes in his ideology for its own sake, because it meets his intellectual demands and satisfies his emotional needs; not for its ability to serve his practical interests or those of the group with which he associates himself. He is prepared, indeed, to disregard and sometimes to negate those practical interests for the sake of his ideology. Undoubtedly there are liberals who are pure ideologues, but it is hard to draw an exact line. Even when the ideologue is utterly sincere in heart, subjectively considered, it will often happen that his ideology will at the same time, in some measure, give an assist to his practical interests, even help fill his wallet. And for some an ideology is no more than a useful masquerade.

It is manifest on the surface that the rough correlations here surveyed between liberalism and one set of social groups, and between non-liberalism and another set, may well have some connection with the differing interests of these diverse groups as well as with the subjective ideas of their members. When we consider the large group of persons whom we call "workers," it is almost impossible to assess the ideological component. Liberalism has, certainly, a warm spot in its ideological heart for workers; and liberals have made the improvement of the condition of the working class one of their persistent aims. The traditional demands of workers for the right to organize, picket and strike and to raise their standard of living are in keeping with liberal doctrine and supported by liberal programs. In the United States the majority of the leaders of the primary organizations of workers—the trade unions—profess to be liberals, and the unions support many liberal policies and proposals in addition to those that are of direct and peculiar proletarian concern. And there is a fairly close relation between many outstanding liberal politicians and the trade union movement.

Nevertheless we may easily exaggerate the ideological liberalism of the mass of workers, perhaps even of the labor leaders. Opinion polls giving results broken down by income and educational level and by occupation seem to back up day-by-day experience in suggesting that most workers do not share the key political and philosophical ideas of liberalism; are, in fact, disturbingly "reactionary" by liberal standards.[1] The workers stick fairly hardheadedly to their practical search for higher wages, better living conditions and increased security; they adopt, and adapt, just enough of liberalism to further their goals, and are not much interested in the remainder.[2]

---

1. As liberals sometimes discover when they delve into the matter. *Cf.* Professor Samuel Stouffer's researches as reported and sadly reflected on in *Communism, Conformity and Civil Liberties.*

2. In Italy and France most of the trade unions are under communist control, and in most of the rest of Europe the trade union leadership is social democratic (of the reformist variety that is similar to the left wing of American liberalism). Even in Italy and France, however, and still more plainly in the other nations of Western Europe and in Britain, the mass of workers is probably not doctrinaire, especially now that Western Europe is joining the affluent society. Accepting arrangements inherited from an earlier historical

It is also true that the trade unions, as organized, active sub-groups of the nation, find liberalism a favorable environment in which to operate. Both the psychological atmosphere generated by the liberal doctrines and the political paths opened up by the procedural rules of the liberals' "open society" give the unions freedom and flexibility for maneuver; and this is no doubt another important factor suggesting to the labor leadership that a public image of liberalism, whether an accurate portrait or not, is useful.

Indeed, liberalism tends to serve the interests, or can be made to serve the interests, of almost any cohesive minority sub-group, as can readily be seen in recent American history in the case of the Roman Catholics, the Jews and most lately the Negroes. It is therefore natural enough that such sub-groups should incline outwardly toward liberal ideology. An overwhelming majority of American Jews is liberal in public profession; and a considerable proportion of the most influential liberal ideologues is Jewish in origin if not always in active faith. The potential of a liberal environment for a cohesive minority may be part of the explanation for the seeming anomaly that we remarked in earlier chapters: the adoption of liberalism by a good many Catholic spokesmen in spite of the difficulty in reconciling Catholic philosophy and theology with some parts of the liberal ideology. The American Negroes are only beginning to develop cohesiveness as a sub-group, but they have had many sorts of internal association for some time; and of the

---

situation, they are able to advance their practical interests through the existing Marxian leadership. Under more extreme social conditions, such as existed in Russia prior to the revolution or in Germany prior to 1933, or now exist in many of the underdeveloped nations, the mass of workers, when spurred by revolutionary activists, may, however, become ideologically intoxicated.

major organizations concerned with Negro interests and composed primarily of Negroes, all except the Black Muslims have in the past been professedly liberal in doctrine and for the most part in leadership. However, as in the case of the trade unions, one must wonder how deep, ideologically speaking, is the liberalism of the generality of members of sub-groups such as these; whether it may not in some measure merely reflect the social position of these sub-groups as minorities in both size and effective power. Where they are an effective majority, or manage to win preponderant power—like the Catholics, for example, in Spain or a number of Latin-American countries or even South Vietnam under the Ngo family regime, or the Jews in Israel, or the Negroes in African nations[3]—they don't seem to be so very liberal. This may be another instance of Veuillot's law.

III

MACHIAVELLI DIVIDED RULERS and aspirants to rule into lions and foxes: the lions who rely on strength, stubbornness and force; the foxes who rely on their wits, on shrewdness, deceit and fraud. Plainly enough, the liberals—especially the two great divisions of liberals recruited from the verbalists and from the employees of governmental agencies and tax-exempt institutions—belong to the foxes. It would occur to no one, surely,

---

3. The reference to Africa may be more doubtful than the others (and all are of course open to question). Catholics in Spain or Peru and Jews in Israel are at least in some socially relevant respects comparable to Catholics and Jews in the United States. But it is not certain whether there are relevant social similarities between African and American Negroes, or, if there are, how far these extend. Contemporary history, including the activities of Negro leaders in both continents, seems to be in the process of expanding them.

to classify Arthur Schlesinger, Jr., Hubert Humphrey, Walt Whitman Rostow or Adlai Stevenson among the lions.

Vilfredo Pareto elaborates this Machiavellian distinction in terms of his theory of "residues." Although he lists six classes of residues, he pays most attention to the first two. Class I amounts to an "instinct for combinations." Persons characterized by Class I residues have a tendency to try to combine and manipulate all sorts of elements from experience. As part of their manipulation of words, they are the ones who put together complicated theories and ideologies. They lack strong attachments to family, church, nation and tradition, though they may exploit these attachments in others. They are inventive, and in economic and political affairs, incline toward novelty and change. In practical conduct, they do not plan very far ahead, but count on their ability to bypass the challenges that may arise, or to improvise answers. These are, in a word, Machiavelli's foxes.

The lions are, in Pareto's terminology, the individuals who are marked by the Class II residues of "group-persistence." They are conservative in attitude, with a deep sense of the objectivity and permanence of family, nation and church. "Family pride," "love of country," concern with "property" as a permanent part of a man's and a family's reality are given emotional force by the Class II residues. In economic affairs, the Class II individuals—the lions—tend to be more cautious, saving and orthodox, more worried over "sound money," than the foxes. They praise "character" and "duty" more often than brains. And they are willing to use force to maintain the entities—family, class, nation, "the true faith"—to which they are attached.

During this century the liberal ideology has gradually increased its influence over the formation of public opinion within the United States, Britain, Italy and to a greater or less degree nearly all the advanced Western nations; and at the same time liberals, or persons accepting the liberal ideas relating to the decisive issues of war and the social order, have come to occupy more and more of the key positions of governmental and social power. This has meant a basic shift in the governing "mix" of Western civilization: the foxes have been getting rid of the lions; the lions, as one of them put it a few years ago, have been fading away; within the governing elite, Class I residues are gaining more and more exclusive predominance over Class II. Pareto summarizes the normal development of such a condition in the following general terms:

> 1) A mere handful of citizens, so long as they are willing to use violence, can force their will upon public officials who are not inclined to meet violence with equal violence. If the reluctance of the officials to resort to force is primarily motivated by humanitarian sentiments, that result ensues very readily; but if they refrain from violence because they deem it wiser to use some other means, the effect is often the following: 2) To prevent or resist violence, the governing class resorts to "diplomacy," fraud, corruption—governmental authority passes, in a word, from the lions to the foxes. The governing class bows its head under the threat of violence, but it surrenders only in appearances, trying to turn the flank of the obstacle it cannot demolish in frontal attack. In the long run that sort of procedure comes to exercise a far-reaching influence on the selection of the governing class, which is now recruited only from the foxes, while the lions are blackballed. The individual who best knows the arts of...winning back by fraud and deceit what seemed to have been surrendered under pressure of force, is now leaders of leaders. The man who has bursts

of rebellion, and does not know how to crook his spine at the proper times and places, is the worst of leaders, and his presence is tolerated among them only if other distinguished endowments offset that defect. 3) So it comes about that the residues of the combination-instinct (Class I) are intensified in the governing class, and the residues of group-persistence (Class II) debilitated; for the combination-residues supply, precisely, the artistry and resourcefulness required for evolving ingenious expedients as substitutes for open resistance, while the residues of group-persistence stimulate open resistance, since a strong sentiment of group-persistence cures the spine of all tendencies to curvature. 4) Policies of the governing class are not planned too far ahead in time. Predominance of the combination instincts and enfeeblement of the sentiments of group-persistence result in making the governing class more satisfied with the present and less thoughtful of the future.... Material interests and interests of the present or a near future come to prevail over the ideal interests of community or nation and interests of the distant future.... 5) Some of these phenomena become observable in international relations as well.... Efforts are made to avoid conflicts with the powerful and the sword is rattled only before the weak....[The] country is often unwittingly edged toward war by nursings of [disputes] which, it is expected, will never get out of control and turn into armed conflicts. Not seldom, however, a war will be forced upon [the] country by peoples who are not so far advanced in the evolution that leads to the predominance of Class I residues.[4]

---

4. Vilfredo Pareto, *The Mind and Society* (New York: Dover Publications, Inc., 1963), Section 2179. Quoted with permission of The Pareto Fund.

FOURTEEN

The Drift of U.S. Foreign Policy

I

UNITED STATES FOREIGN POLICY has seldom been deliberately directed for any length of time toward clearly defined Grand Strategic goals. In this it may be contrasted with many of the great nations and empires of both past and present history. For two centuries, throughout three great wars and decades of confused peace, Rome kept her strategic eye focused on the destruction of Carthage. For even more centuries, the Papacy pursued its battle with the Hohenstaufen until, with the killing of the young Conradin in 1268, the last of that imperial breed was eliminated. Century after century, the Christian Spaniards whittled away at the power of the Moors until Granada fell under the combined weight of Castile and Aragon. Under whatever king at Windsor or political party in Parliament, England remembered the European balance of power, and acted to prevent its overturn. Hitler, in the condensed time scheme of our age, clearly set for his nation the goals, first of smashing the

Versailles Treaty, then of gaining European hegemony. The communist enterprise has always guided its operations in the light of specific objectives for each major phase, all subordinated to the supreme goal of world domination.

Of course, a clear and deliberately chosen goal does not guarantee a successful policy. The goal may be beyond the capability of the man or nation that pursues it, as the history of Napoleon, Hitler and many another sufficiently proves. Or, even if the goal is within the range of possibility, the means, methods and talents brought to bear may be inadequate. But other things being equal, a consciously held objective will assure a more effective utilization of the available forces. It could not be otherwise; without the conscious objective, the available forces will be dispersed, and in at least partial conflict with each other.

Instead of being organized as a consistent program designed to realize a certain objective or coherent set of objectives, United States foreign policy has been, most of the time, a pragmatic amalgam, and in two senses. On the one hand, it is and has been an amalgam of abstract moral ideals with material interests having, in many cases, no intelligible connection with the abstract ideals. This is the double face of United States foreign policy that has so annoyed Europeans, who often, and wrongly, consider the material interests—usually business interests—to be the only genuine part of the amalgam, and the ideals merely a sheen of cynical hypocrisy. In point of fact, the ideals, which in recent decades have usually been drawn from the liberal supply chest, are often solid enough to thwart and negate the material interests. More than one national government or political party friendly to the United States—to recall one set of familiar examples—has been jettisoned by Washington for another that is neutralist or outright anti-Western, but more given to liberal forms and slogans.

United States foreign policy has also been an amalgam in the sense of combining in a single irregular lump a number of quite different, often conflicting tendencies and objectives. Factions, lobbies and influential individuals in the White House, the State Department, the Central Intelligence Agency, the defense establishment, Congress and the lay public push in divergent directions: toward isolationism and toward globalism; for a Pacific-oriented strategy and for an Atlantic-oriented strategy; pro-Britain and pro-Germany; NATO first, the "Third World" first, Moscow first.... Sometimes one of the variants is dominant in the resultant official policy; sometimes it is a shaky attempt at a compromise that is logically as well as practically impossible to achieve; often several divergent policies will operate simultaneously: some in one department of the government, others in another; some in this region of the world, their opposites in that region. Almost always the policy rests on a short-term basis, subject to frequent change and adjustment.

United States foreign policy seldom anticipates events much in advance; and even less often pursues a course designed not only to anticipate events but to control them in the interest of a chosen primary objective. The usual American procedure has been to substitute vague abstractions about "peace," "democracy" and "international law" for serious Grand Strategic objectives; to wait hopefully; and to "react" to problems and crises when they arise.

Probably no other nation, large or small, has been so often "surprised" by international happenings: surprised that Mao or Castro turns out to be a communist; that Japan doesn't surrender or does; that de Gaulle loses power or seizes it, vetoes the British Common Market bid or walks out of NATO; that Khrushchev sends tanks to Budapest or missiles to Cuba; that two billions in grants doesn't prevent a government from supporting Moscow; that African tribes act like African tribes, communists like communists, and human beings, as the ultimate surprise, like human beings. On the occasion of each new surprise there is a frenzied flurry of statements and activity in Washington, while an emergency answer is improvised to meet "the new situation."

This habitual American mode has been much remarked in relation to war. The United States has never been prepared, militarily, politically or psychologically, for its wars. It has always fought them with the narrowly pragmatic aim—apart, that is, from the standard empty abstractions—of "winning the war." And though it has won all but one of its wars, it frequently, as has so often been pointed out, "loses the peace": that is, does not gain the enhancement of national interests that might reasonably have been expected from victory.

The results are not always as bad as might theoretically be expected. Americans are energetic, and possessed of a land fortunate in its size, strategic disposition and natural resources; in order to make out, they do not need to be as intelligent and efficient in foreign policy as the citizens of countries less generously endowed. Besides, the level of intelligence and efficiency in foreign policy has seldom been very high in other nations.

Moreover, the deliberate intent of its leaders is only one and perhaps usually a minor element in determining a nation's international conduct and fate. A nation is pushed and hauled by geography, by economic potential and need, by the inherited weight of beliefs and institutions, by accident and invention, by the shifting pressures of other peoples and societies. The

resultant vector, plotted after the events, can seem to be a coherent course such as would result from pursuit of a deliberately
chosen goal, even though no deliberate goal was ever chosen.

Thus, United States history up to the end of the nineteenth
century has been intelligibly interpreted in terms of the goal of
opening up and consolidating the continental domain. There
were a few leading citizens, Alexander Hamilton prominent
among them, who did see and formulate that goal in advance,
and advocate its pursuit. But there were others who resisted and
rejected it; and many more, the great majority, who merely responded pragmatically to the immediate imperatives of personal, business and political life. The corollary goal—of the isolation and defense of the New World's double continent from
extra-hemispheric intrusions, while the westward thrust of the
mighty new nation was being completed—was brought more
fully into consciousness, partly by being explicitly stated rather
early as a "doctrine."

By the end of the nineteenth century this "continental epoch" was essentially completed. The sovereignty of the United
States was extended and flourishing over the land mass through
to the Pacific; the preeminence of United States power in the
two Americas was established and virtually unchallenged. Most
American citizens would have liked to stop history at about that
point; and most of them even today wish they could get back
there, or dream that they are. But a great nation, like any other
major social enterprise, cannot stop, cannot stabilize. It must
continue up, or start down.

The historical conjuncture at the turn of the century presented the United States with an inescapable challenge: from
its achieved role as the continental power, to become a world
power; and because of its mere size and richness, in the context

of modern technology, to become a world power could only in the end mean to become the first power of the world. This was the perspective lurking behind the idea of "manifest destiny" that flavored the winning oratory of the election of 1900; but few Americans have wished to see clearly along that perspective, still less to work out a serious program to fulfill the destiny of which some of them have spoken. Some have remained, and still remain, within the continental perspective: that is, of isolationism. Others have laced the objective and possible program with the abstractions and the moralizing. Even in 1900, Senator Albert J. Beveridge, leader of the neo-imperialists, was defending the advance of the nation into the western and eastern seas through the Spanish-American War as an act "whose far-off end is the redemption of the world and the Christianization of mankind." As religious rhetoric went out of fashion, the problem of relating the nation to the world became both reflected and confused in changing secular slogans: Make the World Safe for Democracy; Self-Determination of All Nations; Reign of Law; the Four Freedoms; in short, a vague globalism in place of a serious world outlook.

The Spanish-American War can be thought of as an awkward transitional step between the continental and world phases of the nation's history. From the older continental viewpoint, the take-over of the Spanish Caribbean islands and the naval station of Hawaii can be understood as a further consolidation of the continent's defensive perimeter. But from the world viewpoint, the flow of United States power into those positions and on across the Pacific into the Philippines appears as an advance in both directions toward direct involvement in Eurasia—the World Island or Great Continent. The abject apologies for the Spanish-American War made by all liberal American historians in recent decades are a wonderfully pure expression of the liberal guilt. There is a good deal to be said in favor of that war, as wars go.

II

THE FIRST TWO WORLD WARS PROVED that there was no turning back, that for the United States the world role had become unavoidable. According to the revisionist historians of the Left, it was a plot by Morgan & Company, Kuhn, Loeb and British Intelligence that got the United States into the First World War; according to the revisionist historians of the Right, it was a plot by Franklin Roosevelt, General Marshall and British Intelligence that got the United States into the Second. Both sets of revisionists are unwilling to recognize that those plots could succeed only because the United States was indissolubly linked by economic, fiscal, technological and strategic chains to those wars from their beginnings and from before they began. There were just as many plots to keep the nation out of war as there were to get it in. The revisionists never explain why the pro-war plotting succeeded but the anti-war plotting so palpably failed.

In both wars the United States amply indulged its propensity for moralizing. The first was to make the world safe for democracy by alliance with the most reactionary imperialism on earth, by secret deals for carving up nations, peoples and one entire continent, and by enforcement of a Draconian peace on the vanquished. The second was to liberate mankind from totalitarianism by alliance with the major totalitarian power, consignment of a hundred million additional humans to his rule, and adoption of a policy of unconditional surrender implemented by the A-bomb. In strategic terms, the United States was acting jointly with Britain on the traditional British principle of the balance of power: that is, was acting to prevent the consolidation of the European continent under a single sovereignty.

Inside the framework of Western civilization, this principle is intelligible. So long as world power was overwhelmingly concentrated in the Western nations, preservation of a European balance was justifiable precisely in order to uphold Western ideals within the political and social order. These ideals would have been endangered and in some measure destroyed by the premature consolidation of the European continent under the despotic sovereignty of one of the European land powers. But in the twentieth century a formidable power charge was accumulating among peoples outside of the Western structure. The aim of blocking the consolidation of Europe had become obsolescent; the two wars degenerated into an exhausting, incestuous struggle that drained the blood, resources and spiritual energy of the West.

Out of the First World War emerged both Japan and a communist Russia as major non-Western power centers. In the Second World War the United States was compelled to accept, along with the perennial British objective of maintaining the European balance, the further objective of preventing consolidation of the Pacific around a rival power. In that aim the United States was, for the immediate period, successful. Japan was defeated, but in the process of its defeat China moved onto the world stage under the management of the world communist enterprise. At the same time, in the parallel process of Hitler's defeat, Soviet Russia, by extending its empire over Eastern Europe, destroyed Europe's power equilibrium.

The United States is both offspring and organic part of

Western civilization. The religion of the United States, its philosophies, ideals and institutions, its conceptions of man, art, science and technology—the errors and heresies as well as the truths—are all derived from common Western roots, with merely local and secondary variations. The Western heritage is given once and for all, indissolubly; there is no parliament that can authorize the nations of the West to renounce their title, no matter how ardently or basely they may yearn to join an anonymous common humanity. They either remain Western or cease to be. Thus the United States can find its destiny only in and through Western civilization, not outside or against the West. The relation between the United States and England, France or Spain—conflicts and wars as well as friendships—are different in historical kind from the relations the United States can have with Japan, Indonesia, China, Persia or Ethiopia.

The United States issued from the Second World War as unquestioned leader of the West, and this meant a fundamental change in its strategic relation to the world as a whole. So long as the United States was, in effect if not intention, merely bidding as one Western nation among the others for leadership of the West, its base was its own North American continental domain. But as soon as the United States began actually to function, and to the extent that it functioned, as leader of the West, its base became coextensive with that of Western civilization as a whole: that is, with "the Atlantic world." This fact was quickly and unmistakably expressed in the postwar period by formation of the North Atlantic Treaty Organization under United States political domination and military command.[1] It

---

1. In its previous history, as everyone knows, the United States had always avoided peacetime military alliances.

follows—though Americans have not understood or admitted this corollary—that a Western loss, retreat or weakening anywhere in the world, even if accompanied by an apparent strengthening of the United States relative to the other component nations of the West, means a weakening of the basic position of the United States in relation to the world-strategic equilibrium. It is the United States as well as the Poles, Hungarians, Balts and the rest that has suffered a loss in Eastern Europe, because Western civilization lost; the United States as well as the Netherlands, in Indonesia; the United States as well as Britain, in India; the United States as well as France, Belgium, Britain and tomorrow Portugal, in Africa. This interwoven relationship is a common phenomenon in military and political conflicts during the decline of a social formation: the internal struggle leaves X on top, but on top of a structure that by that very struggle has been weakened in relation to external structures.

At the end of the war, the United States was not only the unquestioned leader of the West, but the most powerful force in the world. By virtue of the Eisenhower army still in being, the nuclear monopoly, and a colossal industrial plant not merely untouched but immensely stimulated by the fighting, the United States was in fact immensely more powerful than any other nation or grouping of nations. Through the nuclear monopoly the United States had ready access to more firepower than all the rest of the world, just as through its industrial plant it was producing more than all the rest of the world. There was no precedent for this situation in the world as a whole, though there were a few in the histories of geographically limited "civilized worlds." What was to be done with this power?

Abstractly considered, the full creative response to the challenge then presented would have been to establish a Pax Americana on a world scale. This would have meant a guarantee, backed by the power of the United States acting as the integral leader of Western civilization, of a viable world polity: the key to which would have been the enforcement of the nuclear monopoly and the prohibition of major wars. Such an arrangement might have been worked out in any of several forms, some more palatable than others; as one variant, it could have been handled through the United Nations machinery.

The substance of the proposal for a Pax Americana was stated in different ways by a number of persons immediately following the war. It was put forward, as the appropriate conclusion from what was, I believe, the first systematic analysis of what came to be known as "the Cold War," in my book *The Struggle for the World*, written for the most part in 1944 and published early in 1947. However, this solution was too abstract. Though the opposite of liberal in its content, it was like the typical liberal proposal in conception—"rationalist" in the sense defined by Michael Oakeshott. Though the elements were present from which one could construct a theoretical model of a Pax Americana, it was no doubt impossible in practice. Americans were, and are, too immature for the undertaking, peculiarly untrained by their historical experience and their ideological preferences to fill the role that would have had to be theirs. There was no sizable group within the American governing elite to take the responsibility and leadership that—with the collaboration of associated groups which could, perhaps, have been found in Europe—might have driven the necessary measures through, even granted mass incomprehension. And no doubt the world and man are in any case too intractable for solutions so conveniently neat.

Nevertheless, the dominating military, economic and financial weight of the United States in the postwar equilibrium was a fact. Even though this fact was not deliberately exploited for the sake of creating the conditions that might have made possible a long-lasting Pax Americana, it was of course reflected to some degree in the conduct of United States policy during the early postwar years. The United States did use its military threat as a shield for the protection of Western Europe; did take the initiative in gathering the Western nations into an Atlantic alliance; did draw heavily on its fiscal resources to promote the economic recovery of the Western nations; and did make some attempt for a few years to guide the United Nations along a course compatible with American and Western interests. All of these actions could be understood as consistent elements in a Western-based, American-led world strategy. This, if pursued far and firmly enough and accompanied by the appropriate negative sanctions—against, for prime example, the development of a second nuclear capability—might have yielded international arrangements in which Western civilization would have been reasonably secure. But this Western strategy, besides being incomplete along its own line, was part of the customary American amalgam. It was combined with other and sometimes conflicting strategies as well as with ideologically derived policies having to do with anti-Nazism, anti-colonialism, self-determination, feeding of the hungry, racial equality, peace, disarmament, world law and so on.

THE FOREIGN POLICY AMALGAM that was being juggled by Franklin Roosevelt in the last years of his life contained the principal ingredients that have been combined and recombined in varying proportions since his death.

There was the Western strategy, with the especially close Anglo-American relations as its first premise. During the war, the

Western strategy was basically distorted, of course, by the fact that the war situation defined Germany as enemy, and communist Russia as ally. In the perspective of the Western strategy as it developed after the war, Germany, or at any rate West Germany, resumed its place as an organic part of the Western whole.

There was, second, the "Yalta strategy": that is, the idea of a workable world order guaranteed by a Soviet-American understanding ("condominium"), with Britain tagging along as a junior partner to the United States. This has remained ever since as an element in the policy amalgam. Under the blows of the Cold War it was reduced for a while to a small proportion of the whole, but its relative weight increased rapidly throughout the Kennedy administration and continues its expansion under President Johnson. The Moscow negotiations that produced the test-ban treaty in the summer of 1963 merely extended the line projected by the Yalta conference in the winter of 1945.

It should be observed that the Yalta strategy and the Western strategy are incompatible. The strategic line that led Franklin Roosevelt to Yalta is the same line that brought about the loss to the West of the nations of Eastern Europe with their hundred million inhabitants. And while that line beckoned the Kennedy-Johnson administration toward the Moscow Treaty, it was simultaneously and necessarily producing the cracks in NATO, the quarrel with France, the Italian turn toward neutralism, and so on.

The third ingredient was what might be called "the United Nations strategy," except that this does not designate a single clear-cut strategic line comparable to those of the Western and the Yalta strategies. Theoretically the UN might be used as an organizational form through which to pursue a Western strategy or a Yalta strategy; and on occasion the United States has so used the UN, or attempted to use it. More naturally, however, especially as the membership of the UN has expanded, the UN organization offers itself as an arena in which to promote a "Third World strategy"—that is, a strategy primarily oriented on the regions of the world outside both the communist and the Western boundaries. Geographically, the Third World is equivalent to Africa (except for its southern tip) plus non-communist Asia and—though in a somewhat different sense—most of Latin America. Socially and economically, the Third World is roughly equivalent to the non-communist "underdeveloped nations."

It is the Third World strategy (plus an ample dose of ideology) that has been expressed in United States anti-colonialism, in the political support and moral deference given to the underdeveloped nations, in the massive programs of economic and military aid and so on. This Third World strategy has necessarily been in frequent conflict with the Western strategy, since Third World aspirations have usually been at the cost of the political, military and economic interests of Western nations. It is also in conflict with the Yalta strategy insofar as the communist enterprise and the United States compete for the allegiance of Third World nations. But the conflict between the Yalta and Third World strategies is not irreconcilable. It could be solved by a division of spheres of interest or by being reduced to genuinely peaceful rivalry. And in point of fact the Soviet and American governments have often, especially in recent years, found themselves lined up together on Third World issues against one or more of the European nations.

Along with these three major strategies, there were in the Roosevelt amalgam, and there have continued to be, other secondary strategies directed toward special or temporary objectives or, as in the case of the pro-Israel strategy, imposed by

domestic pressures. All of these have been mixed, often confused and sometimes altogether negated by the moralizing and
ideological trends that have sprung for the most part from the
liberal syndrome.

III

ALTHOUGH THE YALTA STRATEGY lived on in the hopes, il-
lusions or commitments of a large number of American citizens
both in and out of government, and never lost all influence on
the determination of policy, the developments of the immediate postwar period pushed it quickly and rudely, for a while,
into the background. The communists seized all Eastern Europe
without undue trouble from the apostrophes to democracy and
self-determination with which Franklin Roosevelt's aides had
tried to disguise from him and from themselves the strategic
meaning of the Yalta text. In the East, the communists swept
toward power over China, there, too, accompanied by American declarations of faith in compromise, will of the people and
united government representing all tendencies. In Indonesia,
Southeast Asia, India and the Near East, under the stimulus of
native revolutionaries supported and sometimes directed by the
communist enterprise, great regions and hundreds of millions
of persons were breaking away from the Western system. The
communists had thrown Greece into civil war, and were openly
menacing Iran and Turkey.

The United States was compelled to recognize the magnitude
of the Soviet and communist threat, and to undertake a series
of major defensive moves: intervention in the Greek civil war;
backing for the British ultimatum in Iran; guarantee of Turkish
integrity; the Marshall Plan; formation of NATO and the NATO

military force; help to anti-communist governments; rebuilding of United States military strength; fighting in Korea.

Thus, following the 1946-47 transition from the phase of the anti-Nazi front, there was a fairly distinct period lasting from 1947 to 1956 during which the Yalta strategy was only latent. United States policy was dominated by a combination of the Western (therefore both anti-Soviet and anti-communist) strategy and the Third World strategy, together with purely pragmatic responses to troublesome situations as these arose. The development of the Western strategy, particularly in its anti-communist aspect, was by no means uniform; there were several variants contending for precedence, and the result was a rather irregular course.

For a while there was a faction in the United States and some of the European nations—and, conspicuously, among the millions of exiles from the communized areas—that called for an objective of "liberation" or "roll-back": that is, a fundamentally offensive version of the Western strategy, seeking not merely to defend the Western remnant against further communist intrusion, but to regain for the West some and perhaps eventually all of the lands and peoples lost to the communist empire. At the other wing, there were those who believed in what amounted to the appeasement of the communist enterprise, though they preferred to call it "coexistence" or "negotiation"; and this appeasement wing was supported by those who, from honest conviction, illusion or treachery, were in reality opposed to a Western strategy in any form or emphasis. Most of the time, however, the working policy was a center medley that came to be known by the name of "containment" that was first given to it by George Kennan, who as chief of the State Department's policy-planning staff under Dean Acheson had a good deal to do with putting it together.

"The main element of any United States policy toward the Soviet Union," Kennan argued in 1951, "must be that of a long-term, patient but firm and vigilant containment of Russian expansive tendencies." This summary statement, which first appeared in his famous *Foreign Affairs* article (April 1951) under the signature of "X," is far from unambiguous. "Russia" and "the Soviet Union" seem to be equated, and there is no indication where "communism" fits in. However, the general drift of the policy of containment seemed fairly clear. The United States sought to prevent the incorporation of additional territory within the bloc (or empire) dominated by the communist government of the Soviet Union.

From the point of view of the United States and of the West, the desirability of such containment was obvious enough. It should also have been obvious, and it was to at least some persons, that containment was not a sufficient goal for American or Western Grand Strategy. It was purely negative and defensive in conception. It had nothing to say about the vast areas and populations already inside the communist system—which by 1951 included China and Eastern Europe along with the former Russian Empire. It offered no guide to show what action to take when the communist subversion of new territory occurred without overt Soviet intervention. And because the policy was purely negative, it had to win every individual engagement in order to work; it excluded the attempt to achieve a positive gain, and any loss was and remained a loss; but it is impossible to win every time.

Containment was therefore a policy that by its own nature could not succeed over the long run, and that by definition could not make good what the West had already lost. However, at the beginning of this nine-year period, except in the catastrophic instance of mainland China, the application of the containment policy was fairly "hard." In Greece the communist revolt was smashed. The Truman Doctrine in relation to Turkey and Iran amounted to an ultimatum to Moscow. In the Philippines, Malaya and Burma, communist armies were fought and defeated. The communist attack in South Korea provoked a fighting response that for all its tribulations was sufficiently successful in military terms, though the containment rules prevented political exploitation of the military potential. The maneuvers of the Seventh Fleet and the support given the Chinese Nationalist military buildup proved more plainly than diplomatic statements that the communists were not to be allowed to occupy Formosa. The military force of the United States itself was greatly strengthened. During President Eisenhower's first term (1953-57), Secretary of State Dulles' doctrine of "massive retaliation" certainly sounded hard, even though it was never given a critical testing. In those earlier years the policy of containment itself gave modest expression to the idea of "liberation." Mr. Kennan had mentioned, if not very convincingly, a possible eventual liberation of the Eastern European nations as the peaceful result of the good example set by the Western nations in their internal regime. On the practical side, a number of propaganda and political warfare operations implying a liberation objective were actually carried out.

Looking back over the record, however, it seems to be the case that what statisticians would call "the long-term secular trend" of United States foreign policy has been, since the very earliest years of the Cold War, toward ever-increasing softness. The Cold War began when the United States realized that the Soviet Union had broken from the wartime anti-Nazi front and was moving unilaterally to scoop up as much of the world as it could get as fast as it could get it. And it was at the outset, in response to this disillusioning realization, that United States policy was hardest: in Greece and the other applications of the Truman Doctrine, in the Philippines, in the 1948-49 Berlin airlift, in the fighting response in Korea, in the political warfare activities that were begun in those first years. The removal of General MacArthur from the Korean command in April 1951, which implied acceptance of a Korean stalemate, may now be seen as a key symptom that the initial phase of relative hardness had ended. From then on, with an occasional brief upswing as in the 1954 Guatemala action or the fleet demonstrations in the Formosa Strait, the policy has progressively softened.

In a critique of the policy of containment written in 1952, I demonstrated that "at most, containment can be a temporary expedient, a transition. As the transition is completed, containment must move toward one or the other of the two major poles, toward appeasement or liberation."[2] So it has been. Appeasement, which is usually referred to as "coexistence,"[3] is equivalent to what I have called earlier in this chapter "the Yalta strategy." "Liberation," analogously, is equivalent to a positive and fully developed "Western strategy."

IV

WHATEVER CONCLUSIONS we may reach about the hard-soft ratio of the period 1947-56, a discernibly new period, both softer

---

2. *Containment or Liberation?* (New York: The John Day Company, 1953), p. 218.

3. "Coexistence" operates as a "dialectical" term in the sense explained in Chapter XII. From the standpoint of communism, "coexistence" is a mode of revolutionary struggle. From the standpoint of non-communists, "coexistence" means the acceptance of communism; and since communism is in essence aggressive, acceptance means in practice, "appeasement," as experience confirms.

on average and steeper in the rate of softening, may be dated from 1956. October 1956, with the simultaneous crises in Hungary and Suez-Sinai, was a critical turning point in the postwar era and, quite possibly, in world history. As so often, open crisis translated the obscured meaning of a complicated process of development into stark and unmistakable terms.

The United States Government *a)* failed to intervene, with anything other than verbal protests wholly empty under the circumstances, in favor of the Hungarian revolt or against the crushing of that revolt by Soviet arms; and *b)* did intervene vigorously in the Suez fighting, in such a way as to prevent re-establishment of Western control over the Suez Canal and Isthmus.

We may summarize as follows what was involved in this double response:

1. Liberation ("roll-back") was abandoned as in any sense an operative goal. Henceforth it survived only as an occasional rhetorical flourish and as a sop to throw to Eastern European exiles, hard anti-communists among the citizenry, and members of Congress with large numbers of ethnic Eastern Europeans in their constituencies. It should be noted that no better circumstances for some sort of move along the perspective of liberation could be imagined than those existing in November 1956. All of Eastern Europe was stirring with active discontent, and open revolts had been taking place in East Germany, Poland and Russia itself. The post-Stalin regime had not been consolidated. The Belgrade-Moscow break was still sharp. In Hungary the uprising was supported by the overwhelming majority of the population, with such important and sympathetic sectors as the youth and the women prominent among the activists, while at the same time no public image could have been more unsympathetic than

that of the Bolshevik power embodied in alien troops blast-
ing children, mothers and workers with shells from lumbering
tanks. But the United States and the Western nations constrained
to follow its lead and example did nothing; and therefore serious observers knew from then on that the United States was not
going to do anything to help peoples or nations free themselves
from communist dominion.

2. In the Suez crisis the United States not only abandoned its
Western allies, Britain and France, but acted directly against
them even though they were actively engaged on the field of battle. In doing so, moreover, the United States was sacrificing the
general interest of Western civilization: United States intervention made certain that control of the Suez Isthmus, one of the
two or three most important strategic positions on earth, was
lost to the West.

3. In thus abandoning the Western strategy in the Suez crisis,
the United States was orienting its actions along the lines of the
Third World (and United Nations) strategy.

4. In the Suez crisis the United States found itself—in the United
Nations, in diplomacy and propaganda, and in military moves—
acting in almost exact parallel with the Soviet Union, and doing
so at the very same time when the Soviet Union was crushing
the Hungarians. The United States was pursuing, that is to say, a
Yalta, or perhaps better, super-Yalta strategy, along with a Third
World strategy. (We may recall that at the outbreak of the Suez
fighting, Moscow threatened Britain, France and Israel with nuclear missiles if they carried through the Suez and Sinai wars.)

5. In both the Hungarian and Suez crises the United States
proceeded in accord with the rule of "avoiding direct confrontation with the Soviet Union." In the Hungarian affair, this meant
doing nothing, except talking, because taking any practical step

would at once have meant a confrontation. In the Suez affair, the avoidance of confrontation went all the way to collaboration.

6. In both the Suez and Hungarian crises, the United States accompanied its actions, and inaction, with an outpouring of rhetoric drawn from the inexhaustible ideological warehouse of liberalism. Acting against the West in Suez was explained by President Eisenhower and his aides as a triumph for the concept of a single law for all men and all nations, of the renunciation of force and aggression, and of the international authority of the United Nations: and it is even possible that these ideological abstractions did indeed determine United States conduct in the Suez affair. Doing nothing in Hungary was made the occasion for sweeping apostrophes to Freedom, Liberty, the undying Spirit of the People, the inevitable downfall of Tyrants and the future Victory of Freedom, Truth, Justice and Peace.

The shape of the new post-1956 period in United States international policy, which continues with few signs of age as I write this page in 1964, may be seen in the Hungary-Suez double crisis, though its stage of rapid growth and development set in only after the advent of the Kennedy administration in 1961. The policy evolves within the outline fixed by these half-dozen points that I have just listed. There are no surprises in the main trends thus established: support for quick and total decolonization; continuing large foreign aid, with balance shifting from military to developmental; wooing of new nations; heavy emphasis on the United Nations as "the foundation of our foreign policy"; disarmament proposals, negotiations and agreements; pullback of military forces around the communist periphery; frequent support of the Third World in disputes with Western nations; cultural, people-to-people and commercial exchanges with communist countries; shift from stress on containment of

communism to attempts at coexistence and, gradually, collaboration with communism.

The changed attitude toward "neutralism" is an accurate sum-
mation of the basic difference between the 1947-56 period and the
post-1956 period. From 1947-56, neutralism on the part of a government was considered by the United States to be "a bad thing."
If necessary, neutralism was endured; but an effort was made to
influence the neutralist government toward a pro-Western policy.
But in 1956 the neutralist, indeed decidedly anti-Western neutralist, Nasser was supported against not only pro-Western but Western nations. And in the years immediately following 1956 the
idea gradually came to be adopted in official United States circles
that neutralism on the part of a government was quite natural in
many cases, not necessarily a bad thing, and often acceptable.
Under President Kennedy the wheel very nearly completed its circle. As the Laos instance showed most strikingly, it has become
official doctrine that neutralism is, at least sometimes, preferable
to a pro-Western policy; and is certainly preferable to the intransigent pro-Westernism that may upset negotiations with Moscow
or offend the sensibilities of Third World virtuosi.

From the beginning of Franklin Roosevelt's Presidency,
modern liberalism has been on the whole dominant in United
States foreign policy; more decidedly and more consistently, by
a good deal, than in domestic affairs.[4] But it is in the period

---

4. *Cf.* Clifton Brock, *Americans for Democratic Action* (Washington:
Public Affairs Press, 1962), pp. 121 ff. Professor Brock shows, with the help
of statistical tables, that even in Congress, where the influence of liberalism
is much less than in the executive and bureaucracy, the rather extreme liberal
view on foreign policy represented by Americans for Democratic Action has
prevailed by a two-to-one margin. Actually the liberal record is much better
than that if less sectarian criteria than ADA's are used.

of the anti-Nazi war and in this period that became clearly defined under President Kennedy that the liberal influence in the formation, justification and conduct of foreign policy has been most conspicuous. In direction of development—which is in the long run decisive—the ever-softening post-Suez line has been the liberal line, fitting naturally into liberal rhetoric and doctrine. The language and ideas with which the post-Suez line is defended, especially in the most recent years, by officials and diplomats, and by publicists both within and outside the government, are invariably liberal in ideological conception. Many individual conservatives, including not a few in Congress, go along with the line much of the time and support some of its applications, from one motive or another of expediency, confusion or ignorance of any practical alternative. But the line cannot be defended by a conservative kind of argument. A conservative who speaks in its defense invariably sounds like a liberal.

AFTER THE COMMUNISTS had liquidated the Hungarian revolt, the boundary marches between the communist and non-communist regions stabilized. The Western abandonment of the Suez Isthmus opened up the first phase of the African sequence that has still a good many scenes to run. Direct Western power in most of Africa, both north and south of the Sahara, was either destroyed or, in the majority of cases, given up; and Africa joined southern Asia in the Third World. The United States not merely accepted Africa's breakaway from the West but actively promoted it under anti-imperialist liberal slogans of decolonization, self-determination, racial equality, and so on. In this the United States found itself again, and inevitably, acting in tandem with the Soviet Union which, from its own premises, pushed continuously for the African secession.[5] For converse, and equally inevitable, reasons, the United States found itself more and more often opposed to one or more of the Western nations. Both geographically and politically the Western strategic position was cumulatively eroded. In Africa itself, all of the great strategic bases, land, naval and air, with the sole exception of Simonstown at the tip of South Africa, were by 1964 either altogether abandoned by the West or in the process of abandonment.

In 1959-60 the communist enterprise established its first beachhead in the Americas through the revolution led by Fidel Castro in Cuba; and from this the communists mounted expanding guerrilla and paramilitary operations in the Caribbean basin and a vigorous political warfare campaign throughout Latin America. Beginning in 1960, in fact, an increasing fluidity became noticeable in the world situation as a whole. Geographic, political and social alignments in Africa were in continuous flux. Sukarno launched his drive for an empire of the South Seas. Indian imperialism showed itself bold against the West in the take-over of Goa, but hopelessly incompetent when the Chinese made their probing attack across the Himalayas. Nasser renewed his project for an Islamic and Arabian empire.

---

5. The West's abandonment of the Suez Isthmus took the communists by surprise. In their timetable, the revolutionary transformation of Africa was assigned to a somewhat later spot; their preparations had included little more than the writing of some rather abstract theses on the African question and the training of skeleton cadres. When the Suez affair opened the road to Africa, the communists were forced to make up for lost time, and to improvise—often with meager early results. The first sign of the enlargement of communist operations was a "Coordinating Conference" on African problems held in Moscow in February 1957. In 1958 the Soviet Ministry for Foreign Affairs created an African Department.

Under the administration of John F. Kennedy the course of United States foreign policy became more openly and more fully assimilated to liberal ideology, as liberals—some of them conspicuous liberal ideologues—added key advisory and policymaking seats in the government to the opinion-forming and bureaucratic posts they had long occupied. The strategic rule by which the main enemy is sought on the Right was applied with new rigor and intensity—though it was under the bemused eye of Dwight Eisenhower that American power had been used to help oust the pro-Western but right-wing Batista and to ease the path of the left-wing Castro. No United States move was made to hinder Nehru in Goa or Sukarno in west New Guinea; and in relation to Angola it was the Western ally, Portugal, that felt Washington's lash, not the left-wing revolutionaries who, in a Congolese sanctuary protected by the United States as well as the United Nations, trained guerrillas, saboteurs and terrorists. In Yemen, United States influence was quickly thrown to the support of the puppet of the left-wing, anti-Western Nasser against the right-wing, pro-Western Imam. A principle of asylum that had had no previous exception was violated to permit the left-wing Betancourt to avenge himself on the right-wing but firmly pro-American and pro-Western Pérez Jiménez. Any left-wing professor who shambles from the lecture platform into the presidency of a Latin-American state is assured, no matter how total his incompetence, of the applause of the State Department and the open purse of the Agency for International Development; but right-wing military men, no matter how able, who step in to save their country from collapsing will at best get grudging and belated recognition along with liberal oceans of abuse. In the dark and still far from finished Congo episode, United States power and resources were placed at the disposal of the neutralist, anti-Western nations of the Third World in order to smash the relatively right-wing and pro-Western Moise Tshombe. In Laos the United States withdrew all support from the legitimate, pro-Western regime and compelled its leaders, against their urgent desire, to enter into a united front with neutralists and communists that guaranteed immediate communist control over half the nation and an eventual communist take-over of the rest.

Stalwartly "avoiding confrontation" with the supreme leader of the Left,[6] the United States, to the accompaniment of the usual speeches about Freedom, stood aside while the fantastic Wall was built across the middle of Berlin. When the showdown came at the Bay of Pigs, the voice of the Third World and the liberal ideologues proved stronger than the need to close the breach into America's inner strategic zone. With all the 1962 bluster over the communist missiles in Cuba, the armed forces of the United States were again ordered to back away from the confrontation: on their ships and on land the communists successfully defied the demand for direct inspection; the Soviet troops and technicians remained in place; the communist regime was left undisturbed in the island which was being

---

6. It may be remarked that the particular stress on non-confrontation is correlated with Soviet achievement of a nuclear missile capability bringing North America within range, somewhat as the Hungarian stand-aside was correlated with prior Soviet deployment of medium-range missiles bearing on Western Europe. It can be argued that the major turns in policy have been merely the result of such critical changes in the arms balance. However, I am concerned here only with the direction and nature of the drift in United States policy, not with the tides or winds that have caused the drift. I add that changes in military, technical and other material factors are never able of themselves to account, causally, for policy, since policy depends also on what human beings decide to do with and about the material factors. After all, United States policy did not attempt to establish a Pax Americana in the

transformed into a fortress at the same time that it was serving as the dynamic base for continental subversion. In Europe and Turkey, the missiles confronting the Soviet Empire so formidably were withdrawn.

The positive actions undertaken to salvage some remnants of the Western political structure that was toppling in ruins in Southeast Asia, Africa and Latin America, as it had already toppled in the rest of Asia and in Eastern Europe, consisted of the occasional blows at the Right (Trujillo, Pérez Jiménez, the Peruvian, Dominican and other Latin-American military juntas, Boun Oum, Ayub Khan, Tshombe, South Africa, Portugal, Diem) supplemented by social service and welfare programs, as dictated by liberal ideology, to solve the problems by reforming the social conditions: continuing big sums in foreign aid, administered now by the Agency for International Development; huge gifts of surplus food; a $20 billion Alliance for Progress program aiming to save Latin America from communism by bringing the local social systems into accord with liberal doctrine; lavish support of the economic, health, welfare and technical agencies of the United Nations; and—let us not forget the Kennedy administration's most publicized, and revealingly named, contribution to the solving of the world crisis—the Peace Corps.

The Suez affair, the people-to-people exchange projects, the support of African separation from Europe and the varied disarmament talks showed during the Eisenhower administration

---

postwar period, although the material conditions for it—the nuclear monopoly, the industrial and economic predominance—were present. Nor did the Soviet Union soften up just because it was manifestly inferior in arms and available resources. The Bolsheviks, in 1903, set themselves the objective of world conquest when their total armament was half a dozen revolvers.

that the Yalta strategy had never been wholly dropped. Under Presidents Kennedy and Johnson, its relative weight in the policy amalgam has much increased. The neo-Yalta strategy has encouraged more and more bilateral negotiations between Washington and Moscow (with London sometimes permitted to sit in) over the heads of both the Western nations and the Third World. Some of the agreements to which these have led have begun to appear in the open: the neutralization of Antarctica; the special "hot line" opened between Washington and Moscow; the Moscow test-ban treaty; the ban on orbital weapons; the expansion of agricultural and other trade. Presumably such actions as the shutdown of the missile bases in Turkey, Britain and Italy, and the moves toward neutralization of Southeast Asia, are the result of other agreements not openly acknowledged.

Along with the Yalta strategy, the Third World strategy continues to be energetically followed, after the liberal fashion—though favored, too, by many business interests that see European dismissal from the Third World as the chance for large-scale American economic entry. In fact, the ultimate goal implied by a policy based exclusively on a combination of the Yalta and Third World strategies would be a deal between the Soviet Union and the United States to accept and preserve the present division between "the socialist camp" and "the imperialist camp," and to share hegemony in the Third World, administered, perhaps, through the United Nations. But even the liberals, except for the most extreme of the ideologues, are not quite so wholly out of touch with reality as to trust themselves and the nation to so cloudy a vision. The Western strategy, though no longer assigned unquestioned primacy, remains in the mixture, with the Western alliance and its implicit anti-Soviet, anti-communist posture. The three diverse strategies, becoming more nearly equal in the amalgam, more and more interfere with each other. From 1962 on this became especially clear in the case of the Western strategy, which could not be consistently pursued against the counterweight of the Yalta and Third World strategies. The consequence was the appearance of spreading fissures within the Western alliance, clashes of policy among the Western nations brought bluntly into the open by de Gaulle, and a partial breakup of the NATO military command.

In this present period, especially since its more fluid stage began in 1961, the disintegration of the West, after having slowed down for somewhat more than a decade, has speeded up again in a manner comparable in some though not all respects to the process at the end of the war and in the immediate postwar years. Almost all Africa has fallen away. The entire South Seas region is tending to move with Sukarno into the anti-Western front. The Western position in Southeast Asia is crumbling rapidly. The two pro-Western alliances of Asia's southern tier (SEATO and CENTO) are dead, though no one has yet bothered to perform the funeral rites. One after another, the pro-Western regimes among the Third World nations, feeling how the wind blows, change direction or have it changed for them. Votes in the United Nations and the Organization of American States symbolize the breakup of the formerly solid American bloc. British Guiana, Colombia, Venezuela, Guatemala, Nicaragua are in the direct line of revolutionary fire from the hardened communist base in the Caribbean, and beyond them preliminary volleys are reaching Brazil, Bolivia and Chile.

The drift of United States foreign policy, carrying the West with it, is toward continuing disintegration and eventual defeat, or more exactly dissolution. A conclusive demonstration is simple: if the United States has had such trouble handling a small island at its threshold, how can it handle the explosive Third World and the resolute communist empire?

FIFTEEN

Liberalism vs. Reality

I

LIBERALISM IS NOT EQUIPPED to meet and overcome the actual challenges confronting Western civilization in our time.

In its historical practice as well as its ideological doctrine, liberalism has always operated most naturally as a tendency of opposition to the prevailing order, to the status quo, the *ancien régime*, the Establishment in general or in its several parts. Liberalism has always stressed change, reform, the break with encrusted habit whether in the form of old ideas, old customs or old institutions. Thus liberalism has been and continues to be primarily negative in its impact on society; and in point of fact it is through its negative and destructive achievements that liberalism makes its best claim to historical justification.

In post-Renaissance Western society there were a number of deeply imbedded features that were bad on just about all counts; and were, moreover, capable of being eliminated. To get rid of such features, an attitude of skepticism toward custom and tradition, a fondness for change, and a confidence or even overconfidence in the possibilities of human nature were useful and probably necessary. Liberalism expressed that attitude and felt that confidence. Under its banner, reform movements labored successfully to do away with many of the features of the old society or to transform them beyond recognition: many of the bad features, and also of course some of the good features, because liberalism's impulse to tinker with the established order is quite general, and does not stop with this particular feature that we might all agree needs replacement.

Some of the older ways of handling lesser crimes and misdemeanors, for example, were surely barbarous. Torture to secure confessions; hanging for petty thefts; floggings; long prison sentences for minor derelictions, with the sentences almost equivalent to death because of the hideous nature of the jails; the futile and really absurd practice of imprisonment for debt: liberalism had a good deal to do with mitigating these barbarities, and for its humane negative accomplishments to that end liberalism deserves and gets nearly universal approval.

Even in this matter of crime and punishment, though, we should notice that liberalism has not done so well when it has tried to go on from the elimination of past abuses to the constructive job of devising new ways to meet the old conditions that do not disappear because of a change in the methods of dealing with them. Liberalism, applying its usual remedies of education and democratic reform seasoned with optimism concerning human nature, has signally failed to get rid of crime and criminals, or even to lessen the frequency of their occurrence. Liberalism even fosters new sorts of crime through its permissive approach to education and discipline and its provocative egalitarianism; some at least of our fearfully multiplying juvenile delinquency is the logical outcome of liberal principles. In a way, a juvenile delinquent is a youth who takes literally the progressive-educational stress on self-expression and freedom. Nor is our high percentage of multiple offenders much of an endorsement of the liberal schemes for re-educating criminals and giving them plenty of social service along with easy paroles. I have yet to read the account of one of those terrible crimes of sex perversion that take place daily, wherein the savage who rapes and strangles the child or grandmother or both did not have a long record of offenses which in pre-liberal days would have kept him behind solid bars. Pareto remarks that he doesn't much care what theory of punishment people prefer, so long as they are willing to try to keep murderers, thugs and rapists off the streets.

We could make a similar double entry concerning liberalism's past performance in relation to the social position of women, poor laws, abuses in the factory system, electoral practices, business frauds and monopolies, and many other such matters of large and small import: that liberalism has been influential in curing a number of wrongs and grave abuses; and that liberalism has been less successful, has often very dismally failed, in its efforts to construct new procedures and institutions to deal with the perennial problems. And in general, liberalism is better out of power than in power; better at changing than preserving; better at destroying than building.

Am I repeating old clichés? "We need liberals to push through the necessary reforms, and conservatives to make the reforms work..."—that sort of thing? Yes, I readily admit so; and I have great respect, I will add, for many of the old clichés. The plain, platitudinous, common-sense opinion is very often the true opinion, stripped down to essentials. And in this case the platitude is manifestly true, whether we test it by history or by the analysis of ideas. The guilt that is always part of the liberal syndrome swells painfully when liberals gain power and find that the world's sorrows show no tendency to vanish at their sovereign touch. Liberals are uncomfortable, uneasy, when *they* become "the Establishment":

we took note earlier of the desperate lengths to which academic liberals go to prove to themselves that they are non-conformists, even on a faculty every member of which has been formed in the same ideological pod.

Liberalism's inaptitude for power bears directly on the crucial fact: that the primary issue before Western civilization today, and before its member nations, is survival. No one threatened the survival of the West in A.D. 1100: the Crusades were an aggression, not a defense, of the West. No one threatened Western survival in 1500 or 1700 or even so short a time ago in the scale of civilizations as the beginning of this century. But now the threat is present—a clear, immediate and sufficient danger, both from within and from without. Before our time, it was a matter, for the West, of consolidation, growth, adaptation, change, reform, improvement; now it is, first of all and condition of all the rest, survival. Liberalism, and the ideas, sentiments and values to which liberalism gives priority, are not well designed for the stark issue of survival.

Modern liberalism—in this differing from the classical liberalism of the mid-nineteenth century—stands for all-out anti-colonialism, which follows from its emotional bent and value system as well as from its principles. Imperialism of all sorts, and especially imperialism administered by governments of capitalist nations, is wrong, modern liberalism holds; and all colonies, dependencies, subject nations and peoples ought to become free, self-governing, independent states, with seat and vote in the United Nations. The liberal belief in anti-colonialism prevails in all Western nations except Portugal. In the former imperialist powers, the ascendancy of anti-colonialism is a mixed result in which the pressure of colonial revolt has supplemented the spread of liberal ideology. In the United States, which has had a less direct relation to the practical colonial struggle, the anti-colonial attitude is more purely ideological, though its content derives from circumstances of the national history as well as from modern liberalism. In any case, the United States by choice, and all but one of the Western European nations by a combination of choice and coercion, are against colonialism anywhere and everywhere; and in historical fact all but a remnant of Western colonialism has disappeared during these postwar years. But in this actual world we live in—which in the matter of colonialism as in so much else differs so notably from the world of ideology—ousting colonial rule often means destroying the only significant element of social responsibility: as has repeatedly and vainly been demonstrated by ex-colonies in Asia and Africa, and will be more fiercely demonstrated in the years soon to come.

Many of the problems of Latin America overlap those of colonialism. Liberalism, and the United States Government under the spell of liberal doctrine, are against all Latin-American dictators, especially the dictators of the Right; against them even if for a passing while they must be dealt with; and also against the political, economic and social role of the Church, the army, the big landlords and the business oligarchs, since these four groups oppose many of the reforms that Liberalism believes universally obligatory. But in most of the Latin-American countries, when the influence of these four social forces is destroyed or much weakened—as the Alliance for Progress program avowedly aims to do—only a social vacuum remains. The liberals have no replacement for the structure they have so enthusiastically helped to tear down. The vacuum is filled first by chaotic social churning and then, if a qualified dictator doesn't come along to pick up the pieces, quite probably by communism, which does have a method, a will and an apparatus to bring about a reconsolidation on a new foundation. This indicates why the communist and liberal programs agree on most of their negative or destructive proposals. From the communist point of

view, the liberal program *is* the communist program at a preliminary stage in the dialectical unfolding of the revolution.

II

ALL IDEOLOGIES AT EVERY stage in their careers distort reality in some degree, but in its youth and prime a major ideology
remains closely enough in touch with the social world from which
it has sprung to permit it to inspire and guide effective and sometimes creative action. This was the case with the older liberalism
of the nineteenth century and the early years of our own. But the
liberal ideology has by now got so far out of touch with fact that
through its lens it has become impossible to see reality, much less
to act positively on reality. Most of the categories of modern liberalism no longer correspond to anything in the world of space and
time; they are mythical creatures on an Olympus much farther out
in empty space than the residence of the ancient gods, who never
lost their habit of frequently touching down on earth. The liberal
flight from reality is headlong, on every front. It could not have a
purer, or sillier, symbol than the multiplication in this country of
rules that prohibit the designation of race or color on many sorts
of license, document, record and statistic: a classic instance of the
attempt to substitute a satisfying self-generated dream world for a
distasteful reality. It is just as silly, of course, to discuss Peace with
communists, to expect civilized statesmanship from tribal chiefs,
or to imagine you can stop the clock of scientific technology by
signing test-ban agreements.

What are the crucial present challenges to Western civilization?
There are a hundred challenges, certainly, large and small, but let
us narrow down to the challenges that clearly and immediately and
powerfully threaten actual survival. These do not include, contrary

to ritual liberal insistence, mere hunger and poverty. Hunger and poverty are nothing novel and nothing special; in themselves they pose no peculiar problems that haven't been posed a thousand times before. The poor, we were told by a source that the pre-liberal West was once prepared to believe, we have always with us.

The crucial present challenges are, I believe, three: first, the jungle now spreading within our own society, in particular in our great cities; second, the explosive population growth and political activization within the world's backward areas, principally the equatorial and sub-equatorial latitudes occupied by non-white masses; third, the drive of the communist enterprise for a monopoly of world power.

Looking through the glass of liberalism it is impossible, I repeat, even to see these challenges clearly. And liberalism apart, it cannot be easy for people like the author and most readers of this book, who lead, whether aware of it or not, lives carefully sheltered from social horrors, to comprehend the reality of our domestic jungles. Strained headlines thrust it on our attention, but the mechanical repetitions of sensationalist journalism have come to seem almost as meaningless as a TV serial. Now and then I get a front-line report from some unknown correspondent who has happened to read something I have written, like one who wrote from Philadelphia not long after the 1960 election campaign. (In Philadelphia, City of Brotherly Love, the jungle is called just that, "the jungle."):

> The Kennedys and the Nixons and the other out-of-touch young men believe that we must go on civil righting our civilization to death. But they don't know what is happening to the people. I am referring to the little people who ride the buses and street cars and subways; the little people who put up with muggings, rapings, beatings, stabbings and murderings; the

little people who, when the criminals are caught, are told that as culturally handicapped victims of society the criminals had every justification for committing their crimes.

As a man who lives among and is one of these little people, I can aver that the common topic of discussion—just as surely as the sun rises and sets every day—at lodge meetings and sports gatherings and family get-togethers is the increasing savagery of the savages among us. Almost always someone present has been a victim of a savage attack, or has a relative or neighbor who has been a victim.

Last week I heard one cynical neighbor say: "We're in more danger than the pioneers ever were. When night fell, they closed the gates of the stockade. They knew the savages were outside. Nowadays when night falls, we know we've got them roaming around inside with us. What's worse, they're armed, and we're not. And worst of all, one of them is caught attacking a woman and a Civil Liberties lawyer gets him off. The woman victim is maligned by the lawyer as being little better than a prostitute, while the arresting cop is lucky if he gets off without losing his job."

A woman named Marjorie K. McGoldrick, who might have been any of a million others, wrote the *New York Herald Tribune* (October 20, 1962) about the nation's largest and the world's richest city as she was acquainted with it:

Recently our Police Commissioner, Michael J. Murphy, went on record with the statement that there is no reign of terror in New York. Anyone who has eyes which are even drowsily opened for one-twentieth of an inch knows that there is no tranquillity in most parts of this city.

Take for example the recent experiences of the occupants of a five-story building containing six apartments on Riverside Drive between 79th and 80th Streets:

(1) a man from the first floor was coming home around 1 A.M. and was mugged at the outside entrance door;

(2) on the fourth floor a girl and her friend were sitting in the living room one evening when they were suddenly surprised by an intruder who threatened their lives if they didn't cover their heads and toss out their wallets;

(3) a girl on the fifth floor came home one evening to find her apartment burglarized and a number of valuable things missing;

(4) another evening the police were looking for a man on the roof, and later it was found that several windows in the building had been entered, including those of the same fourth- and fifth-floor apartments aforementioned, with many things stolen from the fourth floor;

(5) several days ago the two apartments on the fifth floor were entered, one of them for the third time, and a number of things were taken, with locks jammed and other locks completely broken. Also, two girls in a building near by were raped recently and in another building burglaries occur about once a week.

Do the enumerated occurrences not constitute a reign of terror? Or just what kind of pretty term can be substituted?...

Each time something happened police came, and each time the attitude was one of helplessness and resignation, that this is something which happens every day, is to be expected, and that there is not much to be done about it....

Time (March 22, 1963) began a description of the condition of the capital city of the leading nation of Western civilization:

SUICIDE OF THE WEST

Muggers attack in broad daylight. Churches lock their doors because, as one clergyman explains, "Too many bums come in, wander around and take what they like." Last week a purse snatcher was shot to death by a rookie policeman; a 40-year-old man was beaten to death in his home with a leg wrenched by a couple of intruders from his end table; a bank was robbed and police pursued the bandits through the streets while passers-by scattered to escape the gunfire…

History has a remarkable way of providing striking visual symbols of what is really going on, that tell us much more than the pretentious statistics of the sociologists. In the parks of our great cities, exactly as in all jungles, honest men may no longer move at night; when the sun goes down they must stay near the fires, while the beasts prowl. In those dark jungles and along the jungle paths into which the night transforms so many city streets, huge dogs now join the few hunters still on trail. What have dogs—killer dogs, moveover—to do with men? But dogs are of course appropriate companions in hunting the beasts of the jungle.

For the liberal ideology, the domestic jungles are the merely temporary by-products of a lack of education and faulty social institutions, to be cleared up by urban renewal programs, low rents, high minimum wages and integrated schools—in which regulations forbid physical discipline, expulsion or failing to certify every student to the next higher grade each year.

THE BACKWARD REGIONS of the equatorial zones are only, for liberalism, enlarged slums that will be put to rights by the standard remedies: education, democracy, and welfare in the special form of foreign aid. It is impossible for liberalism, or liberals, to face a truth that is perhaps too terrible for any secular ideology to face: that, with only minor exceptions, there is no chance whatever to cure the hunger, poverty and wretchedness of these two billion human beings in the foreseeable future; that these conditions will, on average, much more probably worsen than improve even in small measure.

Liberalism cannot either see *or* deal with the domestic jungle and the backward regions—the two challenges are closely similar. Liberalism is unfitted by its rationalistic optimism, its permissiveness, its egalitarianism and democratism, and by its guilt. Consider once more the logic of liberalism in relation to the backward regions, bringing it to bear on the question of survival.

From the universalism and democratism of the liberal ideology there follows, as we saw, the familiar one-man, one-vote principle of which so much has lately been made. (The United States Supreme Court explicitly affirmed it in its March 18, 1963 decision on the Georgia voting case.) This principle implies, by simple arithmetic, the subjugation of the West: the members of Western civilization are a small minority—it is as simple as that. The economic egalitarianism of the liberal ideology implies, as we also saw, the reduction of Westerners to hunger and poverty. Of course liberals hide these implications from themselves and from Western public opinion. They dream up some sort of world democracy in which a reasonable world society uses the one-man, one-vote principle to achieve universal freedom, peace and justice, and economic egalitarianism means plenty for all. But that is ideological fantasy. It is the subjugation (or disappearance) of the West, and Western—indeed, universal—hunger and poverty that are the unavoidable end terms of the logic of liberalism.

Naturally this logic is not carried out, or has not yet been carried out, all the way in practice. But in the soul of liberalism, and in the Western civilization that liberalism has permeated, this logic works like a spiritual worm, corrupting the will of the West to survive as a distinctive historical entity, easing the dissolution of the West into the distinctionless human mass. It could not be otherwise. In this case the liberal knows he is guilty, and his guilt is not a mere subjective sentiment. It is a fact that the liberals of the affluent society, by not yielding their power and privileges more fully and more quickly, are guilty: guilty, precisely, of betraying their own principles.

There is only one way to escape the conclusions from these logical deductions: by rejecting at least some of the principles from which the deductions start. There would have to be a rejection, in particular, of the quantitative reduction of human beings to Common Man; and a reassertion of qualitative distinctions. Quite specifically, there would have to be reasserted the pre-liberal conviction that Western civilization, thus Western man, is both different from and superior in quality to other civilizations and non-civilizations, from whatever source that difference and superiority are derived or acquired. And there would have to be a renewed willingness, legitimized by that conviction, to use superior power and the threat of power to defend the West against all challenges and challengers. Unless Western civilization is superior to other civilizations and societies, it is not worth defending; unless Westerners are willing to use their power, the West cannot be defended. But by its own principles, liberalism is not allowed to entertain that conviction or to make frank, unashamed and therefore effective use of that power.

IT IS THE CHALLENGE OF THE communist enterprise that most clearly, directly and immediately threatens Western survival. How clearly may be shown by an elementary extrapolation. If communism continues to advance at the rate it has in fact maintained since it began operating as a distinct organization in 1903, it will achieve its goal of world power before the end of this century: well before that, indeed, because the continuing advance of communism, combined with Western withdrawals from regions not yet communized, would throw the world strategic balance decisively in favor of the communist enterprise some time before the direct extension of its rule over all the world. In fact, there are many indications that the communist high command believes that point to have been reached and passed already.

The challenge of communism is from the Left; and all the major challenges that now bear crucially on survival come from the Left. But liberalism, as we have seen in some detail, is unable to conduct an intelligent, firm and sustained struggle against the Left. Liberalism can function effectively only against the Right.

Jules Monnerot, one of the most remarkable writers on the really serious issues of our time, summed up some years ago the West's discouraging dilemma in the fight against communism: the Left is infected with it, and the Right cannot understand it. Liberalism is infected with communism in the quite precise sense that communism and liberalism share most of their basic axioms and principles, and many of their values and sentiments. In terms of theoretical principle, it is only what remains in modern liberalism of the older individualistic doctrine that sharply differentiates liberalism from communism.

The secular, historically optimistic, reformist, welfare-statish, even the plebiscitary aspects of liberalism are all present in communism. Liberals and communists are, most of the time, *against* the same things and persons—whether Franco or McCarthy, the Chamber of Commerce or the John Birch Society, colonialism or the House Committee on Un-American Activities, big landlords or segregated schools, Tshombe or Arleigh Burke, Diem or Chiang or J. Edgar Hoover. They have the same enemies: and the choice of the enemy is the decisive act in determining the nature of political struggle. What communism does is to carry the liberal principles to their logical and practical extreme: the secularism; the rejection of tradition and custom; the stress on science; the confidence in the possibility of molding human beings; the determination to re-form *all* established institutions; the goal of wiping out all social distinctions; the internationalism; the belief in the Welfare State carried to its ultimate form in the totalitarian state. The liberal's arm cannot strike with consistent firmness against communism, either domestically or internationally, because the liberal dimly feels that in doing so he would be somehow wounding himself.

Though the principles of liberalism and communism thus large-ly overlap in the abstract, communism gives them an altogether different historical content; and communism differs from liberal-ism even more grossly in the methods it employs. Communists are serious, historically serious one might say, in a sense that liberals can neither be nor understand. Liberals cannot believe it when the communists say that they propose to establish a world federation of soviet socialist republics, when they pledge that they will bury us, when they frankly state that they will use *any* means to ac-complish their ends; liberalism cannot believe that every domestic communist is committed on principle to treason. Liberalism can-not help seeing the communists in the mirror of its own doctrine about human nature and motivation—as sharing, fundamentally, the same interests and goals, in particular the goals of peace and universal well-being. Inevitably, therefore, liberalism tries to meet the challenge of communism by means of the approved proce-dures that follow from liberal principles: plenty of talk and free speech—negotiations, as talk between nations is called; the ap-peal to man's better side, his rationality and supposed common interests in peace, disarmament and a lift in the general standard of living; reduction of tensions; avoidance of risky confrontations; exchange and Truth programs to prove to the communists the goodness of our intentions; reform and economic improvement for everybody in the world; in short, peaceful coexistence phasing into appeasement and collaboration.

The communists, since they are serious and since they are irrevocably fixed on their goal of a monopoly of world power, simply turn the liberal-inspired overtures into additional weapons to further their own advance. Shut off from reality by their ideological wall, liberals draw no conclusion from the obvious and frequently documented fact that in every negotiation ever conducted between the communist and non-communist nations, the majority and often the entirety of concessions have always come from the non-communist side; the net political and strategic profit has always gone to the communists. The years' long negotiations on a nuclear test ban provide a textbook case for a rule that has no exceptions. Because the communists are serious, they will have to be stopped, not by getting educated by liberals—the communists know very well what they are doing—but by superior power and will. Just possibly we shall not have to die in large numbers to stop them; but we shall certainly have to be willing to die.

But modern liberalism does not offer ordinary men compelling motives for personal suffering, sacrifice and death. There is no tragic dimension in its picture of the good life. Men become willing to endure, sacrifice and die for God, family, king, honor, country, from a sense of absolute duty or an exalted vision of the meaning of history. It is such traditional ideals and the institutions slowly built around them that are in present fact the great bulwarks, spiritual as well as social, against the tidal advance of the world communist enterprise. And it is precisely these ideals and institutions that liberalism has criticized, attacked and in part overthrown as superstitious, archaic, reactionary and irrational. In their place liberalism proposes a set of pale and bloodless abstractions—pale and bloodless for the very reason that they have no roots in the past, in deep feeling and in suffering. Except for mercenaries, saints and neurotics, no one is willing to sacrifice and die for progressive education, medicare, humanity in the abstract, the United Nations or a ten percent rise in social security payments.

Thus, in relation to the struggle against the communist enterprise, the principles of modern liberalism point inexorably toward the conclusion that has been brought to the surface by the younger people in the pacifist and disarmament movements: *Better Red than Dead!* Once again it is a cliché that goes to the heart of the matter. Unless the members of Western civilization, above all the members of its governing and intellectual elites, are convinced, convinced inwardly and absolutely, of the exact opposite—*Better Dead than Red!*—then their children are most certainly going to be Red, those of them who are not first dead too, for good measure.

III

THERE ARE, THUS, SPECIFIC features of liberal doctrine and habit that explain, in each case, liberalism's demonstrated inability to meet the primary challenges to Western survival. The deficiency can also be related, as I have already suggested, to a more general trait: to the fact that liberalism cannot come to terms with power, in particular with force, the most direct expression of power. It is not that liberals, when they enter the governing class (or when they constitute a revolutionary opposition striving to become the governing class) never make use of force; unavoidably they do, sometimes to excess. But because of their ideology they are not reconciled intellectually and morally to force. They therefore tend to use it ineptly, at the wrong times and places, against the wrong targets, in the wrong amounts.

In all human societies of any magnitude—states, nations, empires, federations, whatever they may be called—force is an inevitable, therefore normal and natural, ingredient: inevitable both for the preservation of internal order and for defense against external threats. From a practical standpoint, everyone knows this, even liberals; a nation wouldn't survive two hours if all its instrumentalities of force and coercion suddenly disappeared. But though liberals know this insofar as they act in practical affairs, their doctrine does not take account of it.

The theoretical recognition and acceptance of the fact that force is integral to the social order presupposes a pessimistic theory of human nature, or at the very least the rejection of any optimistic view. Force is inevitable in society because there are ineradicable limits, defects, evils and irrationalities in human nature, with resultant clashes of egos and interests that cannot be wholly resolved by peaceful methods of rational discussion, education, example, negotiation and compromise. Understanding this, and admitting it, a magistrate will include force in his equations, and will plan in advance how and when to use it effectively; and if he is responsible and reasonably humane, the result may be that a minimum of actual force will be used in practice.

But the liberal is prevented by his ideology from admitting the necessary and integral role of force, and by his temperament he dislikes to plan consciously ahead concerning the ways and means of using force. Moreover, most liberals, as we noted, are foxes rather than lions. They belong to the types, professions and classes who seek their ends by shrewdness, manipulations and verbal skills. What tends to happen, therefore, when liberals become influential

335

or dominant in the conduct of a nation's affairs is that the government tries to handle the difficulties, dangers, issues and threats it faces by those same methods, as Pareto observed in the quotation we earlier considered, and to shy away as much as possible and as long as possible from the use of force. In fact, the liberals tend to employ the social agencies of force—police and army—as above all instruments of bluff. Their actual use of force, which will always be necessary no matter what the theory, becomes erratic and unpredictable, the result not of a prudent estimate of the objective situation but of their own impatience, panic or despair.

This happens in both internal and external relations. In the United States, for example, minority groupings such as trade unions and, more lately, Negroes have incorporated force among their methods. Under the influence of liberal ideas and persons, the authorities have for the past generation or so tried to omit the use of counterforce, and to meet the issues by diversionary maneuvers into bargaining rooms and courts, by manipulating public opinion, by offering compromises, and so on. But every now and then the conduct of a minority grouping gets so outrageous, or so nearly touches some public right or sovereignty, that direct counterforce must be brought into the game. The police get out their clubs, tear gas and sometimes guns to stop a union's reign of terror, open up the public highways, or prevent intimidation of governors or law-makers. But against the background of the pervasive liberal rhetoric and the usual liberal practice in these matters, the appearance of drawn weapons on the scene seems sudden and arbitrary. If strikers or demonstrators get beaten up or thrown in jail, it is the cops and the authorities who seem by the inner logic of liberalism to be the villainous aggressors. And the final outcome is likely to be considerably more blood and bitterness than if a small number of heads had been knocked somewhat earlier on.

In the Kennedy-Johnson administration, liberals, among them ideologues of the first rank, have had a greater voice in international policy than in any previous government of the United States; and it is not surprising that as a consequence the use of force in connection with international affairs has never been so awkward. As a matter of fact, the entire theory of "deterrence" as held at present by official United States opinion—mostly worked out in the largely liberal-staffed "think factories"—is nothing but a gigantic bluff: the purpose of the entire strategic nuclear force is not at all to be used (if that were included in even the possible purpose, a "first strike" echelon, presently excluded, would be part of the strategic force) but merely to make the other side think you *might* conceivably use it. But the awkwardness is more plainly evident in critical episodes that keep arising in one continent after another.

Cuba is of course the prime example. In most of the world, including all the communist countries, the way in which the force available to the United States was mishandled in the Bay of Pigs invasion was quite beyond comprehension. (I happened to be in Manila; and I vividly recall how, when an American semi-official friend and I paid a visit to the floor of the legislature on the critical morning, we were surrounded by fifty or sixty gesticulating members who dismissed the published news as obvious nonsense and demanded to know how quickly the island would be taken.) As was later revealed, and could be readily deduced at the time, the liberal ideologues were the dominant influence on the policy then followed. It was not that they foreswore the use of force: that would have been a decision which, whether correct or not, could certainly be defended. What was so remarkable was that they used just enough force to assure the worst possible result from all possible points of view. It goes without saying that men serious about force, and understanding its functions,

337

would have brought to bear, once they had joined that issue, all the force necessary to finish it.

Laos, Katanga and South Vietnam provide other typical examples. In Laos the United States made available to the anti-communist government insufficient force to deal with the Pathet Lao but just enough to wreck relations between the anti-communists and the neutralists; and then withdrew force from the anti-communists in favor of a compromise that guaranteed continuing conflict in Laos itself and permitted the communists to give uninhibited support to their fighting comrades in South Vietnam. In Katanga, the policy of the United Nations command, so far as the use of force went, was wholly dependent on the decisions of the United States to the extent that the United States chose to decide anything; and in this case conspicuously, as in the case of Cuba, United States policy was the product of the liberal ideologues. Perhaps it was correct to compel Tshombe to knuckle under to the central government. But there has seldom been a more ludicrous spectacle than the eccentric, undirected, sporadic, on-again-off-again use of driblets of force to accomplish that end: with the not unnatural consequence of contributing mightily to the political, social and economic disintegration of that young nation. The force used in South Vietnam is considerably greater, but no less unsurely and inconsistently applied. It is enough to keep the country in a turmoil and to make sure that a good many people, among them Americans, get killed; but not enough, and not used properly, to defeat the communists.

It should not be inferred from examples such as these that liberals never turn to the all-out use of force; merely that they seldom turn to the right amount of force at the right time. It was the liberals who were loudest in demanding war against Hitler, and who invented both the idea and slogan of "unconditional surrender"; and it was a liberal, though he numbered communists among his advisers, who called for the pastoralization of Germany. And it is not inconceivable that a liberal, in a state of panic that cuts through his ideological cover, may press the button that begins a nuclear exchange. Nor is it impossible that a governing stratum of liberals might reach the conclusion that a generalized internal use of force is the only way to assure their prescribed society of peace, justice, well-being and freedom. Georges Sorel, in his study of social violence, warned that

> ...the optimist in politics is an inconstant and even dangerous man, because he takes no account of the great difficulties presented by his projects....If he possesses an exalted temperament, and if unhappily he finds himself armed with great power, permitting him to realize the ideal he has fashioned, the optimist may lead his country into the worst disasters. He is not long in finding out that social transformations are not brought about with the ease that he had counted on; he then supposes that this is the fault of his contemporaries, instead of explaining what actually happens by historical necessities; he is tempted to get rid of people whose obstinacy seems to him to be so dangerous to the happiness of all. During the Terror, the men who spilt most blood were precisely those who had the greatest desire to let their equals enjoy the golden age they had dreamt of, and who had the most sympathy with human wretchedness: optimists, idealists, and sensitive men, the greater desire they had for universal happiness the more inexorable they showed themselves.[1]

---

1. Georges Sorel, *Reflections on Violence*, translated by T.E. Hulme (New York: B.W. Huebsch, 1914; Peter Smith, 1941), pp. 9-10.

SIXTEEN

The Function of Liberalism

I

WHAT, THEN, IS THE PRIMARY function of liberalism in our time? It cannot be supposed that a great ideology, capable of permeating the minds and emotions of tens of millions of human beings, inspiring the programs of governments, and affecting or even dominating public opinion within the major nations of the West, has no function; or that it can be written off by listing its theoretical errors and practical defects; or that it is sufficiently characterized by noting that its doctrines are favorable to the interests of certain social groups, types and classes. Modern liberalism could not have achieved its profound and widespread influence, to which very few citizens of the Western nations are altogether immune, unless it fulfilled a pervasive and compelling need.

We finish our circle at our point of beginning: Liberalism is the ideology of Western suicide. When once this initial and final sentence is understood, everything about liberalism—the beliefs, emotions and values associated with it, the nature of its enchantment, its practical record, its future—falls into place.

Implicitly, all of this book is merely an amplification of this sentence. Let me make sure that in the end there is no doubt left about its explicit meaning.

I have referred in a number of contexts to the several score newly independent states that have appeared in Asia and Africa since the end of the Second World War. Let us consider one special element in the dialectic of independence. On the one hand, we know, every new proclamation of independence is a victory for self-determination, freedom, liberty, the popular will, justice, equal rights, democracy—in sum, for the ideology of liberalism—and is so greeted by the spokesmen of liberalism throughout the world. In most cases, for that matter, liberal opinion and support in the Western world have been important, often indispensable, factors in the achievement of independence.

On the other hand, these moves to independence are at the same time very often—not always, perhaps, but very often—the occasions of tangible and sometimes very substantial losses to the West. Maybe these losses are counterbalanced by indirect or long-term benefits; but the benefits are exceedingly vague and highly speculative for the time being, whereas many of the losses are definite and unmistakable.

Most of these newly independent states were formerly under the political, economic and in some measure cultural control of Western nations. They constitute, therefore, zones of that world contraction of the West that was examined in Chapter I. As was there noted, the completeness of the Western withdrawal differs in different areas; and in some cases a partial or temporary reversal is conceivable. The trend, though, is unmistakable, has not in fact been reversed since it started in 1917, and has already resulted in a world power shift of vast proportions. I suggested in Chapter I that the nature and scope of the trend become dramatically defined if we think in terms of the successive maps of an historical atlas showing by a single color the areas of the world under Western dominion in 1914 and then in each subsequent decade.

Whatever the extent to which in some sense or other Western civilization survives in this or that region no longer under Western political control, the independence march means solid losses to the West that can be pointed to and measured. One set of losses is obvious enough, though it is not ideologically chic to make much of it in liberal assemblies: the billions of dollars' worth of Western property, much of it productive property in land, factories and mines, that has been stolen by the revolutionaries—or abandoned passively by the Western owners. However, the strategic losses are of more lasting and fundamental significance.

The great harbor of Trincomalee, commanding the western flank of the Bay of Bengal, Southeast Asia and the Strait of Malacca, ceases to be a Western strategic base. Gone too are the mighty ports of Dakar and Casablanca, looming over the Atlantic passage. Of the guardian bases of the North African littoral, southern flank of Europe, only Mers-el-Kébir remains, no longer of any importance and scheduled to be soon abandoned. Bombay, overlooking the Arabian Sea; Basra, watching the Persian Gulf and opening toward the northern plateau and the passes from the steppes; the staging areas of the Middle East and those of East Africa guarding the Indian Ocean—all abandoned; Hong Kong, left as a pawn in the arms of communist China; Singapore, shedding its strategic utility for the West as it phases into an independent Malaya; the mighty NATO air base at Kamina in Katanga, air power axis of sub-Saharan Africa, abandoned; the half-billion-dollar system of American-built air bases in Africa's northwest salient into the Atlantic, hub of a great wheel holding within its compass all north and central Africa, the Near East, and Europe right out to the Urals, and linked at its western rim to the Americas: abandoned. Suez, the Canal and the Isthmus: the water passage from Europe to Asia and East Africa, the land bridge between Asia and Africa, abandoned.

We read in 1962 about the units of Gurkhas assigned to the United Nations army in the Congo. Old military hands recalled that the fathers and grandfathers of those Gurkhas, along with the legions of the Sikhs, were among the most stalwart of the soldiers who for generations fought for Britain: nearly two million of them in the First World War and the Second; and there have been few better fighting formations than the elite brigades of Gurkhas or Sikhs trained and led by professional British officers. Those tall, powerful black and brown men that France recruited from a French West Africa and trained in the tradition of Gallieni and Lyautey were nearly as good, though; their weight, too, was felt in the two World Wars; and many American tourists have seen them riding and marching proudly up the Champs-Elysées on July 14th—though they will be seen there no more, as part of a French army at any rate. These splendid fighting men of the Gurkhas, Sikhs, Senegalese and Berbers are not the least of the grievous losses that the West has suffered from the triumphs of decolonization.

It may be objected that civilization is not a matter of military bases, strategic posts and soldiers. True enough, certainly; but without the bases and posts and soldiers, there can be no civilization, there is nothing. The line of the bases and posts, manned by the soldiers, is the *limes* also of the civilization. Its rays of influence may extend beyond that *limes*, but not its full historical reality. South of the wall built across the waist of Britain and guarded by the troops of Rome was civilization—the Chester, Lincoln and

York that still stand today; to the north was only barbarism and the rude hosts of savages. When Arminius destroyed the legions of Varus in the Teutoburg Forest—Arminius, who had been educated at, you might say, Oxford: that is, under Roman teachers, and was much favored by the liberal analogues among the Romans, notably including Varus himself—when Arminius destroyed the legions, Augustus was compelled to order a general withdrawal to the banks of the Rhine. And the Rhine, not the Elbe, became the *limes* of Roman civilization, as we can still see so plainly today when we contrast cities like Trier, still showing their Roman roots, with Nuremberg or Dresden.

What does liberalism do about these terrible, soul-shattering losses, defeats and withdrawals, and the still more searing defeats suffered by the West at the hands of the communist enterprise? Liberalism does not and cannot stop them, much less win back what has been lost; indeed in many instances it has, rather, helped them along. But what liberalism can and does do, what it is marvelously and specifically equipped to do, is to comfort us in our afflictions; and then, by a wondrous alchemy, to transmute the dark defeats, withdrawals and catastrophes into their bright opposites: into gains, victories, advances. Distilled in the liberal alembic, the geographic, political, demographic and strategic losses emerge as triumphs of Freedom, Equality, Progress and Virtue. The troops of a fanatic Arab imperialist, armed by the communist enterprise, stand at the Suez bridge in place of the men of Britain and France? Do not be troubled, fellow Westerners: reactionary imperialism has suffered a deserved setback; self-determination, the equality of races and the rights of small nations have been upheld; a blow has been struck at aggression; the sanctity of one-universal-law-for-all-mankind has been vindicated.

I repeat what I stated in the first chapter: I do not suggest that

SUICIDE OF THE WEST

liberalism is "the cause" of the contraction and possible, on the evidence probable, death of Western civilization. I do not know what the cause is of the West's extraordinarily rapid decline, which is most profoundly shown by the deepening loss, among the leaders of the West, of confidence in themselves and in the unique quality and value of their own civilization, and by a correlated weakening of the Western will to survive. The cause or causes have something to do, I think, with the decay of religion and with an excess of material luxury; and, I suppose, with getting tired, worn out, as all things temporal do. But though liberalism did not initiate the decline and cannot be "blamed" for it, the influence of liberalism on public opinion and governmental policy has become—by obscuring the realities, corrupting will and confounding action—a major obstacle to a change of course that might have some chance of meeting the challenges and of arresting, and reversing, the decline.

Primarily, however, the ideology of modern liberalism must be understood as itself one of the expressions of the Western contraction and decline; a kind of epiphenomenon or haze accompanying the march of history; a swan song, a spiritual solace of the same order as the murmuring of a mother to a child who is gravely ill. There is a really dazzling ingenuity in the liberal explanations of defeat as victory, abandonment as loyalty, timidity as courage, withdrawal as advance. The liberal ideologues proceed in a manner long familiar to both religion and psychology: by constructing a new reality of their own, a transcendental world, where the soul may take refuge from the prosaic, unpleasant world of space and time. In that new and better world, the abandonment of a million of one's own countrymen and the capitulation to a band of ferocious terrorists become transformed into what is called "liberation." The loss of control over the strategic axis of the

Great Continent becomes a vindication of universal law. A crude imperialist grab in the South Seas or the Indian subcontinent becomes a clearing up of the vestiges of colonialism. The failure to retaliate against gross insults and injuries to envoys, citizens and property becomes a proof of maturity and political wisdom.

The novelist Allen Drury has the Secretary of State whom he names "Orrin Knox" meditate on the rituals through which the adepts bring about the ideological metamorphosis:

> At least fifty per cent of the [State] department's laborings, he told himself with a melancholy irony, was devoted to the science of how to make mountains out of molehills that didn't matter, and molehills out of mountains that did. Bright young men, growing somewhat gray and elderly now, educated in the years after the Second World War to accept the idea of their country as not-quite-best, labored with a suave and practiced skill to gloss over the anguish of unnecessary decline. Experienced in the glib rationalization of failure, the smooth acceptance of defeat, they found cogent arguments and reasonable explanations for each new default of will on the part of their government and could always be found hovering at the elbows of those officials, like himself, who still held firm to some vision of America more fitting and more worthy than that. There they smoothly offered their on-the-other-hand's and their let's-look-at-it-from-their-point-of-view's and their but-of-course-you-must-realize-the-people-won't-support-it's. Meanwhile the communist tide rolled on.... [1]

---

1. Allen Drury, *A Shade of Difference* (New York: Doubleday & Co., 1962), pp. 277-78.

Domestic tribulations yield as readily as do foreign to the magical transformation. At the beginning of September 1963, at a moment when the nation's constitutional and social fabric was being torn by generalized racial conflict that was posing issues impossible to settle and therefore certain to become graver and more dangerous over the coming years, the American Psychological Foundation held a large conference in Philadelphia. The *New York Times* (September 2, 1963) singled out for report the address in which Professor Gordon W. Allport of Harvard explained that the "racial demonstrations in America are basically a sign of good national emotional health.... On the whole, it is a wholesome and healthy movement." The Negroes, Professor Allport elaborated further, are "running for home"—a term he adapted from a "goal gradient" theory derived from the observation that "an experimental subject speeds up when approaching the goal presented in a psychological test." It is easy to imagine Professor Allport in late Roman days, explaining how the animals in the Colosseum are generally a playful lot, especially when running for home.

You are worried, citizens, about an active enemy beachhead situated within our strategic periphery? Just let Richard Rovere run the matter through his ideological converter, and you will be relieved to discover that the Cuban situation is, on the absolute contrary, a blessing to be grateful for:

> From the point of view of our over-all policy in Latin America and in the rest of the world, the present occupation of Cuba by Russian troops is not entirely a bad thing. The destruction of Castro and communism by an American occupation would increase sympathy, and perhaps support, for both in other parts of the world; the presence in Cuba today

of Soviet troops can only diminish Castro's personal prestige as a revolutionary leader and the appeal of communism as an expression of self-determination. Moreover, a highly vulnerable Soviet military base in the Western Hemisphere gives us a kind of Soviet hostage—one roughly comparable in numbers and vulnerability to the Allied forces in West Berlin, which the Russians often speak of as a hostage.[2]

As you can easily figure out by extending Mr. Rovere's logic, we shall be able to feel *perfectly* safe as soon as Russian troops reach Chicago.

Mr. Rovere's incantations, though they have a rather wide public reverberation, are at several layers remove from the inner seats of power. Professor Walt Whitman Rostow, as chief of the State Department's policy-planning staff, has stood close to the very center, and has for some years been there in spirit through his books and memoranda. In his most prestigious work, *The Stages of Growth*, presented first as a series of lectures at Cambridge University, then as articles in *The Economist*, most influential magazine of the Western world, then as a full-scale book,[3] Professor Rostow assures us that every society, when "the pre-conditions for take-off" along the industrial path appear, moves upward in a sequence of stages that culminates in "maturity" and "the age of high-mass consumption." That consummation duly arrived at, the aggressive habits of the immature society are discarded, and the populace seeks peace and order in which to pursue its mature goals of more autos, suburban houses and babies. It is no

---

2. Quoted from *The New Yorker*, Mar. 2, 1963, p. 130.
3. Walt Whitman Rostow, *The Stages of Growth* (New York: Cambridge University Press, 1960).

coincidence, you may be sure, since this is why the work exists, that Professor Rostow's most volubly discussed example is the Soviet Union, which, it turns out, is soon to cross, granted forbearance and help from us, that final hump into the peaceful promised land of cars and toddlers.

To debate whether the Rostow "theory of history" is true or not would be a foolish waste of time. Translated from the ideological, what Professor Rostow is saying is: "The stronger our enemy gets, the better for us; and if he gets strong enough—preferably as strong as we or stronger—we shall have nothing to worry about." Nobody needs to be told what a ridiculous statement that is. But what Professor Rostow is up to has nothing to do with truth and falsity about the real world. He is brewing a drug to enable our minds and his own to leave the real world and take refuge in that better world of his ideology where tigers purr like kittens and turn in their claws to the United Nations.

It is as if a man, struck with a mortal disease, were able to say and to believe, as the flush of the fever spread over his face, "Ah, the glow of health returning!"; as his flesh wasted away, "At least I am able to trim down that paunch the doctor always warned me about!"; as a finger dropped off with gangrene or leprosy, "Now I won't have that bothersome job of trimming those nails every week!" Liberalism permits Western civilization to be reconciled to dissolution; and this function its formulas will enable it to serve right through to the very end, if matters turn out that way: for even if Western civilization is wholly vanquished or altogether collapses, we or our children will be able to see that ending, by the light of the principles of liberalism, not as a final defeat, but as the transition to a new and higher order in which Mankind as a whole joins in a universal civilization that has risen above the parochial distinctions, divisions and discriminations of the past.

I do not want to minimize the importance and the value of this function—which is the principal function of modern liberalism; the explanation, in fact, of its widespread present influence in the West, far beyond the circles of those who regard themselves as liberals. It is one of the cardinal works of mercy to comfort the sick and dying, "to let him die at ease, that liveth here uneath."

But of course the final collapse of the West is not yet inevitable; the report of its death would be premature. If a decisive change comes, if the contraction of the past fifty years should cease and be reversed, then the ideology of liberalism, deprived of its primary function, will fade away, like those feverish dreams of the ill man who, passing the crisis of his disease, finds he is not dying after all. There are a few small signs, here and there, that liberalism may already have started fading. Perhaps this book is one of them.

INDEX

Acheson, Dean, 302

Acton, Lord, 42

Adams, John, 42, 148

Agency for International Development, 312, 314

Alexander, Robert J., 238

Algeria, 8; colonial revolt in, 190, 203, 239; dispossession in, 261–62; double standards on, 223, 226–27, 240–41

Alliance for Progress, 68, 221, 314, 323

Allport, Gordon W., 348

America magazine, 45–46

American Association of University Professors, 70, 158

American Civil Liberties Union, 20, 35, 71, 183

American Psychological Foundation, 348

Americans for Democratic Action (ADA), 20, 50, 309–10*n*; *ADA World*, 96, 238; on Castro, 238–39; on disarmament, 90*n*;

egalitarianism of, 82; "faith" of, 52–53; on Franco, 235–36; internationalism of, 80–81, on Kennedy, 45–46; Scoresheets of, 95–96; on Soviet Union, 236; "war against want," 69

American Workers Party, xxi

Anderson, Orville, 24

Angell, Norman, 196

Angola, 190, 223–24, 238–39, 240, 312

Aristotle, 47, 151, 174

Arizona Republican, 23

Arminius, 345

Athens (ancient), 149

Atlanta Constitution, 21

Augustus (emperor), 345

Ayer, A.J. xxix

Ayub Khan, Mohammad, 314

Bacon, Francis, 40, 43, 49

Baldwin, James, 268

Baldwin, Roger, 20, 183–84

Baltimore Sun, 20

Banda, Hastings, 268

Banfield, Edward C., 24

Batista, Fulgencio, 78, 237, 312

Bentham, Jeremy, 41

Berlin airlift, 305

Berlin Wall, 5, 313

Berns, Walter, 24

Bernstein, Eduard, 41

Betancourt, Rómulo, 239, 312

Beveridge, Albert J., 292

Black, Hugo, 20, 71

Black Muslims, 224, 268, 282

Blanshard, Paul, 45

Boas, Franz, 218

Boun Oum, 314

Bowery (N.Y.), 111–13

Bow Group, 279

Bowles, Chester, 20, 35*n*, 69*n*, 81*n*

Brennan, William, 21

Brock, Clifton, 101

Brown, Pat, 21

Brown v. Board of Education, 186–87

Bryant, Joseph, III, xxviii

Buckley, William F., Jr., xiv, xxx, 23, 131

Bulletin of the Atomic Scientists, 20

Burckhardt, Jacob, 42

Burke, Arleigh, 24, 331

Burke, Edmund, 42

Burma, 304

Burnham, Claude, xviii

Byrd, Harry F., 23

Casals, Pablo, 237

Case, Clifford, 19, 21

Case for Modern Man, The (Frankel), 166

Castro, Fidel, 203, 311; favor for, 237–38, 258, 312; prestige of, 348–49; "surprise" of, 289

Catholicism/Catholics, xii, xviii–ix, 30; as a cohesive minority, 281; as majority, 282; on Original Sin, 44–46; papacy, 287

Center for the Study of Democratic Institutions, 20, 64, 90

CENTO, 316

Central Intelligence Agency (CIA), xxviii, xxix

Chafee, Zechariah, 71, 184

Chamberlain, John, 23

Chamber of Commerce (U.S.), 24, 331

Chiang Kai-shek, 236, 331

Chicago Tribune, 21

Childs, Marquis, 23

China, 3, 5, 121, 311; communism in, 239, 294, 301, 303; and Hong Kong, 343

Christianity, 33, 94, 144; clergy in, 22; and communism, 190; on guilt, 212–13, 216*n*, 217, 228; *see also* Catholicism

civil rights, 93, 178*n*, 241; and communism, 251–55; and crime, 325–28

Clark, Joseph, 19

Clark, Kenneth, 107

Clark, Mark, 24

Cohen, Morris R., xx, 172–73

Cold War, 12, 68–69; and containment, 301–5; and *Struggle for the World*, 297; and "Yalta Strategy," 299

colonialism & decolonization, 6–11, 32, 220–21, 310–11, 322–23; liberation movements, 193, 207n, 224, 226–27, 268; and reparations, 218; strategic losses, 342–47

Commager, Henry S., 20, 22, 71, 184

Commentary, 147

Committee for an Effective Congress, 20

Committee for a Sane Nuclear Policy (SANE), 20, 86, 90n, 206n

Committee for Economic Development, 279

Committee for the Separation of Church and State, 45

Commonweal, The, 21

communism, 5–8, 11, 19; Christians under, 190; contradictions in, 251–54; and double standards, 189–90, 233–44; free expression for, 28, 32; and pacifism, 89–90; in Peru, 127–28; and poverty, 68–69; and power, 122; "rationalism" of, 40; in universities, 150; world domination goal, 288, 330–34;

see also Cuba; Soviet Union

Communist Party, 28, 67, 105–6, 243–44

Comte, Auguste, 117

Condorcet, Marquis de, 40, 44, 159; on education, 62; on perfectibility, 49

Congo, 312–13

Congress and the American Tradition, 154n

Congress for Cultural Freedom, xi, xiv, xxix

Cooke, Charles M., 24

Cousins, Norman, 20, 86, 258

criminal justice, 320–21, 325–28

Croce, Benedetto, xxix

Cuba, 8, 203, 206n, 237–38, 311, 312; Bay of Pigs, xi, 313, 337; missile crisis, 290, 313–14; Soviet troops in, 348–49

Czapski, Joseph, 240

D'Arcy, Martin, xix

Deaths in the Forest (Zawodny), 240

Decatur, Stephen, 201

Declaration of the Rights of Man, 35

de Gaulle, Charles, 239, 289–90, 316

Descartes, René, 40, 43, 49

Dewey, John, xix, xxix, 26, 41, 166; on democracy, 169, 170; on "method of inquiry," 73; on socialism, 97–98

Diderot, Denis, 41, 44

Diem, Ngo Dinh, 314, 331

disarmament, 33, 89–90, 196–97, 255–57, 334

Dissent, 226

Dooley, Tom (Dr.), 213

Dostoevsky, Fyodor, 42, 167

Douglas, Paul, 19

Douglas, William O., 19, 71, 242–43

Drury, Allen, 347

Dulles, John Foster, 304

Dupee, Frederick, xx

Eichmann, Adolf, 189, 241

Eisenhower, Dwight D., 304, 308, 312, 315

Eliot, T.S., xx, 147

Ellender, Allen J., 129

Enlightenment, 40, 44, 148, 166, 212–13

Epimenides, 17

Express, L', 26, 201, 226

Fabians, 41, 50, 100

Feiffer, Jules, 173*n*

Fernandez, Ramon, xix

Finletter, Thomas, 20

Fleeson, Doris, 23

food supply, 116–24

foreign aid, 68, 208–9, 267, 308, 314, 328

Foreign Policy Association, 156

Formosa, 304, 305

Fourier, Charles, 40, 117, 159

France, 8, 25; and Algeria, 203, 223, 226–27; communism in, 277, 278, 280*n*

Franco, Francisco, 234–40, 331

Frank, Joseph, xix

Frankel, Charles, 51–52, 166–67

Freeman, Orville, 20

French Revolution, xxv, 50, 62, 246; Declaration of the Rights of Man, 35

Freudianism, 45–46, 165

Friedman, Milton, 24

Fuchs, Klaus, 150

Fund for the Republic, 20, 64

Fustel de Coulanges, N.D., 42

Galbraith, John Kenneth, 20, 29

Germany, 236, 256, 281*n*, 299, 399; Berlin airlift, 305; Berlin Wall, 5, 313; literacy in, 149; *see also* Nazism

Gide, André, 147

Goebbels, Joseph, 150

Goering, Hermann, 150

Goldberg, Arthur J., 19–20

Goldman, Eric, 20, 22

Goldwater, Barry, 23, 92

Goodfriend, Arthur, 69*n*

Great Britain, 8–9, 36, 273; on balance of power, 278, 294; Bow Group, 279; on disarmament, 257–57; and Gurkhas, 344; in India, 9, 296; Liberal Party in, 191*n*; speech limits in, 242; urbanism in, 276; and

Great Britain *(cont.)*
  world wars, 293–94
Great Illusion, The (Angell), 196
Greece: ancient, 150; civil war in,
  301, 304
Gunther, Violet M., 90*n*

Hale, Nathan, 86*n*
Hamilton, Alexander, 291
Harper's, 20
Harriman, Averell, 20
Hartz, Louis, 53*n*
Hayek, F.A., 24
Hazlitt, William, xiii
Heller, Walter, 29
Henry, Patrick, 86*n*, 177
Herblock, 20, 36
Hess, Rudolf, 150
Hiss, Alger, 150, 200
Hitler, Adolf, xxiii, 149–50, 239,
  247, 338; goals of, 287–88
Hobbes, Thomas, xiii, 42
Hoffman, Paul, 21
Hohenstaufen dynasty, 287
Holmes, Oliver Wendell, Jr.,
  74–75, 168
Hook, Sidney, xx, xxi, xxix, 48,
  51, 165
Hooker, Thomas, 42
Hoover, J. Edgar, 244, 331
House Committee on Un-American
  Activities, 71, 243, 331
Hughes, H. Stuart, 20
Hume, David, xv, 42
Humphrey, Hubert, 19, 23, 49;

and ADA, 81*n*; on "change,"
  54–55; as "fox," 282–83; on
  injustice, 51; on negotiation,
  90–91
Hungary, 8, 11, 122, 243, 258,
  306–8
Hutchins, Robert Maynard,
  64–67, 90, 168; on common
  good, 92; "faith" of, 65–66,
  108, 169; on majority decision,
  75; on "universal dialogue,"
  70, 71, 104, 130, 170, 234

India: and Britain, 9, 296;
  communism in, 149; food supply in, 121–22; and Goa, 190,
  224, 311, 312
Indianapolis News, 23
Indonesia, 122, 203, 220, 263–65,
  296, 311
internationalism, 79–81, 179,
  194–96, 205–6
Iran, 301, 304
Isaacs, Stanley, 21
isolationism, 80, 291–92
Israel, 282, 300; and Eichmann,
  189, 241; and Suez, 307
Italy, 277, 278, 280*n*

Jackson, Andrew, 99
Jacobins, 40, 50, 62
James, Henry, xv, 147
James, William, 26, 41
Japan, 3, 289, 294; food supply in,
  118; literacy in, 149–50; and

Japan *(cont.)*
   Pearl Harbor, xxiv, 150
Jaspers, Karl, xxix
Jaurès, Jean, 41
Javits, Jacob, 19, 21, 23
Jefferson, Thomas, 99, 261, 263
Jesuits, 45
Jews, 22, 105, 281, 282
John Birch Society, 131, 331
Johnson, Lyndon, 299, 315
Jones, John Paul, 86–87*n*
Joralemon, Ira B., 118–19*n*
Jowett, Benjamin, xxxii
Joyce, James, 147

Kafka, Franz, 211
Kant, Immanuel, xv
Kassem, Abdul Karem, 239
Katanga, 260, 338, 343
Kautsky, Karl, 41
Kelly, Daniel, xiv, xvii, xviii, xxi–
   xxiii
Kempton, Murray, 173*n*
Kennan, George, 302–3, 304
Kennedy, John F., 116–17, 299,
   308, 312, 315; assassination
   of, 248; Catholicism of, 45–46;
   on hunger, 117; Latin America
   plan, 125, 127; neutralism of,
   310; and Peace Corps, 314;
   peace strategy, 196–97
Kenner, Hugh, 24
Kenya: Mau Mau in, 223; White
   Highlands, 122–24
Kenyon, Dorothy, 20

Keynes, John Maynard, 41, 94
Keyserling, Leon, 29
Khrushchev, Nikita, xxxii, 90, 105;
   and Cuba, 290; on "peace,"
   257–58
Kierkegaard, Søren, 167
Kirk, Russell, 23
Kirstein, Lincoln, xix
Knight, G. Wilson, xx
Korean War, 304, 305
Kuchel, Thomas, 19

laissez faire, 25, 91, 97–98, 129,
   180, 183
Laos, 309, 313, 338
Larson, Arthur, 21, 279
Laski, Harold, 40
Latin America, 125, 127, 273;
   Alliance for Progress in,
   220–21, 314, 323
Lawrence, David, 23
League of Women Voters, 20, 158
Lehman, Herbert H., 20
Lenin, Vladimir, 12–13, 99, 105,
   150
Lerner, Max, 45, 46, 91, 165
Lewis, Fulton, Jr., 23
Liberal Papers, The, 232
Life magazine, 22
Lightner, Marcia, xxii
Lincoln, C. Eric, 107
Lindsay, John, 21
Locke, John, 41–42, 261
Loeb, James I., Jr., 20, 81*n*
Look magazine, 20

Low, Sir David, 36
Lunn, Sir Arnold, 189

MacArthur, Douglas, 24, 305
Machiavelli, Niccolò, xxv, 42,
    282–83
Machiavellians, The, xxiv–xxvi,
    154*n*
MacLeish, Archibald, 20
Maine, Henry, 42
Malaya, 304, 343
Managerial Revolution, The, xiv,
    xv–xvi, xxiii–xxiv
Mann, Thomas, 147
Mao Tse-tung, 236, 243, 289
Maritain, Jacques, xxix
Marshall, George C., 293
Marshall, Thurgood, 107
Martin, Edwin M., 127–28
Marx, Karl, 40, 117
Mauldin, Bill, 20
Mau Mau, 223
McCabe, Ralph, 180*n*
McCarthy, Eugene, 19
McCarthy, Joseph, xiv, xxix–xxx,
    33, 247–48, 331
McGill, Ralph, 20, 124–27
McGoldrick, Marjorie K., 326–27
Menderes, Adnan, 243
Michels, Robert, 163, 208
Mihailovich, Draza, 189
Mill, John Stuart, 41–42, 94, 261;
    on "despotism of custom,"
    58–59, 62; on freedom of
    speech, 71, 72; on government

interference, 91–92
Millis, Walter, 90
minimum wage, 28, 113–16, 328
Modern Age, 23
Monde, Le, 26, 157
Monnerot, Jules, 331
Montaigne, Michel de, 42
Morse, Wayne, 29
Mugabe, Robert, xvii
Murphy, Michael J., 326
Murrow, Edward R., 20
Murry, John Middleton, xx
Mussolini, Benito, 247
Muste, A.J., 258

Napoleon, 288
Napoleonic Code, 261
Nasser, Gamal Abdel, 239, 243,
    312; imperial project, 265, 311;
    neutralism of, 309
Nation, The, 226
National Association for the
    Advancement of Colored People
    (NAACP), 20, 222
National Association of
    Manufacturers, 24
National Review, ix, xiv, xxx–
    xxxi, 23
national sovereignty, 79–81, 179,
    181, 192, 194–99
Nazism, 104, 149–50, 153, 247;
    and double standards, 240;
    Eichmann trial, 189; united
    front on, 232–33
Nehru, Jawaharlal, 224, 244, 312

Netherlands, 122, 203, 220, 224, 263–64, 296
Neuberger, Maurine, 19
New Deal, xxi, 65, 99, 101
New Frontier, 167
New Guinea, 312
New Republic, The, 20, 21, 26, 157
New Statesman, 26, 226
Newton, Isaac, 42
New York Daily News, 21
New York Herald Tribune, 326
New York Post, 20
New York Times, 21, 26, 157; double standards of, 237–38n; on Peru, 126–27
New York University, 221–22
Nichols, William I., 86
Nietzsche, Friedrich, 42, 167
Nkrumah, Kwame, 243, 262–63
North Atlantic Treaty Organization (NATO), 289; fissures in, 290, 299, 316; formation of, 295, 301–2; Katanga air base, 343
nuclear weapons, 12, 178, 179, 206n; and deterrence theory, 337; and Suez crisis, 307; test ban on, 157, 201, 299, 315, 333; U.S. monopoly of, 296–97, 298
Nutter, Warren, 24
Nyasaland (Malawi), 268
Nyerere, Julius, 243, 263

Oakeshott, Michael: on continuity, 203; on ideology, 109; on rationalism, 40, 47–48, 297; on rational utopianism, 53–54; on uniformity, 81–82
Observer (London), 26, 157
Office of Strategic Services, xxvi
Oppenheimer, Robert, 200
Organization of American States, 316
Ortega y Gasset, José, xx
Orwell, George, x, xxiii–xxiv
Owen, Robert, 40, 117

pacifism, 192–93, 195–96, 199, 334; as propaganda tool, 256–57
Pahlavi, Reza Shah, 78
Pakistan, 121, 243
papacy, 287
Pareto, Vilfredo, 171, 336; on motives, 207–8; on public safety, 321; on "residues," 283–85
Partisan Review, xxiii, xxx
Pascal, Blaise, 42
patriotism, 192, 205; rejection of, 85–86, 199–201
Pax Americana, 296–98
Peace Corps, 58, 69n, 208, 314
Pearson, Drew, 20
Pérez Jiménez, Marcos, 312, 314
Perón, Juan, 78, 239
Peru, 124–28
Peter the Great (of Russia), 3
Philippines, 292, 304, 305

Plato, 17, 19

Poland, 8, 11, 122, 306; Katyn massacre, 240

Portugal, 296, 322; and Angola, 190, 223–24, 238, 240, 312

Pound, Ezra, xx, 147

Progressive, The, 20

Proposed Roads to Freedom (Russell), 63

Proust, Marcel, 147, 167

race relations, 56; anti-Semitism, 105, 128; and cohesive minorities, 281–82; discrimination & segregation, 28, 31, 104, 153–54; double standards in, 221–25; innate differences, 106–8; integration, 28, 163–64, 186–87, 204–5, 219; quota systems, 84; and "white guilt," 218–19, 265–69

Radford, Arthur, 24

Rahv, Philip, xxx

Raugh, Joseph L., Jr., 46

Read, Herbert, xx, xxix

relativism, 72–75, 81, 151–52, 199

Renaissance, 41–42, 178, 246, 319

Rhodesia, 239

Ricardo, David, 41

Richards, I.A., xx

Richmond Times-Dispatch, 23

Riesman, David, 20

Roberto, Holden, 241

Robespierre, Maximilien de, 62

Roche, John P., 22

Roman Empire, 2, 3, 7; in Britain, 344–45; and Carthage, 287

Roosevelt, Eleanor, 18, 86, 174; on crime, 68

Roosevelt, Franklin D., xxi, 65, 99; and ADA, 81n; foreign policy strategies of, 298–300, 309; Four Freedoms, 69n; and World War II, 293; and Yalta, 299, 301

Roosevelt, James, 20

Roosevelt, Theodore, 99

Rosenberg, Harold, xx

Rostow, Walt Whitman, 68–69, 197, 283, 349–50

Rousseau, Jean-Jacques, 41, 44, 77

Rousset, David, 153

Rovere, Richard, 247, 348–49

Rowe, David, 24

Russell, Bertrand, xxix, 58, 63

Russia, 3–4, 294; Bolshevik revolution in, 5, 7, 12–13, 105, 203, 281n, 314n; food supply in, 122; literacy in, 149; *see also* Soviet Union

Sacco, Nicola, 189

Saint-Simon, Henri de, 40, 117

Salal, Abdullah al-, 239

Saud, King, 78

Schacht, Hjalmar, 150

Schapiro, J. Salwyn, 158; on free speech, 71–72; on ignorance & error, 43, 54; on reason, 48; on reform, 55, 57, 202; on

Schapiro, J. Salwyn *(cont.)*
  secularism, 88–89; on stagnation,
  229; on universal suffrage, 77
Schlesinger, Arthur M., Jr., xxix,
  20, 22, 51, 131; and ADA, 81*n*;
  on benevolent state, 98–99; on
  conflict or stagnation, 228–29;
  as "fox," 282–83; on radical
  democracy, 167–69; on vital
  center, 244
Schweitzer, Albert, 213
Scientific American, 20
SEATO, 316
secularism, 88–89, 141–42, 212–
  13, 292, 332
Servan-Schreiber, Jean-Jacques,
  201–2
Shirer, William L, 20
Silone, Ignazío, xxix
Singapore, 343
Skid Row, 110–13
Smith, Adam, 41
Smith, T.V., 74–75
Socialist Workers Party, xxii
social security, 34, 185–86, 334
Socrates, 17–18, 271
Sorel, Georges, 339
Sorensen, Theodore, 20
South Africa, 153, 223, 239
South Korea, 243, 304
South Vietnam, 259, 338
Soviet Union: as ally, 299; and
  Berlin, 305, 313; and China,
  201; commerce with, 237*n*;
  concentration camps in, 153;

containment of, 301–5; and
  Cuba, 238, 313–14, 348; and
  Hungarian revolt, 306–8; Katyn
  massacre, 240; military capabili-
  ity, 313–14*n*; negotiation with,
  28, 201, 236, 315; as power
  center, 294; and Spanish Civil
  War, 235; standard of living in,
  68–69; and Suez crisis, 306–8,
  311*n*; and Third World, 300,
  310–11; and Yalta, 299
Spain: Catholics in, 282; Franco
  & Civil War, 234–41, 331;
  Reconquista, 287
Spanish-American War, 292–93
Spengler, Oswald, 9, 10
Spiegel, Der, 226
Stages of Growth (Rostow), 69,
  349–50
Stalin, Joseph, 105, 306
Stevenson, Adlai, 20, 283
St. Louis Post-Dispatch, 20
Stouffer, Samuel, 280*n*
Strauss, Leo, 24
Strauss, Lewis, 23
Strausz-Hupé, Robert, 24
Struggle for the World, The, xxvi–
  xxviii, 297
Suez Canal crisis, 306–8, 310–11,
  344, 345
Sukarno, 122, 224, 243, 263–65,
  311, 312, 316
Susskind, David, 20
Symposium: A Critical Review,
  xix–xxi

Tanganyika, 243, 263
Tate, Allen, xx
Taylor, Allen, 46
Taylor, Harold, 20
Terre Inhumaine (Czapski), 240
Time magazine, 22, 327–28
Tito, Josip Broz, 236–37
Tocqueville, Alexis de, xvi, 42
Tolkien, J.R.R., xviii–xix
Tower, John, 23, 29
Toynbee, Arnold, 2, 9
trade unions, 280–81
Trial, The (Kafka), 211–12, 268
Trilling, Lionel, xx, 147
Trotsky, Leon, xx–xxiii, 105
Trotskyism, xvi, xxi, xxiv, 117
Trujillo Molina, Rafael Leónidas, 314
Truman, Harry S., xxviii
Truman Doctrine, xxviii, 304, 305
Tshombe, Moise, 313, 314, 331, 338
Turkey, 243, 301, 304, 314, 315

United Mine Workers, 216
United Nations, xvii, 205–6, 224, 297, 298; on disarmament, 90; favor for, 20, 28, 86, 139, 200, 201; founding of, 80; on human rights, 35, 78; on Katanga, 338; and Suez crisis, 308; and Third World, 299–300; veto in, 28; Western breakup in, 316
United States Congress, 33, 101; and ADA, 94–96; elections to, 78; and foreign policy, 127, 306, 309n, 310; House Committee on Un-American Activities, 71, 243, 331; seniority in, 56–57, 58
United States Constitution, 100, 261; Bill of Rights, 242–43
United States in the World Arena, The (Rostow), 197
United States Supreme Court, 20, 71, 101, 184; *Brown v. Board of Education*, 186–87; on "deliberate speed," 28, 56; on school prayer, 46; on voting rights, 329
Universal Declaration of Human Rights, 35, 78
University of Chicago, 64
U.S. News and World Report, 21, 23
utilitarianism, 40–41, 54
utopianism, xxi–xxii, 40, 54, 117

Valéry, Paul, xx
Vanzetti, Bartolomeo, 189
Varus, Publius Quintilius, 345
Venezuela, 239
Veuillot, Louis, 269, 282
Vietnam, 16, 164, 259, 338
Vital Center, The (Schlesinger), 98–99, 167–69, 229
vocations: academic, 276–77; business, 275, 278–79; farm, 275; law, 276; medicine, 275–76; military, 272–74; verbal, 277–

vocations *(cont.)*
  79; "workers," 279–81
Voltaire, 40

Wagner, Robert, 21, 114
Wallace, Henry, 81
Wall Street Journal, 21
Warren, Earl, 20
Washington, George, 99, 263
Washington Post, 20, 21, 23, 26, 157
Waugh, Evelyn, xix
Wechsler, James, 20, 23, 46
Wedermeyer, Albert C., 24
Wheelwright, Philip E., xix–xx
Whitman, Walt, 169, 170
Why Men Fight (Russell), 58
Williams, G. Mennen, 20
Wilson, Woodrow, 101
Wittfogel, Karl, 24

World Court, 139, 201
World Food Congress, 117
World War I, 4, 12, 293–94
World War II, xxii, xxiv, xxvi, 5–6, 8, 12; and balance of power, 294; conspiracy theory on, 293; and internationalism, 79–80; Pearl Harbor attack, xxv, 150; and U.S. leadership, 295–98; and Yalta conference, 299, 301
Wright, Quincy, 80
Wyatt, Wilson W., 81*n*

Yeats, William Butler, 147
Yemen, 78, 239, 312
Young, Stephen M., 19

Zawodny, J.K., 240
Zeno, 17

Lightning Source UK Ltd.
Milton Keynes UK
UKHW041328071122
411792UK00002B/58

9 781594 037832